REGIONAL TOURISM

REGIONAL TOURISM

By

Neil Thompson

DISCOVERY PUBLISHING HOUSE PVT. LTD.

NEW DELHI-110 002

First Published - 2011

Reprinted : 2016

ISBN: 978-81-8356-940-8

Regional Tourism

Published by:

DISCOVERY PUBLISHING HOUSE PVT. LTD.

4383/4B, Ansari Road, Darya Ganj
New Delhi-110 002 (India)
Phone: +91-11-23279245, 43596064-65
Fax: +91-11-23253475
E-mail: discoverypublishinghouse@gmail.com
sales@discoverypublishinggroup.com
web: www.discoverypublishinggroup.com

Printed at:
Infinity Imaging Systems
Delhi

PREFACE

Moving from region to region in a train or bus is called regional tourism. Tourism is travel for recreational, leisure or business purposes. The World Tourism Organization defines tourists as people who "travel to and stay in places outside their usual environment for more than twenty-four (24) hours and not more than one consecutive year for leisure, business and other purposes not related to the exercise of an activity remunerated from within the place visited."

Tourism has become a popular global leisure activity. In 2008, there were over 922 million international tourist arrivals, with a growth of 1.9% as compared to 2007. International tourism receipts grew to US$944 billion (euro 642 billion) in 2008, corresponding to an increase in real terms of 1.8%. As a result of the late-2000s recession, international travel demand suffered a strong slowdown beginning in June 2008, with growth in international tourism arrivals worldwide falling to 2% during the boreal summer months. This negative trend intensified during 2009, exacerbated in some countries due to the outbreak of the H1N1 influenza virus, resulting in a worldwide decline of 4% in 2009 to 880 million international tourists arrivals, and an estimated 6% decline in international tourism receipts.

India is a vast country ranging from mighty Himalayas in northern region to far off south Kanyakumari surrounded by three oceans—Bay of Bengal, Arabian Ocean and Indian Ocean. Every state has its own charm and beauty which attracts visitors like nails to magnet. Every village and city in India tells a different story. Each and every state tourism board has its own state tourism packages that cover the entire state and offer a attractive holiday package. Individual states like Kerala, Goa, Rajasthan, Assam, Orissa, Tamil Nadu, Karnataka, Maharashtra, West Bengal, Haryana, Andhra Pradesh, Gujarat, Uttar Pradesh, Uttranchal, Madhya Pradesh, Bihar and other states offer wholesome tourism states package deals. This book is a treasure trove to students pursuing degrees in tour and travel courses. A must read for tourists who wants to know more about regional tourism.

—Author

Contents

Chapter–1

Introduction

Moving from region to region in a train or bus is called regional tourism. Tourism is travel for recreational, leisure or business purposes. The World Tourism Organization defines tourists as people who "travel to and stay in places outside their usual environment for more than twenty-four (24) hours and not more than one consecutive year for leisure, business and other purposes not related to the exercise of an activity remunerated from within the place visited."

Tourism has become a popular global leisure activity. In 2008, there were over 922 million international tourist arrivals, with a growth of 1.9% as compared to 2007. International tourism receipts grew to US$944 billion (euro 642 billion) in 2008, corresponding to an increase in real terms of 1.8%. As a result of the late-2000s recession, international travel demand suffered a strong slowdown beginning in June 2008, with growth in international tourism arrivals worldwide falling to 2% during the boreal summer months. This negative trend intensified during 2009, exacerbated in some countries due to the outbreak of the H1N1 influenza virus, resulting in a worldwide decline of 4% in 2009 to 880 million international tourists arrivals, and an estimated 6% decline in international tourism receipts.

Tourism is vital for many countries, such as Egypt, Greece, Lebanon, Spain, Malaysia and Thailand, and many island nations, such as The Bahamas, Fiji, Maldives,

Philippines and the Seychelles, due to the large intake of money for businesses with their goods and services and the opportunity for employment in the service industries associated with tourism. These service industries include transportation services, such as airlines, cruise ships and taxicabs, hospitality services, such as accommodations, including hotels and resorts, and entertainment venues, such as amusement parks, casinos, shopping malls, music venues and theatres.

HISTORICAL ARCHIVE

The Historical Archive on Tourism (HAT, Historisches Archiv zum Tourismus) is sited in the city of Berlin at the Freie Universität Berlin, housed at the Willy-Scharnow-Institut für Tourismus. The HAT had been founded in 1989; today the length of the shelves amounts to some 500 running meter. The focus of the material is not on "travel" generally but on "tourism" as a special sort of travelling. The HAT is probably the biggest archive in this field, gathering various materials ranging from Baedekers to private photo albums, in particular there is an extensive collection of flyers and other so-called ephemera. Mainly the material stems from Central Europe, in particular from Germany, but nearly all other parts of the world are also represented, e.g. Southern Africa or USA. Over 50,000 leaflets are stored, and some 200 journals and 10,000 books are registered. In addition statistics, posters and maps are gathered. The bulk of the material is from the 19th and 20th century, some books date back to around 1600. No OPAC is installed but short lists are published in the Internet.

WORLD TOURISM

Tourism is a vital source of income for many countries and it generates income through the consumption of goods and services by tourists, the taxes levied on businesses in the tourism industry, and the opportunity for employment in the service industries associated with tourism.

Some of the services offered by these industries include transportation services such as cruise ships and taxis, accommodation services such as hotels, restaurants, bars, and entertainment venues, and other hospitality industry services such as spas and resorts.

The tourism requires having some of disposable income, time off from work and other responsibilities, proper transportation and accommodation facilities and legal clearance for traveling. More than all, sufficient health condition during the course of travel is required.

There are some countries which have legal restrictions on traveling abroad. Any projections of growth in tourism serve as an indication of the relative influence that each country will exercise in the future.

Tourism products have become one of the most traded items on the internet with the advent of e-commerce. Tourism products and services have been made available through intermediaries, apart from direct selling.

Space tourism is expected to be launched in the first quarter of the 21st century and the technological improvement is likely to make it possible for air-ship hotels, based either on solar-powered airplanes or large dirigibles.

There is also an underwater hotel project, such as Hydropolis in Dubai which is expected to be completed by December 2007.

From the year 2000 onwards, there was stagnation for almost 3 years in World Tourism industry. But now again there is an exponential growth since few years and this boom is expected to continue till another decade.

According to preliminary findings presented by the World Tourism Organization (WTO) in January 2007, international tourist arrivals reached an all-time record of 842 million in 2006--an increase of 4.5 percent over 2005.

Tourism growth has occurred in all world regions but was strongest in Africa (+8.1%) and the Asia-Pacific region (+7.6%).

TRAVEL AND TOURISM COMPETITIVENESS REPORT

The Travel and Tourism Competitiveness Report was first published in 2007 by the World Economic Forum. The 2007 report covered 124 major and emerging economies. The 2008 report covered 130 countries, and the 2009 report expanded to 133 countries. The index is a measurement of the factors that make it attractive to develop business in the travel and tourism industry of individual countries, rather than a measure of a country attractiveness as a tourist destination. The report ranks selected nations according to the Travel and Tourism Competitiveness Index (TTCI), which scores from 1 to 6 the performance of a given country in each specific subindex. The overall index is made of three main subindexes: (1) regulatory framework; (2) business environment and infrastructure; and (3) human, cultural, and natural resources. The Report also includes a specific Country Profile for each of the nations evaluated, with each of the scores received to estimate its TTCI, and complementary information regarding key economic indicators from the World Bank, and country indicators from the World Travel and Tourism Council.

Variables

For the 2008 index, each of the three main subindexes is made of the scoring of the following 14 variables, called pillars in the TTC Report. Several changes were introduced in the 2008 TTCI in the definition of the variables as compared to the definitions of the 2007 TTCI. First, the "environmental regulation" pillar was improved with help from the IUCN and the UNWTO, and for the 2008 index was re-named the "environmental sustainability" pillar to "better reflect its components and to capture the increasingly recognized importance of sustainability in the sector's development." Second, the original pillar "natural and cultural resources" was divided into two separate subcomponents: "natural resources" and "cultural resources", thus, allowing to differentiate those countries which do not necessarily have the same strengths or weaknesses in these two different resources. In general, the model was improved with better data and new concepts were introduced. The 2009 report kept the same 14 variables.

WORLD TRAVEL MONITOR

The World Travel Monitor (WTM) / European Travel Monitor (ETM) is a worldwide tourism information system detailing the foreign (outbound) travel behavior practiced by a country's respective resident population.

Origins / Objective

The European Travel Monitor has been continuously surveying the most important data on outbound travel behavior from all European countries since 1988. In 1995, the European Travel Monitor was expanded to the World Travel Monitor to cover all the important overseas markets (USA, Canada, Argentina, Brazil, United Arab Emirates, Saudi Arabia, Japan, China, India, etc.). Data is collected by the architects of the Monitor or by means of working cooperations in the various countries. Today, the World Travel Monitor chronicles nearly 90% of all international travel flows. Conceived and realized by IPK International, the surveys have the objective of tracking all outbound travel of at least one overnight stay, regardless of travel motive. Apart from holiday trips, business trips and all other private trips (e.g. visiting friends or relatives) are also recorded.

The driving impetus behind establishing this information system - initially for Germany (German Travel

Monitor) and Europe - was the fact that it was not possible for decision-makers in the tourism field, based on the information available to them up to that point in time, to gain an overview of the European market or any overseas markets (in the form of a database enabling a direct comparison of aspects such as the volume and structure of outbound trips taken by the Germans, Americans, British, Russians, Chinese, etc.). While various surveys and official statistics were available prior to the introduction of the World Travel Monitor / European Travel Monitor, the individual datasets were virtually impossible to compare because there were major dissimilarities among the samplings as well as among the survey methods used in the individual countries.

The World Travel Monitor / European Travel Monitor are cooperative partnership studies. Main contracting entities include national and regional tourist boards, tourism and economics ministries, tour operators, international hotel chains, advertising agencies, consulting firms, etc.

Methodology

The World Travel Monitor / European Travel Monitor are population-representative surveys; i.e., the composition of the sample corresponds to the composition of the population in the respective countries (over the age of 15). Study respondents are surveyed by computer-supported telephone or face-to-face interviews (the so-called CATI and CAPI methods. The number of interviews conducted varies depending upon the size and significance of a source market (from 2,000 interviews per year in smaller markets up to 24,000 interviews per year in large markets). Altogether, approximately 500,000 interviews are conducted annually on behalf of the World Travel Monitor.

This large sample size translates into better quality and yields a stronger, more profound statistical analysis of the data acquired. It also allows a considerably more precise analytical market segmenting so that reliable information can be furnished even on smaller segments.

All the important parameters of travel are surveyed using a standardized questionnaire, the basic questions of which have remained unchanged since 1988. The questionnaire used for the World Travel Monitor / European Travel Monitor factors in both a determination of travel volume (number of trips taken abroad) as well as numerous individual trip characteristics.Apart from the number of trips/overnights, the following parameters are identified:

- number of outbound trips / market volume
- destination countries (worldwide)
- destination regions / cities
- purpose of trip
- holiday types / segments (sunseekers, tours, specific cities, mountain trips, cruises, winter sports, wellness/ health-motivated, etc.)
- holiday motives / activities
- types of business trips
- length of trip
- means of transportation (incl. low-fare)
- airport of departure / airline
- accommodation types / categories
- booking -behavior / -sites / -products / -period
- internet usage
- travel information sources
- trips with children
- travel season
- travel spending
- target group / traveler profile (gender / age / education / income / children in household / household size)

- regional focus markets
- travel frequency
- travel intensity

Literature

- Conrady, Roland / Buck, Martin: Trends and Issues in Global Tourism 2008, Springer-Verlag (2008)
- Freyer, Walter: Tourismus-Marketing, Oldenbourg Verlag, third edition (2007)
- Fuchs, Wolfgang / Mundt, Jörn.W. / Zollondz, Hans-Dieter: Lexikon Tourismus, Oldenbourg Verlag, first edition (2008)
- Seitz, Erwin / Mayer, Wolfgang: Tourismusmark tforschung, Vahlen Verlag, second edition (2006)

REGIONAL TOURISM POLICIES AND DEVELOPMENT PLANS

The importance of effective tourism planning in ensuring economic benefit and sustainability is now widely recognized. So what are the concepts of national and regional tourism planning and what are the basic approaches, techniques and principles applied. Emphasis is placed on practical techniques and applications in implementing plans. So what are essential principles and techniques of tourism planning, and how to understand tourism development and sustainability. Let us have a discussion on the Regional tourism planning and the development plans. Share your thoughts on this.

World Famous Regional Tourism Spot

Hong Kong

Hong Kong- one of the wonders of the tourist map is an ideal choice for tourists and visitors who want to marvel at the great architecture and technological advancements of modern times and also enjoy the peace and tranquil life of the village life. The beautiful business district offers this great contrast with its offerings which range from great constructions to vibrant coastal life to the serene atmosphere of a peaceful outskirt of the city life.

Italy

Few places in the world an compare to Italy, most won't even make an attempt. The place is a splendid mix of history, art, architecture, mouth watering gourmet experience, sports, fashion and natural beauty at its peak. It is the land of Ceaser, Michelangelo, Galileo, Fellini, Garibaldi and Versace. Italy has been wooing foreign tourists with its rich cultural heritage, aesthetic beauty and diverse offerings catering to the tourists of all tastes and expectations.

Mauritius

Mauritius with its pristine and crystal clear beaches, cool and gentle breeze and extremely friendly people will enchant you with all its glory. The place is a tourists' delight and offers one of the most memorable holiday experiences of life time. The place with its multitude of colors and tastes, its turquoise sea, and peace and tranquility will undoubtedly uplift your moods and make you wish come here again and again to experience a vacation to remember.

Shanghai

Shanghai is perhaps one of the most underrated but exotic holiday destinations offering a great insight and understanding of the Chinese culture and tradition. The place is a melting pot of contrasts with the modern and lavishly built buildings and convention centres on the one hand and the ancient monuments and cultural museums on the other.Chinese gourmet is world famous and you can have some authentic Chinese cuisine being in this wonderful place.Being a major business district, Shanghai is very well connected with most of the European and Asian countries.

New Zealand

New Zealand is a dream destination for holiday makers and tourists. From pristine beaches, stunning snow capped mountains, lush and green forests to steaming volcanoes, sweeping coastlines, deeply indented fiords and lush rainforests, New Zealand offers unique blend of almost everything you can ask for in your holidays. So pamper yourself and book your flight to this beautiful country with rich culture and cosmopolitan way of life.

London

London, the beautiful city, having a rich cultural heritage, truly world class cosmopolitan outlook and one of the most famous galleries of the world is a tourist's paradise and a dream destination. The city attracts millions of tourists from all parts of the world with its breathtaking and mesmerizing atmosphere and sheer variety of top class spots for visitors. Drop your comments on

Florence

Florence, the city of joy, the city with a rich cultural heritage, castles and monuments which will leave tourists and visitors spell bund and the city that is home to great and stunning views of the panoramic landscape and wonderful vegetation is the most beautiful city of Italy. Florence has been the home of the great and mighty of the world such as Leonardo Da Vinci, Dante, Machiavelli and Michelangelo just to name a few.

Regional Tourism Site List

- Abaco Bahamas Green Turtle Club Resort
- Adventure Tours Pakistan
- Agra

- Alabama
- Alberta
- Algarve
- Algeria
- All Oregon
- Amazon Safaris
- Anaheim
- Andaman and Nicobar
- Angola
- Anguilla
- Antigua and Barbuda
- Arkansas
- Arizona (Scottsdale)
- Atlantic City CVA
- Austria/Salzburg
- Austria/Vienna
- Australia
- Australia New South Wales
- Australia Northern Territory
- Australia/Adelaide
- Australia/Brisbane
- Australia/Canberra
- Australia/Darwin
- Australia/Hobart
- Australia/Melbourne
- Australia/Perth
- Australia/Queensland
- Australia/Sydney
- Australia/Victoria

- Australian Capital Territory
- Austria
- Austria/Salzburg
- Austria/Salzburger Land
- Austria/Tirol
- Austria/Vienna
- Austria/Vorarlberg
- Bangladesh
- Bahamas
- Barbados
- Barbados/Bridgetown
- Belgium
- Belize
- Bermuda
- Bhutan/Paro
- Bhutan/Thimphu
- Big Bear Lake
- Brazil/Rio
- Britain
- Brunei/Bandar Seri Begawan
- Calgary
- California
- Cambodia
- Canada
- Canada/Alberta/Calgary
- Canada/Manitoba
- Canada/Newfoundland and Labrador/Saint John's
- Canada/Northwest Territories
- Canada/Nova Scotia

- Canada/Ontario
- Canada/Ontario/Hamilton
- Canada/Ontario/Lennox and Addington
- Canada/Ontario/ Northwest
- Canada/Ontario/Quinte
- Canada/Ontario/Toronto
- Canada/Prince Edward Island
- Canada/Quebec
- Canada/Quebec/Montreal
- Canada/Qu?bec/Qu?bec City & area
- Canada/Saskatchewan
- Canada/Saskatchewan/Regina
- Cape Town
- Canada/Yukon
- Cayman Islands
- China/Beijing
- China/Lhasa
- China/Macau
- China/Shanghai
- Coach House Bed & Breakfast
- Colorado
- Combodia/Phnom Penh
- Combodia/Angkor
- Costa Rica
- Connecticut
- Cote d'Azur
- Croatia
- Cuba
- Cumbria

- Curacao
- Cyprus
- Darjeeling
- Delhi
- Delaware
- Denmark
- Destinations Canada Quest
- Dubai
- Dubai Tourism
- Edinburgh
- Egypt
- Egypt Tourism
- Egypt/Alexandria
- Estonia
- Ethiopia
- Exotic Journeys Group
- Fatih Hotel Alanya
- Fiji Islands
- Finland
- Florida
- France
- France/Arles
- France/Paris
- France/Cote d'Azur
- France/Haute Savoie
- France/Lyon
- France/Riviera
- Grasmere Accommodation, Lake District, UK
- Georgia

- Germany
- Gibraltar
- Goa
- Greenland
- Grenada
- Guadeloupe
- Guam
- Guia Madrid Rural
- Hamilton
- Haute Savoie
- Hawaii
- Himachal Pradesh
- Holland
- Hong Kong
- Honolulu
- Hotel Miray Alanya
- Hungary
- Iceland
- Idaho
- Illinois
- India
- Indiana
- Indonesia
- Indonesia/Bali
- Indonesia/Bandung
- Indonesia/Sumatra
- Israel Vacation Directory
- Israel/Jerusalem
- Israel/Tel Aviv

- Italy
- Italy/Delphi
- Jaipur
- Jamaica
- Japan
- Kauai
- Kentucky
- Kenya/Masai Mara National Park
- Kenya/Nairobi
- Kerala
- Kerala Tourism India
- Korea
- Lanai
- Las Vegas
- Las Vegas Hotels
- Las Vegas Nevada
- Laos
- Long Island New York
- Los Angeles
- Lennox and Addington
- Lyon
- Maine
- Malaysia
- Malaysia Tourism
- Malaysia/Penang
- Maldives
- Maldives Tourism
- Manitoba
- Maryland

- Maui
- Mauritius
- Mauritius/Port Louis
- Mauritius/Rodrigues Island
- Micronesia
- Minnesota
- Missouri
- Mexico
- Montreal
- Molokai
- Montana
- Morrocco/Rabat
- Mumbai
- Myanmar/Mandalay
- Myanmar/Pagan
- Myanmar/Yangon
- Nauru/Nauru
- Nebraska
- Nepal
- Nepal Tourism
- Netherlands
- Nevada
- Newfoundland
- New Jersey
- New Hampshire
- New Mexico
- New York City
- Nicaragua
- North Dakota

- Northern Ireland
- Northwest Territories
- Norway
- Northwest
- Nova Scotia
- Oahu Vacation Rentals
- Oman/Muscat
- Ontario
- Oregon
- Orkney
- Pakistan
- Palestine/Bethlehem
- Palm Springs
- Papua New Guinea/Papua New Guinea
- Pennsylvania
- Peru
- Perthshire
- Philippines
- Travel Poland: Hotels Warsaw, Hotele Warszawa
- Prince Edward Island
- Qatar/Doha
- Quebec
- Qu?bec City & area
- Queensland
- Quinte
- Rajasthan, India
- Regina
- Rio
- Riviera

- Romania/Brasov
- Russia
- Saint John's
- Saudi Arabia/Riyadh
- Salzburg
- Salzburger Land
- San Diego
- San Francisco
- Saskatchewan
- Scotland
- Scotland/Orkney
- Scotland/Dumfries and Galloway
- Scotland/Edinburgh
- Scotland/Perthshire
- Seychelles
- Singapore Tourism
- Somerset
- Sonoma Country Tourism Program
- South Africa
- South Africa Tourism
- South Africa/Johannesburg
- South Africa/Cape Town
- South Africa/Durban
- South Africa/Sun City
- South Africa/Drakensburg
- Spain
- Sri Lanka
- Sri Lanka Tourism
- St. Barthelemy

- St. Lucia
- St. Maarten
- Sweden
- Sweden/
- Switzerland
- Switzerland/Kalmar
- Taj Mahal
- Tanzania
- Tanzania/Mt. Kilimanjaro National Park
- The North America Resort Guide
- Tennessee
- Texas
- The Federated States of Micronesia
- Thailand/Bangkok
- Thailand/Chiang Mai
- Tibet
- Tibet Tourism
- Tirol
- Toronto
- Travel to Russia : All Russian tourism
- Trinidad and Tobago
- Trinidad and Tobago/Port Of Spain
- Tuttovacanze
- Tunisia
- Turkey/Ankara
- Turkey/Ankara
- United Arab Emirates/Abu Dhabi
- United Arab Emirates/Dubai
- UK

- UK/Cumbria
- UK/Somerset
- UK/Weymouth
- UK/Yorkshire
- USA/Alabama
- USA/Arizona
- USA/Arkansas
- USA/California
- USA/Colorado
- USA/Connecticut
- USA/Delaware
- USA/Florida
- USA/Georgia
- USA/Hawaii
- USA/Idaho
- USA/Illinois
- USA/Indiana
- USA/Kentucky
- USA/Maine
- USA/Maryland
- USA/Minnesota
- USA/Mississippi
- USA/Missouri
- USA/Montana
- USA/Nebraska
- USA/Nevada
- USA/New Hampshire
- USA/New Jersey
- USA/New Mexico

- USA/New York State
- USA/North Dakota
- USA/Oregon
- USA/Pennsylvania
- USA/Tennessee
- USA/Texas
- USA/Utah
- USA/Vermont
- USA/Virgin Islands
- USA/Virginia
- USA/Washington
- USA/Washington DC
- USA/West Virginia
- USA/Wisconsin
- USA/Wyoming
- Utah
- Vancouver BC tourism and attractions
- Vermont
- Victoria
- Vienna
- Vietnam/Hanoi
- Vietnam/Ho Chi Minh City
- Virgin Islands
- Virginia
- Vorarlberg
- Wales
- Washington
- Washington DC
- West Virginia

- Weymouth
- Wisconsin
- Wyoming
- Yorkshire
- Yukon

Chapter-2

Regional Tourism Scenario

People in general now view tourism as a way of life rather than a luxury item reserved for the affluent and the elite. Tourism has emerged as the largest service industry globally in terms of gross revenue as well as foreign exchange earnings. The present annual global income from tourism (international and domestic) is nearly US$13 trillion, an amount more than the GNP of all countries except the United States.

According to the World Tourism Organisation (WTO), the number of international travellers has risen to more than 500 million per annum, which means that one out of every ten inhabitants of this planet is a tourist. With rapid developments in the field of transport and communications, the global tourism industry is likely to double in the next decade.

WTO forecasts that there will be 702 million international arrivals in the year 2000, that arrivals will top one billion in the year 2010 and that by 2020, international arrivals will reach 1.6 billion nearly three times the number of international trips made in 1996 which was 592 million.

The 21st century will see a higher percentage of the total population travelling, especially in developing countries, and people will be going on holidays more often, sometimes two, three or four times a year. Travellers of the 21st will also be going farther and farther. The "Tourism 2020 vision" forecast predicts that by 2020 one out of every three trips will be long haul journeys to other regions of the world. Long-haul travel is expected to increase from 24% of all international tourism in 1995 to 35% of all international traffic arrivals by the year 2020.

Tourism is the industry of industries and has a great multiplier effect on other industries. Tourism serves as an effective medium for transfer of wealth because here income earned in places of "residence" is spent in place "visit". It is the highest generator of employment. A total of 212 million persons are now being employed globally through direct and indirect opportunities generated by this industry. This means that out of every nine persons, one person earns a living from tourism. For every million rupees of investment 13 jobs are created in manufacturing industries, 45 jobs in agriculture and 89 jobs in hotels and restaurants. Tourism is therefore considered to be an important area for intensive development for all governments. As the fastest growing foreign exchange earner, specially in developed countries, it is being given priority attention.

WHAT IS TOURISM?

When we think of tourism, we think mainly of people who are visiting a particular place for sightseeing, visiting friends and relatives, taking a vacation and having a good time. 'They may spend their leisure time engaging in various sports, sunbathing, talking, singing, taking rides, touring, reading, or simply enjoying the environment. Furthermore, we may include in our definition of tourism people who are participating in a convention, a business conference, or some other kind of business or professional activity, as well as those who are taking a study tour under an expert guide or doing some kind of scientific research or study.

These visitors use all forms of transportation, from hiking in a wilderness park to flying in a jet, to travelling by rail or going on a cruise. Any attempt to define tourism and to describe fully its scope, we must consider the various groups that participate in and are affected by this industry. Their perspectives are vital to the development of a comprehensive definition. Four different perspectives of tourism can be identified:

The tourist: The tourist seeks various psychic and physical experiences and satisfactions. The nature of these will largely determine the destinations chosen and the activities enjoyed.

The business providing tourist goods and service: Business people view tourism as an opportunity to make a profit by supplying the goods and services that the tourist market demands.

The government of the host community or area: Politicians view tourism as a wealth factor in the economy of their jurisdictions. Their perspective is related to the incomes their citizens can earn from this business. Politicians also consider the foreign exchange receipts from international tourism as well as the tax receipts collected from tourist expenditures, either directly or indirectly.

The host community: Local people usually see tourism as a cultural and employment factor. Of importance to this group, for example, it is the effect of the interaction between large numbers of international visitors and residents.

Thus tourism may be defined as the sum of the phenomena and relationships arising from the interaction of tourists, business suppliers, host governments and host communities in the process of attracting and hosting these tourists and other visitors.

Tourism is a composite of a activities, services, and industries that delivers a travel experience, namely transportation, accommodations, eating and drinking establishments, shops, entertainment, activity facilities, and other hospitality services available for individuals or groups that are travelling away from home. It encompasses all providers of visitor and visitor-related services. Tourism is the entire world industry of travel, hotels, transportation, and all other components, including promotion that serves the needs and wants of travellers. Finally tourism is the sum total of tourist expenditures within the borders of a nation or a political subdivision or a transportation-centered economic area of contiguous states or nations.

WHY IS TOURISM TAKING OVER THE WORLD?

The spurt in tourism has its genesis in economic and social progress.

Technology and science, coupled with industrialisation have brought about higher incomes and longer leisure hours.

The spread of education has fostered a desire to know more about different corners of the globe.

Progress in air transport and tourist facilities have encouraged people to follow their desires.

The basic human thirst for new experiences and knowledge seems to get stronger, as communication barriers are overcome by technology.

Impact of Tourism

As an industry, the impact of tourism is manifold. Tourism industry nourishes a country's economy, stimulates development process, restores cultural heritage, and helps in maintaining international peace and understanding. Tourism at present is India's third largest export industry and the forex earnings is estimated to be about Rs.9186 cores (approx Us $3928 million) in 1995-96.

Employment Potential

The most significant feature of the tourism industry is the capacity to generate large scale employment opportunities even in backward areas, specially to women, both educated and uneducated. Another important feature of tourism is that it contributes to national integration of the people who live in different regions of the country with diverse cultures and languages.

Tourism, the World's Biggest Industry!

What about energy, manufacturing or agriculture?

A survey of 400 policy and opinion makers in 20 countries placed these and three other industries ahead of tourism in global economic contribution, but recently gathered statistics tell a different story.

As a contributor to the global economy, tourism has no equal.

- Tourism employs 204 million people worldwide or one in every nine workers, 10.6 percent of the global workforce.
- Tourism is the world's leading economic contributor, producing an incredible 10.2 percent of the world's gross national product.
- Tourism is the leading producer of tax revenues at US$655 billion.
- Tourism is the world's largest industry in terms of gross output approaching US$304 trillion
- Tourism accounts for 10.9 percent of all consumer spending, 10.7 percent of all capital investment and 6.9 percent of all government spending.

Growth of Tourism in Asia

Furthermore, despite economically and politically induced setbacks threats of terrorism from a variety of global hot spots, recession in Europe, and economic upheaveal in Japan, and the once Communist Eastern Block, the future of tourism is brighter than ever.

Expectations for growth tourism are 6.1 percent, 23 percent faster than the world economy. Travel and Tourism will create 144 million jobs worldwide between now and the year 2005 (112 million in the fast growing Asia pacific.) "In the 21st century" says Geoffrey Lipman, President of the world Travel and Tourism Council, "there will be a surge of Asian travellers in markets around the world, and Asian countries will be the premium destinations."

If tourism is such a major contributor to the world's economic well being, then the question arises, why has tourism received so little attention from domestic policy makers and crafters of international trade agreements?

Tourism a Multicomponent Industry

There is no obvious answer. One explanation is that tourism is a multicomponent industry, many parts of which are inextricably linked to other economic sectors such as airlines to transportation; souvenir shops, concession stands and restaurants to retail or service; hotels and other accommodation to commercial development.

"Broadening the Mind." A survey of the World Travel and Tourism published in the "Economist" offers the following rationale. The size of the travel and tourism business is difficult to comprehend for at least three reasons. First there is no accepted definition of what constitutes the industry, any definition of what runs the risk of either overstating of understating economic activity. Second, tourism is a business, many of whose activities (like tour guides and souvenir sales people) and much of whose income (tips) are well suited to practitioners of the underground economy. In countries with foreign exchange controls (which are always evaded) every official figure on expenditure will be wrong. Third, international travel is bedevilled by astounding differences in the data of different countries. While efforts are underway to bring uniformity to data connection and analysis worldwide, it will likely to be sometime before a consensus is reached and the scope and impact of the tourism industry. However at least two organizations are dedicated to the task of giving travel and tourism its due as the world's largest industry.

The Brussel based World Travel & Tourism Council (WTTC) us a coalition of 65 Chief executive officers from all sectors of the industry. Its goal as stated in WTTC reports is "to convince governments of the enormous contribution of travel and tourism to national and world economic development, to promote expansion of travel and tourism markets in harmony with environment and to eliminate barriers to growth of the industry."

The World Tourism Organization (WTO), on the other hand, is an agency of the United Nations Development Programme, WTO's membership comprises 113 of the world's government and boasts over 170 affiliate members from the travel and tourism industry. It is the only inter governmental organization open to the operating sector. Its mission is the promotion and development of travel and tourism as a means of stimulating business and economic development, and forecasting peace and understanding between nations.

Current Global Tourism Trends

The Travel and Tourism (T&T) industry directly contributes about 3.6% of the world's Gross Domestic Product (GDP) and indirectly contributes about 10.3% to it. As one of the biggest contributors to the global GDP, this industry directly employs nearly 77 million people worldwide, which comprises about 3% of the world's total employment. The T&T industry also contributes to indirect employment generation to the tune of 234 million or 8.7 % of the total employment implying that one in every twelve jobs in the world is in the tourism industry. The industry also represents about 12% of the total world exports.

Global market trends indicate that long-haul travel, neighbouring country tourism, rural and ethnic tourism, wellness and health holidays, cultural tourism, spiritualism, ecotourism, sports and adventure holidays, and coastal tourism and cruises are a few emerging areas of tourist interest. From a geographic viewpoint, there has been a remarkable rise in Asian tourists, particularly from China and East Asian countries. Further, the average age of the international tourist has also been reducing representing a growing segment of young tourists who would typically travel to take a break from increasingly stressful professional lives.

Given the above factors, robust growth in tourism is likely to continue in the coming years. The World Tourism Organisation (WTO) forecasts over one billion arrivals in 2010 versus approximately 693 million today (See Exhibit below). Worldwide long-distance travel is likely to grow faster (5.4% each year) than travel within regions (3.8%). Continuing world prosperity, growing recognition of tourism's contribution to employment and economic growth, availability of better infrastructure, focused marketing and promotion efforts, liberalization of air transport, growing intraregional cooperation, and a growing number of Public-Private-Partnerships (PPPs) are seen as the key drivers for tourism in the next decade.

Exhibit: WTO Forecast for Tourist Arrivals

Further, world tourist arrivals in Asia are likely to grow faster than arrivals in Europe and the Asian market share of world tourism would steadily increase until 2020 (See Exhibit below). The shifts in key trends thus represent greater opportunities for developing economies (since tourism brings with it key benefits of boosting foreign exchange while creating jobs). It also creates avenues to develop niche areas such as coastal tourism, medical tourism and rural tourism to enhance the tourist value of destinations.

Exhibit: International Tourist Arrival Forecasts by Region

Region	Base Year (Million)	Forecasts (Million)		Average Annual Growth Rate (%)	Market Share (%)	
	1995	2010	2020	1995-2020	1995	2020
World	565.4	1,006.4	1,561.1	4.1%	100.0%	100.0%
Europe	338.4	527.3	717.0	3.0%	59.8%	45.9%
East Asia/ Pacific	81.4	195.2	397.2	6.5%	14.4%	25.4%
South Asia	4.2	10.6	18.8	6.2%	0.7%	1.2%

Source: World Tourism Organization

As observed, tourism trends around the world are likely to remain robust and the growth of the T&T industry worldwide will significantly impact tourism flows towards the subcontinent.

Hotel Management & Tourism industry

Hotel Management is closely linked to the tourism industry as such the latter gives a big boost to the former. If tourism industry grows the hotel industry cannot lag behind. Let us have look at this sun rise industry.

World Tourism Scenario

Tourism is the world's largest export industry. According to the World Tourism Organisation, about 567.4 million tourists travelled internationally in 1995 and spent about US$ 372.6 billion. It is estimated that tourism accounts for about eight per cent of the total world exports and more than 30 per cent of international trade in services. In 1995, travel and tourism was expected to provide direct and indirect employment for 212 million people and account for 10.7 per cent of the global work force, according to World Travel and Tourism Council.

International tourist traffic is expected to grow at a compound rate of growth of about 3.1 per cent from 1995 to 2000 and reach 661 million tourist arrivals by 2000 AD. The regions which are likely to experience the maximum growth in tourist traffic in the coming years are East Asia/Pacific (6.8 per cent) and South Asia (6.1 per cent).

The total tourist arrivals in the South Asia region consisting of Bangladesh, India, Iran, Maldives, Pakistan and Sri Lanka were 4.4 million during 1995. This is expected to become about 6.0 million by the turn of the century by a conservative estimate. The factors which are favourable to the South Asia region include the economic liberalisation programme in India and the consequent foreign investment opportunities, development of tourist facilities including expansion of airline services, etc.

The Indian Scenario

The international tourist traffic to the country during 1951 was just 16,829. Over a period of 44 years, the arrivals increased to 2.12 million in 1995 and registered a compounded annual rate of growth of about 17.6 per cent.

However, the mainstay of Indian tourism is domestic tourism. According to the figures available from the state Governments, about 100 million domestic tourists stayed in the accommodation units during 1994. In addition, it is expected that there would be about 150 million pilgrim tourists who did not use paid accommodation.

Tourism is presently India's third largest export industry after ready made garments and gem and jewellery. (In the case of gem and jewellery, the import content is very high). The foreign exchange earnings from tourism during 1995-96 is estimated to be about Rs. 9,186 crore (US$ 3,928 million).

The most significant feature of the tourism industry is its capacity to generate large scale employment opportunities particularly in remote and backward areas. It offers enormous potential for economically utilising the natural attractions like landscapes, mountains, beaches, rivers etc., which would otherwise remain either idle or under utilised. It also applies to a multitude of man made attractions like monuments, palaces, forts and unique rural and city environments.

A desirable feature of the tourism industry is that it employs a large number of women, both educated and uneducated. It has a natural affinity to the nature of the women, as hospitality is an industry in which women have been participating for centuries. In fact, women are in large numbers in hotels, airline services, travel agencies, handicraft making,. cultural activities, and other tourism related activities.

Direct Employment

The direct employment in the sector during 1994-95 was about 7.8 million persons accounting for about 2.4 percent of the total labour force. The labour capital ratio per million rupee of investment at 1985-86 prices in the hotel and restaurant sector is 89 jobs as against 44.7 jobs in the case of agriculture and 12.6 jobs in the case of manufacturing industries. In the case of the tourism industry, taking all individual segments together, the ratio is 47.5 jobs and is still higher than other industries.

Another important feature of the tourism industry, which is of particular significance to India, is its contribution to national integration and environment of social and cultural lives of people. Over 100 million domestic tourists visiting different parts of the country every year return with a better understanding of the people living in the different regions of the country and the cultural diversity of India. Tourism also encourages preservation of monuments and heritage properties and helps the survival of art forms, crafts and culture.

It is also important to note that tourism has become an instrument for sustainable human development including:

Poverty Elimination

Environment regeneration

Job creation

Advancement of women and other disadvantaged groups

Future Prospects

According to the forecasts made by the World Tourism Organisation (WTO), the international tourist traffic to the country by 2000 AD will be about three million. This is based on the input given by us and the assumption that the arrivals will follow the historical growth pattern. However, the National Action Plan for Tourism stipulated a target of five million tourists within five years from 1992. The total number of rooms available in India at present is about 58,000.

The economic liberalisation process initiated by the Government since 1991 has also accelerated the growth of business travel in India. It is, therefore, expected that domestic tourist traffic would grow at an annual growth rate of about 7.5 per cent, from 100 million' to around 170 million, by the turn of the century.

Our Education and Training

We are leaders in hospitality education and training in South Asia, with the largest network of government and private institutions. Indian hospitality skill is now globally sought after. In fact the world's best hotel managers of the future could be from India.

Tomorrow's Tourist - Scenarios & Trends

Based upon first hand cutting edge futures research

Forecasts for world tourism to 2030

Suggests what the tourist will be doing on holiday in 2030

Discusses alternative issues such as climate change, alternative tourism destinations and consumer trends

Shows you how to apply the trends in your organisation

By 2030, China will be the world's largest tourism destination, holidays in Outer Space will be the ultimate luxury experience, extreme Swedish ironing will be an Olympic Sport, embedded technologies will be the norm in future tourists and skiing in the Alps will be no more.

In 1950, 25 million consumers took an international holiday and by 2005 this figure had risen to 803 million. By 2030, it is forecasted that this figure will reach 1.9 billion international arrivals, spending US $2 trillion with US $5 billion being spent by international tourists every day across the world, from US $2 billion in Europe to US $1.5 billion in Asia.

These are some of the changes that will occur between now and 2030 that will change world tourism. Tomorrows Tourist: Scenarios & Trends enables readers to imagine what a future tourist might be, where they will go and what they will do. This is the most comprehensive analysis of how world tourism is changing and what it means for destinations.

Each chapter consists of a scenario about a future tourist, which is then backed up with evidence and trends plus a number of assumptions about the future.

Authored by Ian Yeoman, the world's only futurologist dedicated to tourism, with trend data and analysis provided by the Future Foundation, one of world's leading consumer think tanks.

"Prof. Ian Yeoman has been working for more than a decade in the field of scenario planning for the tourism industry. His thinking outside the goldfish bowl, combined with a sound understanding of the many different areas of the tourism sector, brings new and key contributions to this analysis. This new book presents new insights on how to be better prepared for the future ahead, to be more successful and above all to successfully face the enormous challenges ahead, including new tourists, new markets, climate change and the millennium development goals."

Tourism - Need for Sustainable Approaches

Continuing on the thread left on the last blog post, this one tries to establish with further evidence that Indian domestic tourism can play crucial role in tourism development. I have presented two figures in this blog post. The first one shows how the domestic tourism is growing in the country along with the actual increase in number of domestic tourists from the year 1997 till latest. The other figure presents number of domestic tourists in an index form. A few important features that emerge from the first figure are:

- growth rates fluctuates from year to year due to several reasons; however, it generally maintains a high growth especially in 2000s.
- except 2008, the odd year affected by global recession, the growth rate is mostly over 10% since 2000.
- the actual increase in number of domestic tourists in the country further establishes the contribution of domestic tourists to the country's tourism activities.
- substantial increase in actual increase has been noticed in 2000s compared to the previous decade
- in most of the years in 2000s the actual increases were over 50 million each year, which is a significant addition to the tourism market
- 2009 experienced an increase to the extent of 87 million, despite the fact that economic recovery in the country from global recession was not really visible till the later part of the year. This also suggests the potential of domestic tourism with vibrant growth years

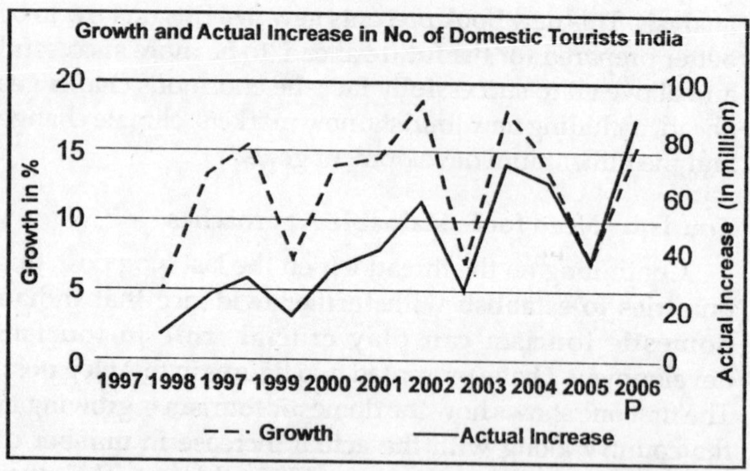

The graph shows the number of domestic tourists in an index form. Year 1997 has been considered as the base year with an index value of 100. A gradual increase has been clearly depicted by the graph over the years and in 2009 the index value reached to 407. This suggests that within a span of about 12 years the domestic tourism has been increased by more than four folds, which is amazingly high compared to any standard. A simple exponential time trend suggests that in another 5 years, by 2014, the total domestic tourists will reach about 1200 million.

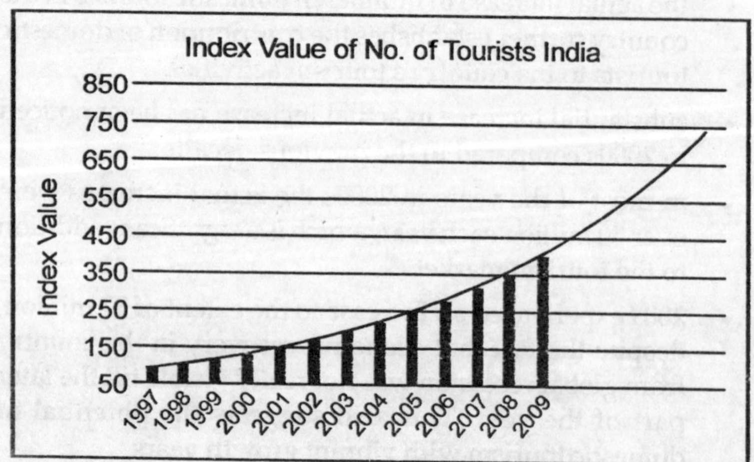

The above points suggest the need for a few important issues that essentially to be addressed by the policy makers to further enrich the tourism activities in the country.

- tourism products should be developed considering the fact the major chunk of the tourism activity will be generated from domestic tourists
- a market segmentation is the need of the hour to understand the requirements as well as develop tourism products catering to these needs
- proper strategy can be developed by the stakeholders to attract domestic tourists from different segments (demographic as well as psycho graphic and others)
- awareness can be developed amongst the tourists towards sustainable tourism so that environmental footprints can be minimized.

To continue the discussion, I will discuss about the tourism market segmentation and its importance to shape a proper tourism market, especially, keeping sustainable tourism development in mind.

The Future

History tells us that war affects tourism. Durie (2003) established that the first tourists came to Scotland because of war in Europe. The first Grand Tours of Scotland, for example, were enjoyed by European tourists who were avoiding France and Germany during the Napoleonic Wars, and tourists chose Scotland rather than Ireland in early Victorian times because Ireland was regarded as barbaric and unsafe for travellers.

The 9/11 attack on targets in New York and Washington in 2001 sent the world into a panic, and the resulting legislation has impacted on US tourism, making it harder for tourists to visit the country because of higher barriers to entry, such asvisas, biometric passports and extra security checks at airports. There is also a perception within potential markets that if people say something negative about the United States then they could face detention (Yeoman, 2007).

As Durie (2003) points out, wars have always happened and will continue to happen. The same can be said about the present debate about global warming. People often forget that the climate has been undergoing change since the beginning of time - in the twenty-first century, we tend to believe that climate change is a new phenomenon and the world may be coming to an end.

Taking the Long View

If people's time horizon encompasses only 1 day in the past and 1 day in the future-then their perception of the future will be the same as their understanding of the present. If we cannot see beyond tomorrow, then we shall not have the ability to anticipate change, nor take relevant action in response.

If our time horizon is only yesterday and we do not consider circumstances of long ago, then we cannot understand the cycle of events when they re-occur. The long view is about 'picturing' what the world could look like as a consequence of change. Taking the long view is important because the consequences of unfolding trends can be 'pictured' only over a time period of 10, 20, or 30 years, whether it be the impact of demographics or technologies.

Taking the long view is the secret ingredient of success, because without doing that the business world cannot prepare for the future. Today, the pace of change in the modern world is frightening as the line between fact and science fiction becomes blurred.

If you want to understand the future of technology, you have to take a science-fiction approach in order to imagine the imaginable - such is the pace of change. The nature of work, consumer expectations and the environment are all shifting radically, making it difficult for society and businesses to plan ahead and to prepare adequately for future challenges. Indeed, in our age of hyper-change, many people have no notion of what sort of world they should prepare for.

Taking the well-considered long view or having sufficient foresight, in contrast to accepting fatalistically what will happen, gives us increased power to shape our future, even in the most turbulent times. People who can think ahead will be prepared for the rapid social and technological progress that is affecting every aspect of our lives.

Many of the best-known techniques for long-term planning were developed by US military planners, because the post-World War II nuclear age made it critical to 'think about the unthinkable' and prepare for whatever might happen.

Pioneering futurists at the RAND Corporation (the first think-tank) began to seriously consider what new technologies might emerge in the future and how these might affect the security of the United States. The RAND futurists, along with others, refined a number of ways of thinking about the future.

Futurists recognise that the future is continuous with the present, so we can learn a great deal about what may happen in the future by looking systematically at what is happening now and what has taken place in the past. The key is not simply looking at events but rather scrutinising trends, such as long-term shifts in population or the increase in the processing power of technology.

Futurists develop these trends into scenarios, as a way of thinking about the future. Scenarios are not predictions but are a way of setting the scene (or scenes) so as to state in a credible way what could happen in the future. Scenarios help us think about what the future may bring and help us react or adapt to circumstances in a relevant way.

A useful technique is trend analysis, which is an examination of the causes, the speed of developments and the impact they may have. This is one of the techniques that has been used throughout this book; for example, a longer lifespan is one of the key drivers of change in a number of chapters:

- As society ages, medical discoveries extend people's lifespan and consumers also become more interested in well-being therapies.
- As society ages, people become interested in sporting activities in order to stay healthy and live longer.
- As the population ages, people's attitudes and outlooks change, and they desire earlier retirement or second/ holiday homes or more time with grandchildren.

This book is based on a combination of different disciplines and methodologies.

The thinking about scenarios has required an appreciation of history in order to understand the future; it means recognising the macro drivers that are shaping the world and what impact they may have on tourism. The thinking has also necessitated a comprehensive understanding of economics and demographics in order to envisage future purchasing power and the impact on tourist flows and destination choice.

We have used the application of psychology and sociology in order to understand what the future tourist will do on holiday. Scenarios also consider barriers to growth, such as people's need for security and the impact of climate change.

The strength of argument in this book lies in the methodology and analysis behind it, which seek to explain through trends where the tourist will go on holiday in 2030 and what they will be doing with the use of a little bit of creativity and imagination.

As well as providing scenarios for the future, this book gives an insight into how change is occurring, by using data from the Future Foundations Changing Lives Survey.

Changing Lives is a comprehensive survey of European households, which since 1980 allows futurists or researchers to understand how change has taken place over a period of time. In addition, the data which comes from such a survey allows futurists to put forward projections of trends in order to find out what the impact of those trends would be.

Some of the chapters vary in size depending on the complexity of the subject. They can be read in whichever order you prefer, but I would recommend that the first section is read first - it just reads better that way.

MARKET RESEARCH FOR THE TRAVEL AND TOURISM INDUSTRY

Euromonitor has the world's most comprehensive research on the travel and tourism industry. We monitor and analyse industry trends in travel and tourism globally, including in-depth data on market share and market size - from the "big picture" down to specific category levels. Categories in travel and tourism include:

- Car rental
- Health & wellness tourism
- Tourism flows domestic
- Tourism flows inbound
- Tourism flows outbound
- Tourist attractions
- Transportation
- Travel accommodation
- Travel retail

Euromonitor data and market analysis advances your knowledge of the industry and its competitive environment, ensuring accurate and focused strategies for your business. Our market research can be used throughout your entire organisation, including strategic development, marketing, mergers and acquisitions, and brand management.

Chapter-3

Regional Tourism Organisations (RTO)

Regional Tourism Organisations (RTOs) are responsible for promoting their regions to domestic and international visitors. There are currently 29 RTOs in New Zealand and these vary in size, structure, and scope of the activities they undertake. Some are funded in part or in full by local council, others by annual membership fees. All 29 however, act as a bridge between tourism operators, national tourism bodies, and local and central government.

North Island RTOs

- Destination Northland
- Tourism Auckland
- Tourism Coromandel
- Tourism Bay of Plenty
- Hamilton & Waikato Regional Tourism
- Destination Rotorua
- Tourism Eastland
- Destination Lake Taupo
- Visit Ruapehu
- Venture Taranaki
- Venture Hawkes Bay

- Discover Wanganui
- Destination Manawatu
- Destination Wairarapa
- Nature Coast Enterprise
- Positively Wellington Tourism

South Island RTOs

- Destination Marlborough
- Nelson Tasman Tourism
- Tourism West Coast
- Christchurch and Canterbury Tourism
- Destination Mount Cook Mackenzie
- Central South Island Tourism
- Tourism Waitaki
- Destination Queenstown
- Lake Wanaka Tourism
- Tourism Central Otago
- Tourism Dunedin
- Destination Fiordland
- Venture Southland Tourism

DESTINATION NORTHLAND

To assist Northland businesses and communities to maximize and manage the sustainable economic benefits of increased visitor numbers through partnership

Destination Northland, the Regional Tourism Organisation, is responsible for marketing and promotion of the region, nationally and internationally, as a visitor destination through partnerships with industry and through cooperative and direct marketing and promotion.

DNL ensures that tourism's interests are promoted and considered at all levels in the regional environment and acts on Northland's behalf in national forums to promote Northland's tourism interests. For the local industry DNL facilitates tourism communications and information flows, creates marketing partnership opportunities for tourism operators and coordinates an events programme.

Its primary role is as a facilitator and planner, rather than as a funder and operator and its marketing role is strategic and generic rather than product specific, achieving outcomes for the benefit and promotion of the Northland destination and brand.

Goals

- To increase and manage the growth of visitor numbers to the region
- To increase visitor nights and expenditure within the region, resulting in positive economic development
- To assist industry and communities to enhance the quality of the visitor experience in Northland, and the flow on of financial benefits
- To work in partnership with Maori to increase their involvement in tourism throughout Tai Tokerau Northland
- To facilitate and assist with the delivery of the key priorities from the 2003 Northland Tourism Strategy
- To assist identification of, and encourage the development of viable new visitor products
- To promote the Twin Coast Discovery Highway concept to encourage a greater regional spread of visitors throughout the region

To encourage new tourism investment from public and private sectors

The Coromandel

The Coromandel is where Kiwis go on holiday! Renowned worldwide for its natural beauty - misty rainforests and pristine golden beaches, the Coromandel is blessed with hundreds of natural hideaways, making it an ideal place to slow down, relax and unwind.

Dig your own hot spa pool in the sand at Hot Water Beach, explore the Coromandel Forest Park, or cruise the islands by boat. Use this official Coromandel website to plan your Coromandel holiday, from accommodation to activities, events and festivals.

The Coromandel has quality accommodation at affordable prices for your New Zealand rugby holiday. Transport options within 2 hours of 18 of the 2011 rugby world cup matches in New Zealand (or 1 hours drive from Auckland international airport) you can be enjoying your holiday in the Coromandel. Include iconic Coromandel events into your 2011 rugby road trip while visiting New Zealand. Framed by native Pohutukawa trees on the western side, beautiful white sandy beaches on the east and divided by ranges cloaked in native rainforest, the Coromandel's 400kms of coastline offers the visitor a truly distinctive blend of experiences. Keep up to date with Coromandel events, accommodation and activity travel deals. Sign up the Coromandel monthly newsletter

Plan Your Travel to The Coromandel

There is a great selection of quality accommodation, activities and transport within 2 hours of the Auckland International Airport. Within 2 hours of downtown Auckland is a scenic ferry tc Coromandel town. The Coromandel is renowned for producing homegrown food that contributes to the dining experience. The key feature of The Coromandel is the locals, living towns linked by thePacific Coast Highway.

Accommodation

Part of the pleasure of travel is choosing where to stay. Do you want a room with a view, a luxury suite or a campsite for your motorhome? The Coromandel has a superb range of accommodation from luxury lodges, to intimate B&B's, self contained holiday homes and plenty of more accommodation options.

Whatever your accommodation option you can be sure of a memorable holiday when you're staying in New Zealand's favourite holiday destination - The Coromandel.

Activities & Attractions

Land Activities

Adventure

Farms

Fun Activities

Guided Sightseeing Tours

Gardens

Golf Courses

Horse Riding

Hot Springs

Motorbike Tours

Nighttime Activities

Wineries

Water Activities

Diving & Snorkelling

Fishing

Scenic Boat Cruises

Sailing

Sea Kayaking

Arts, Culture, Heritage & Food

Arts, Crafts and Galleries

Museums

Gold Mining Attractions

Local Food Outlets

Activities & Attractions

Land Activities

Adventure

Farms

Fun Activities

Guided Sightseeing Tours

Gardens

Golf Courses

Horse Riding

Hot Springs

Motorbike Tours

Nighttime Activities

Wineries

Water Activities

Diving & Snorkelling

Fishing

Scenic Boat Cruises

Sailing

Sea Kayaking

Arts, Culture, Heritage & Food

Arts, Crafts and Galleries

Museums

Gold Mining Attractions

Local Food Outlets

The Coromandel stands out from the rest of New Zealand.

Located just one and a half hours from Auckland International Airport the Coromandel is a world away from the urban sprawl. Its unique landscape and relaxed lifestyle make it an ideal destination for both New Zealanders and international visitors. There is plenty to do in the Coromandel and plenty to learn about.

Along with its natural beauty - misty rainforests and pristine beaches - it's historical past is rich and colourful. Captain Cook visited the area in 1769 and observed the transit of the planet Mercury across the face of the sun hence the names of some of the region's beaches and bays - Mercury Bay and Cook's Beach.

In the nineteenth century the peninsula teemed with human activity associated with the exploitation of timber, gold and kauri gum. Eventually the kauri and the accessible gold were exhausted and the gum market destroyed. The Coromandel lapsed into an economic and social decline that was eventually halted by the gradual growth of farming, fishing, horticulture, and tourism. The land slowly "mended" and a new era of people moved into the area, one that valued the environment. Thirty four percent of the land on the peninsula is now administered by the Department of Conservation.

Many visitor attractions have been developed so that visitors can reflect on the region's former days. The Coromandel's history is captured in the many museums around the region. Guides are available to take visitors into the bush to view the remnants of the gold mining and logging era.

The Coromandel is a walker's paradise with many coastal walkways and inland bush walks ranging from several hours to several days. Huge kauris that were saved from the loggers' saws still remain and can easily be viewed.

Many artists and craftspeople have made the Coromandel their home, inspired by the region's idyllic setting. Visitors can follow an arts and crafts trail from one side of the peninsula to the other following the popular Pacific Coast Highway.

Other tourism operators have established themselves to take advantage of the clear waters and many kilometres of coastline and islands surrounding the Coromandel. Choose from the numerous water activities available - fishing, sailing, kayaking, snorkelling or swimming. Take a few days to enjoy this exceptional part of New Zealand - it is too good to miss.

The Coastal Bay of Plenty

The coastal Bay of Plenty, one of the country's top holiday destinations for Kiwis, offers a great mix of accommodation, activities, scenic attractions, culture and top dining experiences. Whether you're after adventure, beach life or a bit of indulgence, the Bay of Plenty has all the bases covered. Located along the picturesque Pacific Coast Highway, the region is home to a beautiful landscape in which to enjoy a full range of activities year-round. The region's main centre is Tauranga and the coastal suburbs of Mount Maunganui and Papamoa have long been popular with visitors. The region is also home to the heart of the kiwifruit industry in Te Puke, the art-loving town of Katikati, quiet coastal village of Waihi Beach, historic Maketu and the tourist activity centre of Paengaroa. There are plenty of things to do in Tauranga and the Bay of Plenty. Choose from water adventures like white-water rafting, kayaking, dolphin encounters, parasailing and jetboating. There's also skydiving, scenic flights, blokarting (a locally-invented land sailor), horse treks, cultural experiences, golf courses and a variety of gardens and museums to peruse. The range of accommodation includes waterfront hotels, motels and apartments, holiday parks in great locations and lodges set amongst orchards and hills. From the beaches and harbour to a thriving kiwifruit industry and Maori culture, the coastal Bay of Plenty is a great holiday destination.

ROTORUA

Whether seeking to experience Maori culture, geothermal earth forces, spa rejuvenation, thrills and adventure, or any of the other natural assets such as 16 lakes, some of the world's best mountain biking trails, fantastic trout fishing and myriad forest walking tracks - Rotorua delivers it all!

This site, Rotorua's official website, details all essential Rotorua information including attractions and activities, tours and daytrips, the vast range of accommodation choices, what's on now plus upcoming events, and how to get here. We also showcase our art, culture, history, legends, personalities, buildings, population and weather.

"Rotorua - feel the spirit - Manaakitanga" is our catch-cry . . . and it holds a pretty powerful promise as well as an invitation to experience our extraordinary slice of New Zealand. A deep-rooted Maori cultural concept, Manaakitanga places a responsibility on us as your hosts to give you the best of ourselves, our time and our history.

Great Lake Taupo, Turangi, Tongariro and Mangakino— Located in the heart of New Zealand's North Island, Great Lake Taup? is undoubtedly one of the world's most unique and picturesque areas. The film location for The Lord of The Rings movie, the region is centred around the majestic Lake Taup?, the largest freshwater lake in Australasia. Activities available in the area are as diverse as the landscape itself, which boasts beautiful geothermal scenery, breathtaking waterfalls and world heritage listed forest reserves. You'll see spectacular steaming cliffs, geysers, boiling lakes, bubbling mud pools and many thermally heated hot pools as well as the mighty Huka Falls, New Zealand's most visited natural attraction. For adventure lovers the region is ideal, with activities ranging from bungy jumping, skiing, mountain biking, rafting, jet boating not to forget world class trout fishing.

Where Adventure Begins

It is within this natural playground that you'll be inspired and captivated by the majesty of the region. Dominating the landscape are the dramatic volcanic mountains of Ruapehu, Tongariro and Ngauruhoe. Skiing and riding enthusiasts flock to Mt Ruapehu' s Whakapapa or Turoa ski areas during the ski season (June - November). The Tongariro National Park, which is also a World Heritage area is home to the famous Tongariro Alpine Crossing. There is no better region for mountain biking that Ruapehu. The region is proudly home to not one but two of the National Cycle-way trails; Central North Island Rail Trail and Mountains to the Sea, amongst others. Navigate the deep gorges, surrounded by rich flora and fauna bush areas of the Whanganui River, at your leisure. Surrounding the region are the urban settlements of Taumarunui, National Park, Ohakune and at the far eastern reaches, the army town of Waiouru.

Taranaki

With Taranaki's epic surf, spectacular gardens, great events, legendary mountain and countless outdoor and cultural adventures it's easy to see why the region prides itself on being a destination 'like no other'. This site features up to date information on the region and its many attraction, event and accommodation options. Enjoy your visit.

Kapiti Coast & Horowhenua

Known as the Nature Coast for good reason, the Kapiti-Horowhenua region offers a stunning natural environment on the lower west coast of the North Island, where the mountains meet the sea. Kilometres of unspoilt beaches, forest walks and a hinterland that is rich in both Maori and European history are melded with a temperate climate and innovative entrepreneurs and artists.

NELSON NEW ZEALAND TOURIST INFORMATION

To visit Nelson region is to discover azure skies and wide open spaces, beaches and lakes, spectacular national parks and unique landforms, vineyards and gourmet cafes, artists and galleries, entrepreneurs and boutique shopping experiences...a uniquely Nelson way of life.

Nelson region combines the finest elements of the New Zealand experience and delivers them across stunning geography, sun-ripened at the perfect latitude under New Zealand's highest sunshine hours.

Nelson Accommodation

At the heart of an enjoyable Nelson holiday is welcoming and hospitable New Zealand accommodation. Nelson accommodation options range from backpacker originals to luxury lodges, and everything in between.

visitor information for Rugby World Cup 2011 . . .

NelsonNZ.com is the official tourism site for Nelson Tasman region. This site contains complete visitor services, including destination information, maps, trip itineraries, accommodation, dining, events, conferences and booking services. It is your one-stop visitor service where you can find everything you need to ensure a safe, successful visit to our beautiful part of the world for Rugby World Cup 2011.

VISIT OAMARU & WAITAKI DISTRICT

A district of stunning natural beauty, lush rolling farmland, ancient marine landscapes and the Moeraki Boulders. Ensure a close encounter with our precious wildlife; view Blue Penguins, the worlds smallest. in their natural environment. Close by visit one of the worlds rarest penguins, the Yellow Eyed (Hoiho). View priceless Maori artefacts, grand Victorian Architecture, plus a unique colonial heritage that shaped the nations wealth. This is our district!

South Coast Regional Tourism Organisation

South Coast Regional Tourism Organisation Inc. (SCRTO) is the RTO for the South Coast of New South Wales and is made up of six Local Government Areas (LGA): Wollongong City, Shellharbour City, Kiama Municipality, Shoalhaven City, Eurobodalla Shire and Bega Valley Shire. The area covered by the Regional Tourism Organisation is, therefore, from Helensburgh in the north to the Victorian border in the south including Jervis Bay Territory.

WORLD TOURISM ORGANIZATION

The World Tourism Organization (UNWTO/OMT) is a specialized agency of the United ?Nations and the leading international organization in the field of tourism. It serves as a ?global forum for tourism policy issues and a practical source of tourism know-how.?

UNWTO plays a central and decisive role in promoting the development of responsible, ?sustainable and universally accessible tourism, paying particular attention to the ?interests of developing countries.?

The Organization encourages the implementation ?of the Global Code of Ethics for Tourism, with a view to ensuring that member ?countries, tourist destinations and businesses maximize the positive economic, ?social and cultural effects of tourism and fully reap its benefits, while minimizing its ?negative social and environmental impacts.?

Its membership includes 154 countries, 7 territories and over 400 Affiliate ?Members representing the private sector, educational institutions, tourism associations ?and local tourism authorities.?

Direct actions that strengthen and support the efforts of National Tourism ?Administrations are carried out by UNWTO's regional representatives (Africa, the ?Americas, East Asia and the Pacific, Europe, the Middle East and South Asia) based at ?the Headquarters in Madrid.?

UNWTO is committed to the United Nations Millennium Development Goals, geared ?toward reducing poverty and fostering sustainable development.?

Aims

The World Tourism Organization plays a role in promoting the development of responsible, ?sustainable and universally accessible tourism, paying particular attention to the ?interests of developing countries?. The Organization encourages the implementation ?of the Global Code of Ethics for Tourism, with a view to ensuring that member ?countries, tourist destinations and businesses maximize the positive economic, ?social and cultural effects of tourism and fully reap its benefits, while minimizing its ?negative social and environmental impacts. UNWTO is committed to the United Nations Millennium Development Goals, geared ?toward reducing poverty and fostering sustainable development.

History

The origin of the World Tourism Organization stems back to 1925 when the International Congress of Official Tourist Traffic Associations (ICOTT) was formed at The Hague. Some articles from early volumes of the Annals of Tourism Research, claim that the UNWTO originated from the International Union of Official Tourist Publicity Organizations (IUOTPO), although the UNWTO states that the ICOTT became the International Union of Official Tourist Propaganda Organizations first in 1934.

Following the end of the Second World War and with international travel numbers increasing, the IUOTPO restructured itself into the International Union of Official Travel Organizations (IUOTO). A technical, non-governmental organization, the IUOTO was made up of a combination of national tourist organizations, industry and consumer groups. The goals and objectives of the IUOTO were to not only promote tourism in general but also to extract the best out of tourism as an international trade component and as an economic development strategy for developing nations.

Towards the end of the 1960's, the IUOTO realized the need for further transformation to enhance its role on an international level. The 20th IUOTO general assembly in Tokyo, 1967, declared the need for the creation of an intergovernmental body with the necessary abilities to function on an international level in cooperation with other international agencies, in particular the United Nations. Throughout the existence of the IUOTO, close ties had been established between the organization and the United Nations (UN) and initial suggestions had the IUOTO becoming part of the UN. However, following the circulation of a draft convention, consensus held that any resultant intergovernmental organization should be closely linked to the UN but preserve its "complete administrative and financial autonomy".

It was on the recommendations of the UN that the formation of the new intergovernmental tourism organization was based. Resolution 2529 of the XXIVth UN general assembly stated:

The general assembly believes that a formula that would allow agreement to be reached more readily among governments for the establishment of an international tourism organization of an intergovernmental, particularly to assist the developing countries would be:

(a) The conversion of the International Union of Official Travel Organizations into an intergovernmental organization through a revision of its statutes: (b) The establishment of operational links between the United Nations and the transformed Union by means of a formal agreement.

In 1970, the IUOTO general assembly voted in favor of forming the World Tourism Organization (WTO), based on statutes of the IUOTO, and after ratification by the prescribed 51 states, the WTO came into operation on November 1, 1974.

Most recently, at the fifteenth general assembly in 2003, the WTO general council and the UN agreed to establish the WTO as a specialized agency of the UN. The significance of this collaboration, WTO Secretary-General Mr. Francesco Frangialli claimed, would lie in "the increased visibility it gives the WTO, and the recognition that will be accorded to [it].Tourism will be considered on an equal footing with other major activities of human society".

As of 2010, its membership included 154 member states, seven associate members (Flemish Community, Puerto Rico, Aruba, Hong Kong, Macau, Madeira, Netherland Antilles), two observers (Holy See, Palestine). 15 of these members have withdrawn from the organization for different periods in the past: Australia, Bahamas, Bahrain, Canada, Costa Rica, El Salvador, Honduras, Kuwait, Malaysia, Nicaragua, Panama, Philippines, Qatar, Thailand and Puerto Rico.

Non-members are: Suriname, Guyana, United States, Belize, Trinidad and Tobago, Dominica, Grenada, Barbados, Antigua and Barbuda, Saint Lucia, Saint Kitts and Nevis, Saint Vincent and the Grenadines, Liberia, Somalia, Comoros, Ireland, Iceland, United Kingdom, Denmark, Sweden, Finland, Belgium, Luxembourg, Liechtenstein, Estonia, United Arab Emirates, Myanmar, Singapore, New Zealand, Palau, Micronesia, Marshall Islands, Cook Islands,

Tuvalu, Nauru, Niue, Kiribati, Solomon Islands, Samoa, Tonga and the rest of states with limited recognition.

Additionally there are some 350 affiliate members, representing the private sector, educational institutions, tourism associations and local tourism authorities. The frequent confusion between the two WTOs - World Tourism Organization and the Geneva-based World Trade Organization - officially ended on 1 December 2005, when the General Assembly approved to add the letters UN (for United Nations) to the start of abbreviation of the leading international tourism body in English and in Russian. UNWTO abbreviation remains OMT in French and Spanish. UNWTO General Assembly concluded its work at its 16th session in Dakar, Senegal, on 2 December 2005.

Secretaries-General of UNWTO

- 1975-1985 - Robert Lonati (France)
- 1986-1989 - Willibald Pahr (Austria)
- 1990-1996 - Antonio Enriquez Savignac (Mexico)
- 1998-2009 - Francesco Frangialli (France)
- 2010-present - Taleb Rifai (Jordan)

Structure

General Assembly

The General Assembly is the supreme organ of the Organization. Its ordinary ?sessions, held every two years, are attended by delegates of the Full and Associate ?Members, as well as representatives from the Business Council.? It is the most important meeting of senior tourism officials and high-level ?representatives of the private sector from all over the world.

Regional Commissions

Established in 1975 as subsidiary organs of the General Assembly, the six Regional ?Commissions normally meet once a year. They enable member States to maintain ?contact with one another and with the Secretariat between sessions of the General ?Assembly, to which they submit their proposals and convey their concerns. Each ?Commission elects one Chairman and its Vice-Chairmen from among its Members ?for a term of two years commencing from one session to the next session of the ?Assembly.??

Executive Council

The Executive Council's task is to take all necessary measures, in consultation with ?the Secretary-General, for the implementation of its own decisions and ?recommendations of the Assembly and report thereon to the Assembly.? The Council meets at least twice a year.? ?The Council consists of Full Members elected by the Assembly in the proportion of ?one Member for every five Full Members, in accordance with the Rules of Procedure ?laid down by the Assembly with a view to achieving fair and equitable geographical ?distribution.? The term of office of Members elected to the Council is four years and elections for ?one-half of the Council membership are held every two years. Spain is a Permanent ?Member of the Executive Council.

Committees

World Committee on Tourism Ethics ?*Programme Committee ?*Committee on Budget and Finance ?*Committee on Market and Competitiveness

- Committee on Statistics and the Tourism Satellite account
- Sustainable Development of Tourism Committee
- Committee on Poverty Reduction
- Committee for the Review of Applications for Affiliate Membership

Secretariat

The Secretariat is led by Secretary-General ad interim Taleb Rifai of Jordan, who ?supervises about 110 full-time staff at UNWTO's Madrid Headquarters. He is assisted ?by the Deputy Secretary-General. These officials are responsible ?for implementing UNWTO's programme of work and serving the needs of Members. ?The Affiliate Members are supported by a full-time Executive Director at the ?Madrid Headquarters. The ?Secretariat also includes a regional support office for Asia-Pacific in Osaka, Japan, ?financed by the Japanese Government.

CANADIAN TOURISM COMMISSION

The Canadian Tourism Commission (CTC) was created in 1995 to promote Canadian tourism in order to capitalize on a major international industry. The CTC states that it "is dedicated to promoting the growth and profitability of the Canadian tourism industry by marketing Canada as a desirable travel destination and providing timely and accurate information to the Canadian tourism industry to assist in its decision making." The CTC is a public/private sector partnership.

The CTC states that it "recognizes that the greatest source of tourism knowledge and expertise rests with the tourism industry itself. Therefore, the CTC designs, delivers and funds marketing and research initiatives in partnership with provincial and regional tourism associations, government agencies, hoteliers, tour operators, airlines and attractions managers." The CTC markets Canada in the United States, Mexico, Japan, China, Australia, Germany, the United Kingdom, France and South Korea.

COMPAGNIA ITALIANA TURISMO

CIT, the Compagnia Italiana Turismo, was an Italian travel agency and tourism promotion quango, privatized in

1996. It was established by royal charter in 1927 as the Fascist tourist promotion agency, in contrast to the Liberal ENIT and the bourgeois Touring Club Italiano. Its first president was Ezio Maria Gray, an enthusiastic Fascist and corporatist. Its goal was to promote Italy as an international tourist destination and to support Italian foreign tourism. To do this, it created a network of travel agencies in Italy and worldwide. Its founding members were the Ferrovie dello Stato, the Banco di Sicilia, the Banco di Napoli, and ENIT (the Italian national tourist board).

CARIBBEAN TOURISM ORGANIZATION

The Caribbean Tourism Organization's main objective is the development of sustainable tourism for the economic and social benefit of Caribbean people. The CTO provides to and through its public and private sector members, the services and information to accomplish this goal. The CTO, with headquarters in Barbados, comprises 32 member countries, including English, French, Spanish and Dutch countries and territories, as well as private sector allied members. These include the Caribbean Hotel Association, companies, organizations and persons providing products and services to the Caribbean tourism industry. CTO's offices are located in the USA, UK, Canada and Barbados. CTO Chapters are located in France, Germany, Holland, across the U.S. and in the Caribbean.

CTO was established in 1989 with the merger of the Caribbean Tourism Association (founded in 1951) and the Caribbean Tourism Research and Development Center (founded in 1974). The body is primarily involved in the joint promotion and marketing of Caribbean tourist destinations in North America and Europe.

KOREA TOURISM ORGANIZATION

The Korea Tourism Organization (KTO) is a statutory organization of the Republic of Korea (South Korea) under the Ministry of Culture and Tourism and is commissioned to promote the country's tourism industry. The Korea Tourism Organization (KTO) was first established in 1962 as a government-invested corporation responsible for the Korean Tourism industry according to International Tourism Corporation Act. The organization primarily promotes Korea as a tourist destination to attract foreign tourists. Starting in the 1980s, domestic tourism promotion also became an important function of the KTO. Increased living standards , increased disposable income, and enhanced public transportation systems have contributed to increasing public tourism demand. By following current tourism trends, the KTO helps develop tourism in Korea. Inbound visitors totaled over 6 million in 2006 and the tourism industry is said to be one of the factors that has influences on Korean economy.

JAPAN TOURISM AGENCY

The Japan Tourism Agency, abbreviated JTA, is an organization which was set up on October 1, 2008 as an extra-ministerial bureau of the Ministry of Land, Infrastructure, Transport and Tourism. Japan Tourism Agency seated itself with intentions to stimulate local economies and to further international mutual understanding, following legislation of Basic Act on Promotion of Tourism Nation (in December 2006, to wholly revise Tourism Basic Act), committee resolutions in both Houses of the Diet in the legislation process, and decision at a Cabinet meeting of Basic Plan (in June 2007) which was drawn as provided by the Basic Act. One legal basis of the Agency is Act for Establishment of the Ministry of Land, Infrastructure, Transport and Tourism.

The two committee resolutions (of almost the same contents) are made by the Committee on Land and Transport of each House of the Diet, to point out eight issues on which the government should take appropriate measures when it enforces the Basic Act. In the issue No. 8 it was stated that the government should make efforts to set up tourism agency or so.

In the Basic Plan, five fundamental targets are set, whose substances are, respectively, to increase the number of

a. foreign tourists visiting Japan;
b. international meetings held in Japan;
c. nights for stay in accommodations per one Japanese during domestic sightseeing tours;
d. Japanese tourists to overseas;
e. expenditure in Japan on sightseeing tours.

All the five targets each have numerical value. Many among the total of 25 various targets each have some numerical value.

JAPAN NATIONAL TOURISM ORGANIZATION

The Japan National Tourism Organization or JNTO provides information about Japan to promote travel to and in the country. Its headquarters are in Yurakucho, Chiyoda, Tokyo. It operates Tourist Information Centers (TICs) as well as a website. The JNTO disseminates information about transportation, lodging, food and beverage, and sight-seeing. It distributes photographs of Japan suitable for computer wallpaper or printing for personal use.

JNTO is an Independent Administrative Institution of the government of Japan. Its publications and website assist in preparing travel itineraries within Japan, providing a wide range of travel information in English and other languages on transportation, accommodations, shopping and events. The materials are updated frequently.

While traveling in Japan, visitors may take advantage of the nationwide "i" Information System, which numbered 113 outlets in 2004. Each "i" center is an information source for the area it represents. The "i" centers are ordinarily located at railway stations or in city centers, and are easily recognized by their logo, a red question mark with the word "information" printed underneath.

JNTO sponsors a Goodwill Guide Program, through which some 47,000 bilingual volunteers assist visitors from abroad. They earn the right to wear the program's identifying badge, a white pigeon superimposed upon a globe. Throughout Japan, there are 77 Systematized Goodwill Guide groups (SGG) consisting mostly of students, housewives and retirees who engage in a variety of activities using their foreign language skills. Some groups offer a free preset walking tour, for which the visitor only needs to go to a pre-established place at a certain date and time, while others are available to meet tourists on request. There is no charge for the service of the Goodwill Guides, as they are volunteers, only their travel expenses and their admissions to tourist facilities, and for shared meals.

Services of professional guides and interpreters may be retained through the Japan Guide Association or the Japan Federation of Licensed Guides. A total of some 1,550 licensed guide-interpreters are registered with these organizations.

CROATIAN NATIONAL TOURIST BOARD

The Croatian National Tourist Board (CNTB) (Croatian: Hrvatska turisti?ka zajednica) is a national tourist organization founded with a view to promoting and creating the identity, and to enhance the reputation of, Croatian tourism. The mission also includes the planning and implementation of a common strategy and the conception of its promotion, proposal and the performance of promotional activities of mutual interest for all subjects in tourism in the country and abroad, as well as raising the overall quality of the whole range of tourist services on offer in the Republic of Croatia. It's office is located in the Empire State Building in New York City.

The European Institute of Cultural Routes

The European Institute of Cultural Routes (EICR) was established as a European public service and technical body as part of a political agreement between the Council of Europe and the Grand Duchy of Luxembourg (Ministry of Culture, Further Education and Research). Since 1988 the Institute has worked in close collaboration with the Council of Europe in carrying out its responsibilities, namely to ensure the continuity and development of the programme of the Cultural Routes in the 51 signatory countries of the European Cultural Convention and, depending on the geographical and historical requirements of the themes, in those countries which have had and continue to have close relations with Europe.

The EICR resides in the Centre Culturel de Rencontre - Abbaye de Neumünster, in Luxembourg. It retains all relevant documentation and maintains a specialist library on the routes. The Institute regularly welcomes those in charge of the networks of the routes as well as project managers, researchers, students and members of the general public. The EICR is also charged with participating in European training, research and analysis programmes concerning cultural tourism, for the European Commission and various governments and project managers. The Institute organises themed symposiums and specialist training, collaborates in the setting up and running of the Routes, and participates in specialist exhibitions while promoting a greater awareness of the links between culture, tourism and the environment.

From 2004 to 2006 the Institute managed the visibility and communication work of the European research programme PICTURE (Proactive management of the impact of cultural tourism on urban resources and economies).

In 2008 the European Commission (Directorate-General Education and Culture) named the EICR as a body active on a European level in the field of Culture, in recognition for its essential role in creating a coherent programme of sustainable cultural tourism initiatives promoting the "Destination Europe" and encouraging Europeans to discover their common roots and history through travel and the exploration of material and immaterial heritage.

The Institute is a member of NECSTOUR, an association of European regions working to develop competitive and sustainable tourism, and has signed an agreement with the Cité de la Culture et du Tourisme durable to provide distance-learning and to study the sustainability of introducing tourism to the cultural routes. The Institute is currently working with the Council of Europe and the Tourism Unit of the European Commission on a study into the impact of the cultural routes on small and medium businesses.

In 2011 the Institute should welcome a Partial Agreement aimed at combining the voluntary contributions of those member countries of the Council of Europe who wish to increase the funds available to the cultural routes.

Since the opening up of Europe to the East, the Cultural Routes have enabled, and continue to enable (particularly by expanding to include the Southern Caucasus), the creation of a real dialogue between Eastern and Western Europeans. The opening of a resource centre for the Cultural Routes in Sibiu, in the Casa Luxembourg, in liaison with the European Institute of Cultural Routes in Luxembourg and the Mioritics Association is testament to this.

EUROPEAN TRAVEL COMMISSION

The European Travel Commission (ETC) is the organization responsible for the promotion of Europe as a tourist destination. Its members are the national tourism organisations (NTOs) of thirty-eight European countries, including all EU member states, as well as Croatia, Georgia, Iceland, Monaco, Montenegro, Norway, San Marino, Serbia, Switzerland, Turkey and Ukraine. The national tourism organizations of all sovereign states in Europe are eligible for full membership of the European Travel Commission. Regional cross-border organizations and tourism-related bodies may join as associate members. The European Travel Commission is neither part of the European Commission nor an institution of the European Union.

History

ETC was established in 1948 in Norway. Between World War I and World War II, Europe became aware of the importance of tourism.

1925-The establishment of national tourism organizations rapidly led to the creation of the "International Union of Official Tourist Publicity Organizations": its first mission was the launch of a joint publicity campaign named "Europe Calling".

1947-This union became the International Union of Official Travel Organisations (IUOTO), which is today known as the World Tourism Organization, WTO.

1948-In its first General Assembly, the IUOTO adopted the principle of Regional Commissions: 19 European countries were represented and those countries decided to establish the first such Commission. Since its creation, ETC, has been a results-oriented organisation working closely with government agencies and all segments of the industry to achieve practical objectives. First priority was given to making governments aware of the importance of tourism in their national economies, which had been deeply disturbed by World War II. That is why ETC has always supported an international co-operation, a collective action and the building of a European solidarity.

Constitution

Henri Ingrand (France), the first chairman of the ETC had settled the basic principles for its operations. The second one, Arthur Haulot (Belgium) drafted in 1958, its official statutes in accordance with the Belgium law. When the Commission was transferred to Dublin in 1965 with Timothy O'Driscoll as chairman, these statutes remained the only "legal" constitution of the ETC. New statutes were drafted in 1987 when the headquarters were transferred to Paris under the chairmanship of Walter Leu (Switzerland). In 1996, when the ETC moved to Brussels a new version was adopted to the Belgian legislation under the chairman Walter Leu (Switzerland). Constitution was modified and adopted at the General Meeting n°66 following the 2002 law.

Membership

In 1948, the original membership of the European Travel Commission was 19 countries. At that time Eastern European countries, members of IUOTO were invited to participate. None of these countries accepted, apparently due to political reasons. Germany, Yugoslavia, Malta and Cyprus joined the Commission a few years later.

Mission

ETC sees itself as a virtual organisation marketing Europe as a tourist destination in global markets, primarily by means of the internet. The three principal focuses of the Commission's work are electronic marketing, market intelligence and operational excellence. ETC seeks to provide added value to members by encouraging exchange of information and management expertise and promoting awareness about the role played by national tourism organisations.

Organisation & Budget

The members elect a President, three Vice-Presidents, a Board of Directors, a Chairman of the Market Intelligence

Group and a Chairman of the Marketing & Technology Network for revolving two years terms.

ETC is entirely financed by Members' contributions, calculated according to a set of agreed criteria. Additional financial support for specific campaigns is raised overseas. Long-standing local industry support for ETC's activities is proof of its credibility in the field.

ETC is registered in Belgium as an 'association internationale sans but lucratif' (or aisbl) - a non-profit making international association.

Overseas

The representatives of the overseas offices of the European national tourism organisations operating in the various long-haul markets join together to form an ETC Operations Group and elect a Chairman. They decide on a programme of joint activities for the promotion of Europe for the year ahead, propose a budget, and seek local industry support.

In Europe

This programme is submitted for approval to ETC's Members in Europe, who meet twice a year (in Spring and Autumn) for a General Meeting.

Activities

ETC currently promotes and markets "Destination Europe" around the world through its operations groups in the United States, Canada, Asia (Japan) and Latin America (Brazil). ETC also plans to extend its activities to emerging markets such as China, India and Russia.

Vital to ETC activities are its Market Intelligence Group and Marketing & Technology Network. The Market Intelligence Group commissions and produces market intelligence studies, handbooks on methodologies and best practice, and facilitates the exchange of European tourism statistics on "TourMIS".

The Marketing & Technology Network provides information and expertise about the use of digital media by national tourism organisations, produces the "New Media Review", and organises an e-Business Academy once a year. The work of all operations groups is carried out by experts from member NTOs.

visiteurope.com is the official website of the European Travel Commission (ETC). ETC markets Europe as tourist destination on behalf of its 38 member countries. Under a pair of soaring wings, a symbol of travel and discovery deeply rooted in Europe's myths and history, visiteurope.com brings the excitement of a European vacation to potential guests around the world with localised versions in a number of major languages. The content of visiteurope.com is brought jointly by ETC and the 38 national tourism organisations.

GERMAN NATIONAL TOURIST BOARD

The German National Tourist Board (abbreviation: GNTB) is a national marketing organisation and has worked with the Federal Government of Germany to promote tourism in and to Germany. It represents Germany throughout the world as a destination for holidays, business travel and visits to friends and family.

The GNTB is a eingetragener Verein which was founded in 1948. The head office is situated in Frankfurt am Main, Germany. The marketing organisation is mainly financed by the German National Ministry of Economy & Technology.

Since 1999, the German National Tourist Board has also been responsible for the marketing of domestic tourism from one region to another. Its strategic goal is the responsible marketing of inter-regional Vacation Themes in Germany.

The GNTB works in close cooperation and economic partnership with all levels of the tourism industry in Germany.

HONG KONG TOURISM BOARD

The Hong Kong Tourism Board (HKTB) (Traditional Chinese:) is a Government-subvented body founded in 2001. The Board replaced the Hong Kong Tourist Association (HKTA) (Traditional Chinese) established in 1957. It has 15 branch offices and 5 representative offices around the world, and its primary mission is to maximise the social and economic contribution that tourism makes to the community of Hong Kong, and consolidate the city's position as a desired destination. In fulfilling this, it works with the Government, travel industry and other partners to market and promote Hong Kong worldwide, improve the range and quality of visitor facilities and tourism service standards, and enhance the experiences of visitors once they have arrived.

MAHARASHTRA TOURISM DEVELOPMENT CORPORATION

Maharashtra Tourism Development Corporation, commonly abbreviated as MTDC, is a body of the Government of Maharashtra responsible for development of tourism in the Indian state of Maharashtra. It has been established under the Companies Act, 1956, (fully owned by Govt. of Maharashtra) for systematic development of tourism on commercial lines, with an authorized share capital of Rs. 25 crore. Since Inception it been involved in the development and maintenance of the various tourist locations of Maharashtra. MTDC owns and maintains resorts at all key tourist centers and having more resorts is on the plan.

NORTHERN IRELAND TOURIST BOARD

The Northern Ireland Tourist Board (the N.I.T.B.) is an non-departmental public body of the Department of Enterprise Trade and Investment. Its primary objective is to promote Northern Ireland as a tourist destination. It provides a service to the public for information on tourist destinations within Northern Ireland, public transport, accommodation and the various tourist attractions throughout Northern Ireland. The board operates in close cooperation with equivalent agencies in the rest of the United Kingdom and Fáilte Ireland in the Republic of Ireland.

POSITIVELY CLEVELAND

Positively Cleveland (formerly the Convention and Visitors Bureau of Greater Cleveland, Inc. and originally the Convention Board of the Cleveland Chamber of Commerce) is the convention and visitor bureau for the Greater Cleveland area. It was incorporated as an independent organization in 1934 and adopted the Positively Cleveland name in 2007. Positively Cleveland is a non-profit organization that works to bring conventions and tourists to Cleveland, Ohio. Each year, 14.05 million convention and leisure visitors bring $4.53 billion into the local economy. That makes the convention and tourism business one of the largest industries in Cuyahoga County. Positively Cleveland's offices are located in the historic Higbee Building on downtown Cleveland's Public Square. A Visitor Information Center is also housed and operated in the building. The staff of Positively Cleveland is responsible for marketing the City of Cleveland and the Greater Cleveland region to vacation travelers, business travelers, meeting planners, and group travel planners. Additionally, the convention sales and services staff assists meeting planners with selecting meeting facilities, hotels for meeting attendees, unique venues and support services. Positively Cleveland is a member organization, promoting over 600 members from the hospitality industry, including restaurants, transportation, hotels, events, attractions and entertainment.

LIMPOPO TOURISM AND PARKS BOARD

Limpopo Tourism and Parks Board is a governmental organisation established in 2001 and responsible for maintaining wilderness areas and public nature reserves in Limpopo Province, South Africa.

RAJASTHAN TOURISM DEVELOPMENT CORPORATION

Rajasthan Tourism Development Corporation (RTDC) is an agency of Government of Rajasthan set up in 1978 to develop tourism in the state. It manages many restaurants, cafeterias, motels and bars. The Corporation also organises package tours, fairs, festivals, entertainment, shopping and transport services. In collboration with Indian railways it runs the luxury tourist train Palace on wheels. RTDC has hotels/motels at all majour tourist places in Rajasthan.

SEOUL TOURISM ORGANIZATION

The Seoul Tourism Organization (STO) is a public-private joint venture company primarily funded by the Seoul Metropolitan Government and is commissioned to promote the city's tourism and convention industries. The STO was established on February 4 2008 as a public-private invested corporation responsible for the Seoul tourism industry. The STO is focused on promoting and enhancing the attractiveness of Seoul as a destination for international visitors. The STO seeks to increase the numbers of foreign visitors through promotional campaigns backed by incentive programs to international conventions. Marketing efforts includes retail approaches for individual tourists such as their retail souvenir shop, location in Insadong, Jungno Gu and the Seoul Center for Culture and Tourism located in Myeongdong, Jung-gu Seoul. The main office and Jeodong Seoul Tourism Center are located in the Jung-gu district (near Myeongdong) in downtown Seoul.

Major Functions

1. International Marketing: The Seoul Tourism Organizations provides overseas marketing services, technical support for international conventions and incentives for investors in the tourism sector. The company is a central source for overseas tourist information concerning Seoul and develops and distributes merchandise linked to city promotions.
2. Development: In addition to helping plan new hotels, performance facilities, convention complexes and theme parks, the Seoul Tourism Organization advises on the development of the city's transportation, restaurant, and entertainment industries. The organization supports also tourism in fields that include medical treatment, cultural events and international sports.
3. Meetings, Incentives, Conventions and Exhibitions (MICE): Employing incentive programs to draw major international gatherings to Seoul, the Seoul Convention Bureau (SCB) under the STO, promotes a broad spectrum of activities, known as MICE businesses. In close cooperation with the Seoul Metropolitan Government, the Seoul Tourism Organization is a key player in the city's effort to become a destination of exceptional value for meeting planners from around the world.

SINGAPORE TOURISM BOARD

The Singapore Tourism Board is a statutory board under the Ministry of Trade and Industry of Singapore, tasked to promote the country's tourism industry. The board was first established in 1964 and was called the Singapore Tourist Promotion Board. In that year, there were 91,000 visitors. The primary task of STPB was to coordinate the efforts of hotels, airlines and travel agents to develop the fledging tourism industry of the country.

Later, STPB began to initiate new marketing ideas to promote Singapore's image aboard. The board created the Merlion, a symbol based on a Singapore mythical legend, that became an icon of the Singapore destination. The board also has been providing travel agent licensing and tourist guide training.

STPB actively promotes the development of infrastructure, including the building of hotels and tourist attractions such as the Jurong Bird Park and Sentosa which now becomes a popupar resort island for both tourists and local visitors. The board also market the city as a convention venue and organised events to attract visitors.

In the 1980s, several historic and cultural significant areas such as the Chinatown, Little India and Arab Street were earmarked for preservation. These places express Singapore's cultural diversity and became popular tourist destinations. The Singapore River underwent a major cleanup program and the areas along the river were developed for restaurants and other tourists amenities. The board was renamed as Singapore Tourism Board in 1997.

UNITED STATES TRAVEL AND TOURISM ADMINISTRATION

The United States Travel and Tourism Administration (USTTA) has been operating the country's official travel and tourism offices world wide. In 1996, the U.S. government decided that this country would no longer need such and closed all offices. Since, there are some Visit USA Committees in countries where many U.S. tourism companies have offices, but their focus is on the main markets represented by their member companies, a neutral marketing platform also promoting "off site" destinations is missing.

VIRTUALMALAYSIA

Virtualmalaysia.com is an official e-portal for the ministry of tourism malaysia. It features articles on background and lifestyle, tourism, and festivities in Malaysia. There is also a comprehensive directory of restaurants, businesses, hotels, and more in Malaysia. Endorsed as the Official e-Portal for the Ministry of Tourism Malaysia on October 2006, its establishment aims to rigorously promote the country as one of the premier destinations to be visited worldwide as well as extending the global industry players with a unique platform to network with the global market. VirtualMalaysia.Com develop Packages2Go, an e-platform for the travel agencies to convert them as potential clients. VirtualMalaysia.Com constantly enhances its e-initiatives by recently launching its e-hotel hub as a platform for hotels to reach the network and sell both B2B and B2C.

Awards-

APMITTA - Asia Pacific MSC, IT and Telecommunication Award (Best Content Development - Year 2000)

APICTA - Asia Pacific IT Award (Best Tourism Applications- Year 2001 and 2005)

Prime Minister Award (ICT Premiere Award - 2003)

TOURISM NEW ZEALAND

Tourism New Zealand is the national institution tasked with promoting New Zealand as a tourism destination internationally. It is the trading name of the New Zealand

Tourism Board, a Crown entity established under the New Zealand Tourism Board Act 1991. It is the marketing agency for New Zealand, while the New Zealand Ministry of Tourism is the government department tasked with policy and research.

New Zealand was the first country to dedicate a government department to tourism, when in 1901, the Department of Tourist and Health Resorts came into being. Through most of the 20th century, its role was tactical - it ran hotels and put together itineraries around New Zealand as well as advertising. After reorganisation and the selling off of assets in the late 1980s, the organisation, as Tourism New Zealand, now focuses on marketing of New Zealand.

Its main marketing tool is the award-winning "100% Pure New Zealand" campaign, which had its ten year anniversary in 2009. The campaign uses advertising, events, the internet and work with international trade and media to get the 100% Pure NZ message across to potential visitors.

To achieve the best efficiency, from limited resources, the campaign is mainly directed to travellers who will enjoy the New Zealand experience the most, who are most likely to "enjoy the authenticity of the New Zealand experience" and are willing to pay for quality experiences.

Recent activities (2007) have included a NZ$7 million campaign in China, concentrating on Shanghai, cooperating to produce a New Zealand tourism layer for Google Earth, the first country to receive such a treatment, and placing a Giant Rugby Ball venue in front of the Eiffel Tower in Paris. The Rugby Ball subsequently was sited in London and visited by the Queen.

Tourism New Zealand also took over YouTube homepage in 2007, to launch the latest iteration of its 100% Pure New Zealand campaign, featuring the theme of New Zealand being the 'Youngest Country' in the world - the last major habitable landmass to be discovered.

TELLURIDE TOURISM BOARD

Telluride Tourism Board is a community non-profit organization that is funded by the Town of Telluride, Mountain Village and San Miguel County in Colorado, USA. The Telluride Tourism Board is dedicated to providing visitors with the most up-to-date information and ensuring that vacations to the Telluride region are easy, efficient and enjoyable. The Telluride Tourism Board also oversees operation of the Telluride Visitor Center and Telluride Central Reservations.

This tourism hub's story first began with the Ute Indian's summer migrations to the area, followed by the silver mining boom in the late nineteenth century. Telluride Historic District is listed on the National Register of Historic Places and is one of Colorado's 20 National Historic Landmarks.

In the winter months, Telluride tourism revolves largely around skiing and snowboarding at Telluride Ski Resort, but the area boasts a wide range of other winter activities for locals and tourists alike, including ice climbing, ice skating, ice fishing, sledding, snowmobiling, nordic skiing and more.

When summer rolls around, most tourists flock to the region to enjoy one of the many outdoor festivals that pack Telluride's festival and event calendar. Telluride's signature summer events include the Telluride Film Festival, Telluride Bluegrass Festival and Mountainfilm in Telluride. Other summer activities involve mountain biking, camping, golfing, hiking and more.

IRVING CONVENTION AND VISITORS BUREAU

The Irving Convention and Visitors Bureau, also known as the ICVB, exists to direct individuals traveling to Dallas/ Fort Worth for business conventions and for leisure. It is a $1.5 Billion dollar a year hospitality industry which includes hundreds of restaurants and 75 hotels with more than 11,000 rooms. The Irving CVB is not a membership-based organization. Irving was founded in 1903 by J.O. Schulze and Otis Brown. After purchasing 80 acres (320,000 m2) of land which is now Irving, the first two town lots sold in December 1903 at the public auction. The Irving Convention and Visitors Bureau is an independent not-for-profit organization which is funded by: Irving's hotel/motel tax collections

Location

Irving CVB building is located immediately adjacent to Dallas/Fort Worth International Airport alongside Las Colinas. It is located in between Dallas and Fort Worth.

Awards

Gold Service Award from Meetings and Conventions Magazine

Awards of Excellence from Corporate & Incentive Travel Magazine

Successful Meetings' Pinnacle Award

CHICAGO CONVENTION AND TOURISM BUREAU

The Chicago Convention and Tourism Bureau, or CCTB, exists to promote Chicago to the global leisure travel and convention industries. The CCTB works in partnership with the Metropolitan Pier and Exposition Authority, the Chicago Office of Tourism, the City of Chicago, and the Illinois Department of Commerce and Economic Opportunity's Bureau of Tourism, as well as many other related associations in Chicago. It is the only entity selling McCormick Place and Navy Pier for conventions and trade shows. The CCTB was founded in 1970 with the merger of the Chicago Convention and Visitors Bureau and the Tourism Council of Greater Chicago. It was made the principal sales agent for McCormick place by the Metropolitan Fair and Exposition

Authority in 1980.

Funding

The CCTB is an independent not-for-profit organization, which receives its funding from several sources, including:

- A percentage of Chicago's hotel/motel tax
- Grant monies from the State of Illinois for development of local conventions and tourism
- Membership dues from local hospitality-related businesses
- Grant money from the MPEA

DESTINATION MARKETING ASSOCIATION INTERNATIONAL

Destination Marketing Association International (DMAI) is a professional organization representing destination marketing organizations and convention and visitor bureaus worldwide. As the world's largest resource for official destination marketing organizations (DMOs), Destination Marketing Association International represents over 1,500 professionals from 658+ destination marketing organizations in more than 25 countries. They provide members - professionals, industry partners, students and educators - with educational resources, networking opportunities and marketing benefits available worldwide. They maintain an online bookstore and resource center, an e-mail discussion lists for members, professional certificates and designations (PDM, CDME), an accreditation program and an official online travel portal: OfficialTravelGuide.com. DMAI also owns the Meeting Information Network (MINT), the meetings and convention database. Destination Marketing Association International (DMAI) is a professional organization representing destination marketing organizations and convention and visitor bureaus worldwide.

As the world's largest resource for official destination marketing organizations (DMOs), Destination Marketing Association International represents over 2,500 professionals from 650+ destination marketing organizations in more than 30 countries.

They provide members - professionals, industry partners, students and educators - with educational resources, networking opportunities and marketing benefits available worldwide. They maintain an online bookstore and resource center, an e-mail discussion lists for members, professional certificates and designations (PDM, CDME), an accreditation program and an official online travel portal: OfficialTravelGuide.com. DMAI also owns the empowerMINT.com, formerly called Meeting Information Network (MINT), the meetings and convention database.

DMAI's mission statement is To enhance the professionalism, effectiveness, and image of destination marketing organizations worldwide.

DMAI was founded in 1914 as the International Association of Convention Bureaus (IACB) to promote sound professional practices in the solicitation and servicing of meetings, conventions and tourism. In 1975, the association changed its name for the first time to become the International Association of Convention and Visitors Bureau (IACVB), to reflect the growing importance of consumer travel. In August of 2005, the association changed its name for the second time to become Destination Marketing Association International.

DESTINATION MARKETING ORGANIZATION

A destination marketing organization is an entity or company, which is promoting a tourist destination, in order to increase the amount of visitors to this destination. They promote the long-term development and marketing of a destination, focusing on convention sales, tourism marketing and services.

Australia

The Association of Australian Convention Bureaux (AACB) consists of 15 city and regional bureaux, dedicated to marketing their specific region as premier Business Events destinations to intrastate, interstate and international markets. The bureaux also recognise their responsibility to promote Australia as a whole.

Germany

The German Convention Bureau (GCB) represents the interests of the German tourism industry. The GCB markets Germany as a destination for conventions, meetings, events and incentives, both on a national and international level and is the place to contact for anybody planning an event in Germany.

Korea

Korea Tourism Organization (KTO) is a statutory organization of the Republic of Korea (South Korea), under the Ministry of Culture and Tourism and is commissioned to promote tourism in South Korea.

United States

DMO's are represented in the United States by convention and visitor bureaus (CVBs), which are paid by bed taxes or just from their members. Every U.S. state and almost every larger city and county has its own CVB.

Examples of United States DMOs:

- Baton Rouge Area Convention and Visitors Bureau(BRACVB)
- Panama City Beach Convention & Visitors Bureau(PCBCVB)

- Fairfax County, Virginia Convention & Visitors Corporation (Visit Fairfax)
- Loudoun Convention & Visitors Association(LCVA)
- Bradenton Area Convention & Visitors Bureau(BACVB)
- Minneapolis, Official Convention + Visitors Association
- River Parishes Tourist Commission
- Auburn-Opelika Tourism Bureau
- Tunica Convention & Visitors Bureau (TCVB)
- North Carolina Division of Tourism
- Ventura California Visitors & Convention Bureau
- Oakland Convention & Visitors Bureau
- Jersey Shore Convention & Visitors Bureau(JSCVB)

Puerto Rico

The Puerto Rico Convention Bureau (PRCB) is a non-profit organization that markets tourism in Puerto Rico, as a meetings and conventions destination.

Scandinavia

TravelG8 and Travelgate.net, Destination Marketing anno 1994, promotes all major countries looking for Scandinavian travellers. Scandinavia & Nordic countries (Sweden, Norway, Denmark, Finland and Iceland) is the third largest market in Europe.

CHAPTER-4

REGIONAL TOURISM INFRASTRUCTURE

Investment in infrastructure is viewed as the pump primer for floundering economies. While investment in roads, ports, airports and urban amenities have a cascading effect creating the virtuous cycle of stimulating demand, production, employment, consumption surplus and more demand, the impact is the quickest and most spread out through investment in tourism infrastructure.

Tourism involves activities of persons traveling to and staying in places outside their usual environment for leisure, business and other purposes. Tourism Infrastructure demands for goods and services, and the establishments which provide such services are considered as part of the tourism industry. Further, the Tourism Infrastructure also includes establishments whose products are mainly sold to visitors, though they do not form a major share of tourist consumption. Several infrastructure sectors like power,telecommunication, water supply, roads and some production sectors like travel items, sports equipment, photographic materials, medicines and cosmetics are included in this category along with Tourism Infrastructure.

The infrastructure for tourism thus includes basic infrastructure components like airports, railways, roads, waterways, electricity, water supply, drainage,sewerage, solid waste disposal systems and services. Moreover, facilities like accommodation, restaurants, recreational facilities and shopping facilities also comes under the ambit of Tourism Infrastructure. Planning for sustainable development of Tourism Infrastructure, therefore, involves the integrated development of basic infrastructure and amenities along with all the tourism facilities in a balanced manner.

Tourism is acknowledged as a 'high growth' industry globally with over 700 million tourist arrival internationally, the sector accounts for more than US $ 500 billion by way of receipt. Besides, the sector possesses immense income, employment and foreign exchange generation potential, thereby, providing a multiplier effect to the economy. The tourism industry is widely regarded as having the ability to generate high levels of economic output with relatively lesser levels of capital investment.

The potential and benefits of the tourism sector become more relevant especially for developing economies like India, where capital availability is scarce and need for economic and employment generation activity is high. With a mere 0.4% share of international tourist arrivals and a large volume of domestic travellers - mainly in the religion/ pilgrimage segment - the sector still accounts for 5.6% of GDP while providing direct employment to 20 million people. However, compared to global averages, the industry has not scaled up to its full potential. Geographical smaller countries have managed successfully to generate much higher levels of revenue from this industry . This is borne out by the fact that globally, the industry contributes approximately 11.6% to the GDP.

Delhi, the capital of India, has its origin from 1450 B.C. and has been in continuous existence for over a thousand years now. It is a site of many historic capital cities, traces of ten of which survive even today. The city is significant for the role it has played throughout history, having been the centre of an empire for the majority of this millennium. It is an important city in the Indian subcontinent and comparisons have often been made to other great cities of the world. However, very few cities carry with them, to such an extent, the weight of several layers of continuous history. In spite of this rich and diverse cultural heritage, Delhi is used only as a gateway for travelling to Jaipur, Agra and other cities of tourist interest. Though, Delhi has the highest number of tourist arrivals, it is only used as entry point to the country.

Delhi being National Capital Territory, receives 62% of foreign travellers and NRI visiting India. There has been no concerted effort to project Delhi as a Tourism Destination, with attractions to provide the visitors 2 - 3 night stays. There is an emergent need to make Delhi a historical city, a convention center, environmental and eco friendly destination and cultural destination and to spread awareness among tourists as well as its citizens regarding its glorious past. To achieve above goals, there is a need to develop the basic infrastructure, accessibility to the tourist destination, local facilities and identification of thrust areas of tourism promotion.

In order to boost the tourism activity in these UTs, OIDC has taken up many ambitious projects.

To unveil the creativity and to encourage the local artisans of Dadra & Nagar Haveli, we contributed a seed capital of Rs. 1 lakh for the promotion of local tribal artifacts and handicrafts. Diu has been declared as a special tourism area because of its beautiful beaches, churches, forts and cultural heritage.

Realising the potential of Diu as an up market tourism destination, we strived hard to contribute towards tourism infrastructure at Diu. Due to its strategic location and scenic beauty, we developed several tourist destinations in Diu. We leased out Pelican Resort at Jallandhar Beach and land for Indian Style Health Resort at Nagoa Beach to private entrepreneurs.

The schemes, which are to be taken up under the major head, "TOURISM INFRASTRUCTURE" are as under:

Water Sports Tourism Complex at Bhalswa

Delhi Tourism is in possession of Bhalswa Lake Over the past decade; Delhi Tourism has developed facilities for outdoor leisure by undertaking water sports and allied activities in the lake. Such recreational activities have added to the civic life of capital. Recreational-boating through pedal boats, hovercraft, water scooter, shikara and sports boats like kayaking, canoeing and rowing has already been introduced by the Corporation. In the recent past DTTDC has constructed an earthen bandh around the lake and fixed sluice gate between the lake and supplementary drain to maintain the water level in the lake. Indian Kayaking and Canoeing Association has given proposal to organize national and international level competition at this lake. At present the facilities for tourists/ visitors are very limited. DTTDC proposed to add some facilities like open shed, change room, water cooler for drinking water for visitors/ tourists .

Besides, the Government of NCT of Delhi has a plan to develop this area as an integrated tourist complex by creating infrastructure facilities like water sports, golf course, amusement rides and various other adventure activities. It is an ambitious project and could be developed as a centre-point for sports lovers from all over the world.

Establishment of Wayside Amenities

At present, the arrival of foreign tourists in Delhi is approximately 13 lacs annually with the growth rate of 5% p.a. With the introduction of modern techniques of dissemination of tourists information identification of new destinations, better marketing and services, it is contemplated that growth rate shall be progressively stepped up and by the year 2008, number of tourists visiting Delhi shall be approx. 25 lacs. In addition, domestic tourists shall be double within the next five years.

In the present scenario, no wayside amenities are available at the national highways around the city. The nearest wayside amenities provided by the adjoining states are at a distance of 40 km or more from the entry point of Delhi. The Corporation is in possession of land measuring 2.08 acres at Delhi-Jaipur Road, National Highway No. 8. The Corporation has a plan to provide these amenities to the tourists and commuters through developing this site into a unique project.

The concept/ design of the project has been finalized. The construction work of the project will start soon. However, the boundary wall, earth work and boring of two tube wells, have been done.

Development of Dilli Haat type projects in different parts of Delhi.

The Corporation has set up a Dilli Haat at INA, Sri Aurobindindo Marg, which is an upgraded version of traditional part offering a delightful amalgam of craft, food and cultural activities with a major difference-while the Village haat is a mobile, flexible arrangements, here it is the craftsmen who are mobile and ever changing there by offering ponaramic view of the richness and diversity of Indian handicrafts and artifacts. The project has already won heritage and cultural award i.e. PATA gold awards.

In view of its wide success and in pursuance of govt. policy of promoting and preserving our immense heritage of human skills, the Corporation has decided to set up more Haats in the Capital. The Corporation is in the process of identifying the sites for the purpose. The DDA has been approached by DTTDC for identification of suitable sites to set up these projects.

One site measuring 7.2 acres at Pitampura near TV Tower has been allotted to DTTDC for this purpose.

Restoration of Denotified Monuments

Delhi, being a city of monuments consisting historical importance, rich heritage and religious tradition and culture, attracts a large flow of tourists towards it. There is a series of denotified monuments that have remained neglected, unknown and unvisited due to absence of proper maintenance, hygienic conditions, publicity and better accessibility. Since 1996, Delhi Tourism has undertaken the restoration of such denotified monuments through INTACH. A study has been conducted by INTACH in the area and identified over 80 monuments. The Corporation has restored 34 denotified monuments in Mehrauli area and the work at 4 more monuments is in full swing.

Refurbishment of Monuments

Delhi being a city of monuments has rich cultural heritage and its glorious past. There is an emergent need to make aware the tourists visiting capital territory about these buildings/ monuments through wide publicity, more accessibility and providing infrastructure facilities like drinking water, public conveniences, food kiosks, telephone facilities, souvenir shop, tourists information counter, path ways, land scrapping, hark system etc.

Signage at monuments and other historical places for identification and awareness of tourists.

There is lack of information and awareness amongst the tourists and residents of Delhi for the cities with historic past. There are a large number of monuments in the Maurauli heritage area and other parts of the city that has tremendous historical significance but unveiled. In order to provide more detailed information on the rich architecture of the buildings, their historic importance and other aspects, DTTDC proposes installation of signage aesthetically designed at these monuments. Department of tourism, Government of India has sanctioned a scheme for installation of signage at monuments/ historical buildings in Delhi.

Accessibility to destination through trail etc.

Integrated conservation and landscape development of Mehrauli is a project that attempts to consolidate the scattered ruins of the settlement into a comprehensive scheme to preserve the monuments and potential archaeological sites and provide the city populace with a meaningful, multifaceted recreation space following the image of an ideal 'City Forest'. The management of the natural and historic environment being the prime objectives, the proposal aims at developing a series of pathways for access and maintenance, suitably treated to uphold historic authenticity and serving to heighten the perception of the complex natural setting for an enhanced interpretation of the site. With the stretch around the Jamali Kamali being the present focus and scope of the project, the process once initiated would go for a long way to reintegrate the historic area through positive intervention with the socio-cultural and economic processes of the city so as to make it an active part of the system, imparting it a new relevance within the contemporary scenario.

Illumination of Monuments

Many tourists are visiting Delhi from India and abroad. There is much to see during daytime but hardly any thing for the evenings. To enhance the beauty of Delhi during evenings proposed to illuminate the ancient monuments, which are visible from the roads while driving.

Development of Lakes

In spite of having more than 30 big ancient lakes, Delhi does not offer sufficient outdoor leisure facilities for tourists and its residents, as most of the lakes have been disappeared due to change in use of land and non-retention of water. Delhi, acrossing range of Aravali hills, particularly in Mehrauli area of South Delhi had underground water level at 50 feet. Now, the water level has drastically gone down to

200 feet deep, which is not only disastrous from agricultural point of view but also for tourism potential. Water bodies with recreational facilities provide ample attraction to the tourists. These facilities have added to the civic life of capital. For the purpose, infrastructure for various types of amusement could also be developed on the embankment of the lakes. There is an emergent need for development, preservation and maintenance of existing water bodies to beautify the city and to keep it at par with the other major cities of the world and to cater to the widening demands.

Recently Delhi Tourism has taken over the possession of Sanjay Lake at Mayur Vihar and Shahdara Lake for recreational water sports activities through Boats, water scooter, Jetty, Shikara, bungee jumping, etc. the Hovercraft facilities at Sanjay Lake & Bhalaswa Lake are also being considered and battery operated eco-friendly boats at Nazafgarh drain at Chhawla and Kanganheri .

Setting up of soft adventure park with Bungee Tower at Sanjay Lake - Trans Yamuna Area

Sanjay lake is one of the biggest lake of Delhi and is abound 2.5 k.m. long. The lake is mainly rain fed. leisure boating activities at Sanjay Lake are available since September 2004. There is a huge scope for setting up of soft adventure park at Sanjay lake consisting of obstacle courses, spider web, tarzan rope, Burma bridge, trampoline, zapping. The area has scope for construction of high bungee tower made of concrete structure. It is also proposed to construct a restaurant at the top of Bungee tower. This Bungee tower will also support an artificial rock climbing wall.

Soft Adventure Park at Purana Quila

Purana Quila is situated at main Mehrauli Road and is surrounded by important land marks of Delhi like Delhi Zoo and Trade Fair ground. Leisure boating activity at Purana Quila and is also provided and it is proposed to develop soft adventure park in the land around Purana Quila .

Development of Coffee Homes in Different Parts of Delhi

Coffee Homes at Connaught Place, Laxmi Nagar, R.K. Puram and Ajmal Khan Park were set up to provide clean hygenic wholesome food to Delhi ties/visitors at reasonable rates.These coffee homes have become very popular and propose to extend these facilities in other parts of the city.

Installation of Sport Climbing Wall

Delhi, being an urban city, the government has more emphasis to spread awareness through education in all spheres of life like social economical political, technical, to educate every citizen of the city. Besides, tourism and its various streams like Adventure Tourism has become an important activity to promote tourism potential, revenue generation, and employment generation among the youth of Delhi. To promote the adventure activities, DTTDC intends to install four Rock Climbing

Walls atleast in four corners to the city to facilitate the students and youth during 10th five-year plan. Recently, DTTDC has set up an artificial (Fibre) Rock Climbing Wall at Azad Hind Gram. It has been observed that small school children a slightly scared to climb the Fibre Rock Climbing Wall. It is proposed to put up two inflated Rock Climbing Wall at Azad Hind Gram specially for small children. These walls can also be carried out for demonstration to various schools of Delhi.

Setting up of Night Bazaar

The life at National Capital Territory has become more and more busier day by day. The Delhites have no time of amusement, entertainment and to cater the daily needs as per demand of progressive living standard. Moreover, the tourists visiting the city stay two or three nights in Delhi as they use this city only as an entry point to the country by them. To facilities these visitors, DTTDC intends to set up

Night Bazaar in Delhi to keep Delhi at par with the world's most popular cities.

Delhi Tourism proposes to organize Night Bazaar on the corridors of the State Emporiums commencing from Gram Ship Emporium up to Phulkaari Emporium at Baba Kharak Singh Marg. Bazaar is proposed to be organzed on weekends instead of weekdays. The timing of the Bazaar will be from 8.00 P.M. to 04.00 A.M. The objective for holding Bazaar is to showcase the rich art, culture and heritage of India and to provide quality leisure time to the tourists (foreign as well as domestic) and Delhities along with the shopping experience. It has been proposed to have stalls of easily dismantable items such as, Octonorm exhibition panels or fabric walls. Stalls shall display Handloom and Handicraft items, souvenir, Boutiques, books on culture and heritage of India etc. Toys, traditional/ ethnic jewellery, Indian food especially from Walled City, Puppet show, Magic show, classical music and dance performances and performance of folklore of India etc.

Consultancy of Tourism Projects Tourism Research and Development

Many agencies are involved in promoting tourism in city through its various roles. The thrust areas of tourism potential are identified for establishment of tourism projects. Due to lack ness at various corners, these projects have not attained success at requisite level. Therefore, the proficiency and technical expertise are required while identifying the thrust areas and conducting techno-feasibility study of the tourism projects.

It Application

The potential of Information Technology for promotion of the tourism is only limited by the imagination. The world is in the midst of an Information and Technological revolution and the opportunities for the Government are enormous. it is not enough to simply automate their current ways of doing business. With the new tools of a networked society, Delhi Tourism is rethinking and engineering its IT infrastructure. By taking full advantage of the information revolution, we can both provide better services to the tourists and use our unique position to promote competition and innovation-thus improving the quality of services for the tourists. Delhi Tourism may like to produce more information material on the electronic media such as interactive, theme based and Virtual walkthrough based CDs. Besides Delhi Tourism may like to extend and expand the computer networks by way of new technology and software systems. The frontiers of Internet are to be explored further for better information dissemination and facilitation.

Chhawla & Kanganheri Project

The Corporation identified two sites measuring 2.77 and 11.44 acres at Chhawla and Kanganheri on Najafgarh Drain respectively for setting up of Adventure Sports Complex and Eco Park with leisure facilities. Memorandum of Understanding is being finalised with Irrigation and Flood Department to transfer the land to DTTDC. The preparation of concept/design of the project is under process and soon after the approval of GNCTD. the project may go ahead with the preliminary work like Development of site and other services i.e. construction of boundary wall, earth work, levelling and dressing of site etc.

Adventure Park at Azad Hind Gram

DTTDC owns around six acres of land on National Highway No. 10 at Tikri Kalan on Rohtak Road before Bahadurgarh Border. DTTDC has already set up a museum and smark on Netaji Subhash Chandra Bose at Azad Hind Gram. Public convenience, snack bar, restaurant, banquet facilities are already in existence in this complex.The process of setting up an artificial rock climbing wall is already completed. In the remaining portion of this complex, DTTDC plans to set up a permanent adventure park where tourist would be given courses in soft and hard adventure. The tourist will also be provided with night stay after completion of their soft and hard adventure games.

TRAVEL AND TOURISM COMPETITIVENESS

Tourism competitiveness is an important economic indicator. It is a major element in economic stimulation packages. Tourism is among the largest employers in most countries and also a fast-lane vehicle into the workforce for young people and women. Encouraging travel boosts consumer and business confidence, it strengthens two-way trade and promotes export income.

"Managing in a Time of Turbulence" is an apt reflection of the many difficulties the international travel and tourism industry faces. A combination of a commercial downturn brought about by the global financial crisis, the rise in price of fuel and natural occurrences such as the Icelandic Ash Cloud have combined to heap pressure onto the industry.

All these pressures must be overcome to ensure strong sectoral growth in the future. The current situation is captured by the topics covered in the analytical chapters, exploring issues such as the impact of oil prices on the tourism industry and the importance of price competitiveness for attracting tourists.

Switzerland, Austria and Germany have the most attractive environments for developing the travel and tourism industry, according to the third annual Travel & Tourism Competitiveness Report. France, Canada, Spain, Sweden, the United States, Australia and Singapore complete the top ten.

"Our study aims to measure the factors that make it attractive to develop the travel and tourism industry of individual countries. The top rankings of Switzerland,

Austria, Germany, France and Canada demonstrate the importance of supportive business and regulatory frameworks, coupled with world-class transport and tourism infrastructure, and a focus on nurturing human and natural resources for fostering an environment that is attractive for developing the travel and tourism sector," said Jennifer Blanke, Senior Economist of the World Economic Forum's Global Competitiveness Network.

This cross-country analysis of the drivers of competitiveness in travel and tourism provides useful comparative information to make business decisions and to add value to governments wishing to improve their travel and tourism environments.

The rankings are based on the Travel & Tourism Competitiveness Index (TTCI) covering 133 countries around the world. The TTCI uses a combination of data from publicly available sources, international travel and tourism institutions and experts, as well as the results of the Executive Opinion Survey, a comprehensive annual survey conducted by the World Economic Forum, together with its network of Partner Institutes (leading research institutes and business organizations) in the countries covered by the report. The survey provides unique data on many qualitative institutional and business environment issues.

"For the past four years, the World Economic Forum has engaged key industry and thought leaders through its Aviation, Travel & Tourism Industry Partnership Programme to carry out an in-depth analysis of the travel & tourism (T&T) competitiveness of economies around the world. The goal is to construct a platform for multistakeholder dialogue to ensure the development of strong and sustainable national travel and tourism industries capable of contributing effectively to international economic development," noted Klaus Schwab, Founder and Executive Chairman of the World Economic Forum.

CHAPTER-5

REGIONAL TOURIST ATTRACTIONS

ALBEMARLE CHARLOTTESVILLE HISTORICAL SOCIETY

The Albemarle Charlottesville Historical Society nurtures and promotes awareness and appreciation of local history by encouraging the identification, collection, study, and preservation of the materials of history; by striving for excellence and quality in research and interpretation of collections and local history; and by disseminating knowledge through educational activities, so that the past may shed light on the present and the future.

Activities toward which the efforts of the Albemarle Charlottesville Historical Society are directed include but are not limited to:

- Encouraging the collection and preservation of manuscript and printed materials and other physical remains pertaining to the history of Charlottesville and Albemarle County;
- Promoting historical programs, lectures, exhibitions, and other educational activities;
- Facilitating writing and reporting upon local history in its relation to the local community, the Commonwealth of Virginia, the Nation, and foreign countries; and
- Exhibiting such material in its own or other museums or elsewhere and maintaining and operating a library and museum for housing and displaying historic materials.

History

Founded in 1940, the Albemarle Charlottesville Historical Society (Society) is a private, non-profit educational organization (IRS 501 (c) 3) that seeks to study, preserve, and promote the history of Charlottesville and Albemarle County, Virginia. The Society is a membership organization, open to all, and receives no continuing operating support from federal, state or local governments but rather relies on membership fees, gifts and donations, and grants from private foundations.

The Society's research library, administered by a librarian on the staff of the Jefferson-Madison Regional Library, contains over 2,000 books and bound periodicals, as well as manuscripts, maps, pamphlets, newspapers, and vertical files relating to the history of our community. Additionally, the archival collection contains over 1,500 artifacts of historical significance to Charlottesville and Albemarle County in addition to over 60,000 photographic images.

The Society is located in downtown Charlottesville in the historic McIntire Building. Designed in the Beaux Arts style by architect Walter Dabney Blair, the McIntire Buidling was completed in 1921 and donated by local civic benefactor Paul Goodloe McIntire to the City of Charlottesville as the city's first municipal library. Following an extensive renovation by the Society of this city-owned building in 1993 and the Society moved into it in January 1994.

BLENHEIM VINEYARDS

Established in 2000 by owner Dave Matthews, Blenheim Vineyards is a family-operated winery located 20 minutes southeast of Charlottesville. With two vineyard sites growing five European varietals, the goal at Blenheim Vineyards is to make high quality wines that reflect the climate, soil, and beauty of the surrounding piedmont landscape.

CENTRAL VIRGINIA CIVIL WAR

On to Richmond" was the battle cry of Northern politicians, military leaders and newspapermen as the war began. A quick, powerful thrust would cast aside Southern resistance, topple the Confederate capital and end the war. So went the promise.

Maps made it look easy. Only 100 miles or so separated the two warring capitals. But maps don't show the quality of the resistance. Maps don't show the ineptness and genius of leaders.

The most direct road to Richmond was straight south. Northern armies under Gens. McDowell, Burnside, Hooker and Meade tried that road and found it blocked, most times by determined Confederates under Robert E. Lee. Finally, in the spring of 1864, U.S. Grant took command and drove relentlessly south. His soldiers marched into Richmond nearly a year later.

The countryside west of the Tidewater and east of the Blue Ridge Mountains between Washington and Petersburg is the most bloodsoaked in the country. Thousands died fighting at places no one had heard of before, places like Cold Harbor, Chancellorsville, Malvern Hill, Spotsylvania, Brandy Station and the North Anna River. More fell during encounters at places that had no name.

Their earthen fortifications, memorials to their deeds, and their graves still mark the landscape.

VIRGINIA'S VALLEY & MOUNTAINS

Bordered on the west by the Allegheny range and the east by the Blue Ridge Mountains, the Shenandoah Valley dramatically combines beautiful landscapes with extraordinary Civil War history.

The Valley is described often as an avenue of invasion directed to the head of the Federal government at

Washington D.C. More importantly, it was a vital (and vulnerable) granary for the Confederacy and a worrisome flank for both sides during operations around Richmond.

In 1862, the great Stonewall Jackson played the Valley's terrain like a fine-tuned instrument when his "foot cavalry" embarrassed three Federal armies sent against him. Jackson's efforts pinned down troops that might have joined Gen. George McClellan's drive against Richmond.

Confederate control over the Valley eroded in the spring, then evaporated in the fall of 1864. After deep Federal forays at New Market and Lynchburg were repulsed, Union Gen. Philip Sheridan took over and, after hard fighting at Cedar Creek, pushed Gen. Jubal Early's Confederates out of effective contention.

Although it's possible to follow day-by-day the various Valley campaigns, the trip plan would look like a corkscrew and would plow the same ground several times. A more logical plan is to start at one end of the Valley and work your way to the other.

Key to that idea is U.S. Route 11, which generally follows the path of the old Valley Pike. This will take you "up" the Valley - north to south. You also may want to explore two other corridors full of scenic beauty as well as interpreted Civil War sites. Tours are outlined here along Route 250 and Route 340.

TIDEWATER VIRGINIA CIVIL WAR SITES

The Tidewater area of Virginia is defined by tidal rivers - primarily the James, York and Potomac - that flow from the Chesapeake Bay into the interior of the state. These rivers made the Confederate heartland, including Richmond, vulnerable to attack by water or water-supported land assault.

Most of the Civil War sites in this area are related to the 1862 Peninsula Campaign, which was an attempt by a Union army under Gen. George McClellan to march to Richmond using the "Peninsula" created by the York and James Rivers.

A visitor center at Lee Hall Mansion in Newport News helps explain the Peninsula Campaign. A Virginia Civil War Trails map/brochure is available there and at most visitor centers in Tidewater.

Northern Virginia

When Virginia seceded, the Federal government in Washington D.C. found itself virtually surrounded by a hostile foreign country. Abraham Lincoln moved swiftly to occupy a comfort zone around his capital.

Farther away from Washington, however, Union control was less certain. Confederate John Singleton Mosby was a feared raider of Union patrols and supply lines. Citizen loyalties were almost always in question.

Today, many of the forts built by Union engineers during the war still exist in parks. The bloody battlefields at Manassas have been preserved in a National Park, which is an oasis in a rapidly growing area of development. Farther west, the countryside remains much the same as Mosby might have found it.

Firsyt Colony Winery

Firsyt Colony Winery is nestled in beautiful Albemarle County, the heart of Virginia Wine Country. Owner Randolph McElroy, Jr. has created a truly spectacular winery by producing exceptional wines in the classic European style. Old world traditions abound at First Colony with a French winemaker, whose focus is on producing world class wines.

OPEN DAILY FOR TASTINGS-Monday-Friday 10am-6pm, Saturday and Sunday 11am-6pm

Frontier Culture Museum

The Frontier Culture Museum tells the story of the thousands of people who migrated to colonial America, and of the life they created here for themselves and their descendents. These first pioneers came to America during the 1600s and 1700s from communities in the hinterlands of England, Germany, Ireland, and West Africa. Many were farmers and rural craftsmen set in motion by changing conditions in their homelands, and drawn to the American colonies by opportunities for a better life. Others came as unwilling captives to work on farms and plantations. Regardless of how they arrived, all became Americans, and all contributed to the success of the colonies, and of the United States.

To tell the story of these early immigrants and their American descendents, the Museum has moved or reproduced examples of traditional rural buildings from England, Germany, Ireland, West Africa, and America. The Museum engages the public at these exhibits with a combination of interpretive signage and living history demonstrations. The outdoor exhibits are located in two separate areas: the Old World and America. The Old World exhibits show rural life and culture in four homelands of early migrants to the American colonies. The American exhibits show the life these colonists and their descendents created in the colonial backcountry, how this life changed over more than a century, and how life in the United States today is shaped by its frontier past.

HISTORIC GARDEN WEEK IN VIRGINIA

Welcome to Historic Garden Week in Virginia's 78th anniversary season. This spring, visitors will step through the gates of more than 250 of Virginia's most beautiful gardens, homes and historic landmarks during "America's Largest Open House," April 16-23, 2011. Three dozen Historic

Garden Week tours present a rich mosaic of some of the country's finest properties at the peak of Virginia's springtime color. Sponsored by The Garden Club of Virginia, local events are scheduled from the Atlantic Ocean to the Allegheny Mountains and will span the centuries from the early 17th through the early 21st.

For those interested in horticulture, there will be formal gardens, walled gardens, cottage gardens, cutting gardens, annual and perennial gardens, herb gardens, water gardens, and even secret gardens. Visitors interested in architecture and interior decorating will see beautifully renovated historic properties as well as stunning contemporary residences, exceptional artwork, and some of the country's best collections of glass, china, and American, European and Asian antiques. Many houses have interesting family histories intertwined with the Revolutionary War, the Civil War and the Victorian era.

Historic Garden Week is the oldest and largest statewide house and garden tour event in the nation. Sponsored by The Garden Club of Virginia, tours benefit the restoration of important historic grounds and gardens throughout the state. Each event offers an engaging variety of five to six local houses and gardens, most open to the public for the first time for Garden Week.

A number of historic James River plantations will have special openings during Garden Week. Tuckahoe Plantation, a boyhood home of Thomas Jefferson with exquisite gardens, will be open. The National Park Service's National Register of Historic Places in partnership with the James River Plantations of Charles City County, Virginia, the Virginia Department of Historic Resources and the National Conference of State Historic Preservation Officers, invite you to explore the James River Plantations. Information about other plantations will be outlined in the Historic Garden Week in Virginia guidebook.

Information about overnight accommodations can be obtained by calling the Virginia Tourism Corporation 1-800-VISITVA for a free "Virginia is for Lovers" travel guide and state highway map.

The Hatton Ferry

Hatton Ferry is located outside of Scottsville and runs from Saturday 9-5 and Sunday Noon- 5 from mid-April through mid-October. Call the Albemarle Charlottesville Historical Society (434-296-1492) or check out the Hatton Ferry on Facebook to make sure the ferry is in service.

The Hatton Ferry is the last pole operated ferry in America. America moved west on these ferries and it is only fitting that the last one is still working on America's River, the birth place of the first permanent English settlement, Jamestown on the James River. The ferry has crossed the river for over 140 years. It has carried farm products, the mail and vehicles both horse drawn and motorized from Buckingham County to Albemarle County and back. This is living history worth saving for future generations.

The Hatton Ferry is a non-profit organization that relies on donations to save this piece of American history. We urge you to help us with this worthy cause. Any assistance you can give us will be greatly appericated.

Standing on the banks of the James River at Hatton Ferry next to the flat-bottomed ferry anchored at the river's edge, you get the sense that the sounds of the rapids and the expansive view upstream haven't changed much over time. The fact is, 200 years ago more than a thousand poled ferries carried people across rivers throughout this country, but today the Hatton Ferry is the very last.

Hatton Ferry's history begins in September of 1870 when Buckingham County authorities issued a court order to maintain a public ferry across the James River to the Albemarle lands of Thomas P. Gantt, an Albemarle distiller, near Totier Creek. Three years later in December 1873, Gantt sold 18 ¾ acres of river front property to James A. Brown (1835-1896), who built a general store there. With the land purchase came the ferry rights established by Buckingham County. Brown, however, ran into trouble with the land owners on the Buckingham side of the river when they informed him and their county board of supervisors that they did not want ferry traffic across their property. Although Brown sought legal help, the Buckingham land owners continued to protest. In January 1874, Brown and Gantt were asked by Buckingham County to show cause why the ferry should not be discontinued. The County then ordered ferry service to cease.

Unable to turn that opposition around, Brown moved his store and ferry upstream to its current location which was also near Lock 24 of the James River and Kanawha Canal. The site became known generally as Brown's, Brown's Store, or Brown's Landing.

Over the ensuing years, Brown's became a thriving transportation hub on the James River. In 1881, Richmond and Allegheny Railroad established a train stop there. In July 1883, Albemarle County authorized a public road to be built from Brown's Landing to an established county highway. A few months later, a post office began operating from Brown's Store. However, the post office's arrival necessitated a new name because there was already a Brown's Post Office operating in northwestern Albemarle County. The name chosen was Hatton. By the late 1890's, Brown's ferry, too, was more commonly referred to as the 'ferry at Hatton' or Hatton Ferry.

Each Hatton business thrived because of the totality of services provided at this location: timber and farm produce were ferried across the river and loaded onto freight trains at Hatton; at the store, ferry customers picked up mail and merchandise shipped into Hatton via train; and the ferry itself provided a vital transportation link between Buckingham and Albemarle Counties.

When Brown died in 1896, Hatton operations were continued by Brown's daughter, Cora, and her husband, Edwin Raine. In 1906, James Benson Tindall, Sr., of Buckingham County rented Brown's Store and renamed it J.B. Tindall's Groceries. He enlisted Eugene Layne, an old Buckingham friend, as his business partner. On September 7, 1914, Tindall purchased from Cora Brown the store, the landing on both sides of the river, and all ferry boats, lines, and oars; the store, and about five acres of land surrounding the store and land. Jim's brother, Lewis Tindall, became his new partner in 1916 when Eugene Layne returned to Buckingham farm life. Tindall Sr. managed it until his death in 1945. The Tindall's in latter years lived on the hill above the store. The Tindall family managed Hatton Ferry operations until 1940 when James B. Tindall, Jr. deeded the ferry to the State of Virginia.

By 1970, the cost of operating and maintaining Hatton Ferry exceeded its revenue, and there was much talk of discontinuing service by Albemarle and Buckingham, who shared the Hatton costs equally. In 1972, Hurricane Agnes destroyed the ferry and almost ended service. An interested public led by James B. Tindall, Jr., Bernard Chamberlain of the Albemarle County Historical Society, Peter Way of Albemarle County Board of Supervisors, and other Albemarle citizens persuaded authorities to continue this historic ferry. A new ferry was built by the Virginia Department of Transportation, and it was rededicated in September 1973, with the assistance of Richard Thomas, star of the TV series, "The Walton's."

By the mid 80's, VDOT was again contemplating the discontinue of service, but once again Hatton Ferry was saved thanks to efforts of the Albemarle Charlottesville Historical Society who persuaded Albemarle County to allocate funding to operate the ferry, thus allowing VDOT to return it to service. So until 2009, VDOT, Albemarle County, and the Historical Society all supported various functions of the ferry operation.

The Historical Society took on the aspects of promoting it and renovated the ferryman's hut. It was redesigned it to return it to its original appearance and added a historical kiosk. Now it s a place for visitors to view history as well as a place for the ferrymen to store life jackets and other things needed to run the ferry.

In 2010, ownership of America's last poled ferry was transferred to "Hatton Ferry", a non-profit corporation established by the Albemarle Charlottesville Historical Society to operate the ferry. Now a group of interested citizens from both Albemarle and Buckingham Counties are working together to continue the long tradition of ferry service across America's River - the James River.

Interesting Tidbits-In the ferry's early years, wagons, buggies, horses, cattle, sheep, farm equipment, lumber, and farm produce were carried across the river. Ferrymen operating Hatton Ferry have included Joe Napier, Bolling Bryant, Monroe Napier, Luther Randolph, Harvey Briddle, Raymond Hackett, Ned Hocker and Ashley Pillar.

On March 9, 1918, the General Assembly authorized the construction of a bridge at Hatton.

The former Brown-Tindall Store was built on a strong foundation comprised of large stones that Brown took from the James River and Kanawha Canal lock #24 about one-half mile away. Rail service ceased in 1950. The Hatton Post Office closed on February 28, 1975.

James Madison Museum

The James Madison Museum houses exhibits on James and Dolley Madison, featuring one of the nation's most outstanding collections of Madisonia. The focal point of the Madison Room is Madison's favorite chair, a campeche chair given to him by his good friend, President Thomas Jefferson. Also on display are a number of Madison's personal items, papers and furnishings.

Thomas Jefferson called James Madison "the best farmer in the world" and to pay respect to Madison the farmer, the Museum's Hall of Transportation & Agriculture displays an interesting collection of antique farm tools. Also featured are a 1924 Model T Ford, 1922 Velie, and the Arjalon Price House, a 1733 "patent" or "cube" house. The house is partially reconstructed so that visitors will be able to see first-hand the building practices of the day.

The museum also features a small gift shop where items related to James Madison, Virginia Agriculture, and Orange County may be purchased.

The structure where the museum now resides was originally built in 1928 as the Powell Nash car dealership. Adjacent to, and now owned by the museum, is the former Hill Top Restaurant (which in the early century served as a gas station).

Mission-The mission of the James Madison Museum is to serve the community by: Collecting and preserving the artifacts and cultural heritage of 18th, 19th, and 20th century rural Virginia; and promoting an awareness and appreciation of the lives and achievements of James Madison and others who made a unique contribution to the region.

The Sporting Life

During earlier times, hunting, fishing, and trapping were necessities of life and means of survival for both the indigenous peoples and the settlers who came to this new world. Over the years, agriculture was established, providing food and other products used in daily life. Individuals were no longer dependent on their prowess in securing food and other necessities from the wild. Hunting, fishing, and (to some extent) trapping evolved into recreational activities enjoyed by many.

This exhibit includes items from both the past and present times. There are arrowheads and early handmade fishing and trapping implements. There are samples of the guns used for various types of hunting. They range in time from the early 19th century percussion cap musket to the much more recent Sears and Roebuck Shotgun. The importance of the hunting dog is illustrated in the various prints and paintings as well as the books on dog training. Varieties of fishing equipment include a collection of beautifully hand-tied flies. And a part of the taxidermy collection of John Johnson gives a wonderful feeling of the wild in which all these activities occur. Objects on display are from the Museum collection and from local collections. The exhibit continues until July 1, 2007.

The Madison Room-The Madison Room features the personal belongings of James and Dolley Madison, including furniture, correspondence, clothing, books, and other period artifacts. The focal point of the exhibit is Madison's favorite chair-a Campeche chair given to him by his good friend, President Thomas Jefferson.

Hall of Transportation and Agriculture-To honor Madison the farmer, the museum's Hall of Transportation & Agriculture displays an impressive collection of antique farm tools. And, to provide a record of local culture, the hall displays a partially reconstructed 1733 "cube" house and examples of evolving modes of transportation including an original 1924 Model T Ford and a rare 1922 Velie.

The Hall's main exhibit is titled: Planting a Legacy. Farming in Orange County. The goal of the exhibit is to present the local impact James Madison had on farming communities while providing objective views of the culture for you to explore.

Special Exhibits-The museum also presents special exhibits changing quarterly, with an emphasis on Madison's Orange County (which once stretched to the Mississippi and included seven states). Focus of Exhibits include: area history, popular culture, and historical collections. Pictured: Musical instruments from the exhibit "People of the Blue Ridge".

Visitor Information

Hours: The museum is open Monday through Saturday from 10:00 a.m. to 4:00 p.m. and Sundays 1:00 p.m. to 4:00 p.m. all year. The Museum is closed New Year's Day, Easter, Thanksgiving and Christmas.

Rates: Admission to the museum is $5 for adults; $3 for senior citizens over 60 and AAA members; and $1 for children ages 6 to 16. There is no admission fee for museum members, Orange County school children, and children under 6.

Once again the James Madison Museum is participating in the Time Travelers program for students. For more information on this wonderful program visit their website. All Time Traveler students will be eligible for a 50 cent admission price to the museum.

Group Tours: Tours are self guided and available for groups of all ages at special rates. Please call the Museum at (540) 672-1776 weekdays between 9 a.m. and 5 p.m. for additional information.

Directions: The James Madison Museum is located at 129 Caroline Street, in the town of Orange, Virginia.

James River Reeling and Rafting

Come float the historic James River with the Premier Outfitter and create dreams you will always remember and share with family and friends. Relax on the bank of the James River while our professional staff readies your equipment for your pleasure. Have the time of your life spending that relaxing day on the wild and scenic James River that courses through the wooded foothills of the Blue Ridge Mountains. Bring your fishing tackle along for the best small mouth bass fishing on the east coast or simply unwind with a packed cooler for that picnic and let the James River take you away. As the tall, woodland banks slip past, look for the Deer, Blue Herons, Ospreys and Bald Eagles.

We are pleased to offer self-guided float trips for kids and adults of all ages, from the beginner to the more adventurous. Class I, II, and III Rapids available. Family owned and operated by Kevin and Geneva Denby for the past 19 years, we have something for everyone here on the James River in Scottsville. Gift Certificates are available and make the perfect gift for that hard-to-shop-for adventurer in your life!

Tourism in Budapest

Budapest became one of Central Europe's most popular tourist attractions in the 1990s. Attractions in the city include Buda Castle which houses several museums including the Hungarian National Gallery, the Matthias Church, the Parliament Building and the City Park. The city has many museums, three opera houses, and thermal baths. Buda Castle, the Danube River embankments and the whole of Andrássy Avenue have been recognized as an UNESCO World Heritage Site.

Hungary has an estimated 1,300 thermal springs, a third of which are used at spas across the country. Hungary's thermal waters and spa culture are promoted to tourists. Only France, Japan, Iceland, and Italy have similar thermal water capacity. Hungary's thermal baths have been used for 2,000 years for cleansing, relaxation and easing aches and pains. The Romans were the first to use Hungary's thermal waters in the first century, when they built baths on the banks of the Danube River. Budapest lies on a geological fault that separates the Buda hills from plains. More than 30,000 cubic metres of warm to scalding (21° to 76°C) mineral water gushes from 118 thermal springs and supply the city's thermal baths. Budapest has been a popular spa destination since Roman times. Some of the baths in the city date from Turkish times while others are modern. They have steam rooms that utilize the healing properties of the springs. Most of the baths offer medical treatments, massages, and pedicures. The most famous of Budapest's spas were built at the turn of the 19th century.

There are two hundred known caves under Budapest, some of which can be visited by tourists and are a popular tourist attraction. In the Buda hills there are caves that are unique for having been formed by thermal waters rising up from below, rather than by rainwater. The Pálvölgy Stalactite Cave is a large and spectacular labyrinth. Discovered in the 1900s, it is the largest of the cave systems in the Buda hills. The Szemlohegy Cave has no stalactites and has fewer convoluted and claustrophobic passages than the Pálvölgy Cave. The walls in this cave are encrusted with precipitates formed by warm water dissolving mineral salts. The air in the cave is very clean and its lowest level is used as a respiratory sanatorium. The Matyas Cave in the outskirts of the city has a crawling-room-only section called the "sandwich of death."

Regional Tourism

Lake Balaton in western Hungary is the largest freshwater lake in Central Europe. It is the second most important tourist destination in Hungary. 2.5 million tourists visited the lake in 1994. Hungary's other tourist attractions include spas, excellent facilities for activity holidays, and cultural attractions such as the villages of the Great Hungarian Plain and the art treasures found in Budapest. Hungary has more than 400 camping grounds. There are more than 2,500 km of dedicated bicycle lanes in the country.

Fishing is popular in Hungary and almost half of the country's 130,000 hectares of rivers and lakes are used by anglers. The country has excellent opportunities for birdwatching, and horse riding and hunting are also popular.

TOURISM IN ALBANIA

Tourism in Albania, although still underdeveloped, has seen an impressive increase in recent years. Official data showed that 2,089,538 tourists had entered Albania from abroad during the first six months of 2008, which was a 23 percent increase compared to the same period of the previous year. Lonely Planet recently listed Albania 1st on its top 10 list of countries to visit for 2011.

Citizens of the following countries do not require visas to enter: Andorra, Argentina, Australia, Austria, Belgium, Brazil, Bulgaria, Canada, Chili, Croatia, Cyprus, Czech Republic, Denmark, Estonia, Finland, France, Germany, Great Britain, Greece, The Netherlands, Holly See, Hungary, Ireland, Iceland, Israel, Italy, Japan, Kosovo, Latvia, Liechtenstein, Lithuania, Luxemburg, Macedonia, Malaysia, Malta, Monaco, Montenegro, New Zealand, Norway, Poland, Portugal, Romania, Russia, San Marino, Serbia, Singapore, Slovakia, Slovenia, South Korea, Spain, Sweden, Switzerland, Turkey, United States of America, and Ukraine.

Albania has been visited sporadically by important figures including Lord Byron, Edith Durham and others through history. However, during the communist regime tourism was not allowed to be established. Groups of Western tourists were first permitted to visit in the 1980s. Since the fall of communism, visiting restrictions have been greatly eased.

Some of the most visited cities include:

- Berat, the town of a thousand and one windows
- Durrës, the old port city of Dyrrhachium

- Gjirokastër, the city of stone
- Krujë, the balcony over the Adriatic sea
- Tirana, the capital
- Vlorë, beach city of Vlora (the city of olives and grapes)
- Lezha, the historic diplomatic capital of Albania
- Pogradec, the poet's city
- Sarandë, the honeymooners' city
- Shkodër, the city that is home, among other, to the Rozafa castle

Some increasingly popular natural features include:

- Albanian Riviera, the coastal area along the Ionian Sea encompassing some of the above cities
- Albanian Alps, part of the Prokletije range in extreme northern Albania

Albania has been dubbed the "New Mediterranean Love".

UNESCO World Heritage Sites

Albania is home to three World Heritage Sites:

- Butrint, an ancient Greek and Roman city
- Gjirokastër, a well-preserved Ottoman medieval town, together with Berat, the 'town of a thousand and one windows'

Issues Affecting Tourism

Some of the problems holding back foreign tourism include illegal construction which is ruining some popular areas. Its proximity to Kosovo on the northeast border means that unexploded ordnance may be a hazard for unguided tours into the countryside of that border region. At present the security situation in Albania is much improved however.

Poor infrastructure greatly limits tourism. Electrical power outages are still common. Independent bus and minibus (furgon) operators provide inexpensive transport between most large communities, but schedules and prices are not fixed. Train service is also limited and sporadic.

In 2006, the Albanian government imposed a moratorium on motor-powered sailing boats on all lakes, rivers, and seas of Albania to curb organized crime. The only exemption to the rule are government owned boats, foreign owned boats, fishing boats, and jet boats. In 2010, the moratorium was extended for 3 more years, until 2013.

Beggers are a problem in every large city, and Albania is no exception. Often using their children as persistent panhandlers, parents will sit on sidewalks and in crowded squares nagging passersby for money.

Despite the above problems, Albania is making progress. Foreign tourists are not uncommon. International hotel chains are established in Tirana and organised day trips are available from Corfu to Sarandë and nearby Butrint. Club Med has proposed a development between Vlorë and Sarandë.

South of Durrës, there is a long, uncoordinated beach development popular with Albanians. There are other, off-the-track beach areas, locally popular, with acceptable food and facilities.

TOURISM IN AUSTRIA

Tourism forms an important part of Austria's economy, accounting for almost 9% of the Austrian gross domestic product. As of 2007, the total number of tourist overnight stays is roughly the same for summer and winter season, with peaks in February and July/August.

In 2007, Austria ranked 9th worldwide in international tourism receipts, with 18.9 billion US$. In international tourist arrivals, Austria ranked 12th with 20.8 million tourists.

Vienna attracts a major part of tourists, both in summer and winter. Salzburg receives about a fifth of tourist overnight stays compared to Vienna, which ranks it 2nd in the summer season. In the winter season, a number of winter sport resorts in western Austria overtake Salzburg in the number of tourist overnight stays: Sölden, Saalbach-Hinterglemm, Ischgl, Sankt Anton am Arlberg, and Obertauern.

Visits to Austria mostly include trips to Vienna with its Cathedral, its "Heurigen" (wine pubs) and romantic Waltz music events. Worth a visit are Salzburg, birthplace of Mozart, Innsbruck, capital of Tyrol surrounded by the Alps, and the Danube valley with its vineyards, for example the Wachau or Dunkelsteinerwald, which are between Melk and Krems. In the western part of the country the province Vorarlberg reaches the Lake Constance, in the eastern part Neusiedler See. The three most visited landmarks in Austria are Schönbrunn Palace (2.590.000 visitors per year), Tiergarten Schönbrunn (2.453.987 visitors) and Mariazell Basilica (1.500.000 visitors).

Of great touristic importance are the Austrian skiing, hiking and mountaineering resorts in the Alps as well as family-friendly recreation areas (e.g. the Witches's Water in Tyrol). The same applies to the numerous Austrian lakes (e.g. Wolfgangsee and other lakes in the Salzkammergut east of Salzburg or Wörthersee in Carinthia).

For visitors interested in Media Art, there is the Ars Electronica Center in Linz. Since 1979 this center has organized the Ars Electronica Festival and presented the Prix Ars Electronica, the worldwide highest-ranked prize for media art.

Tourism in Serbia

Serbia stretches across two geographic and cultural regions of Europe: Central Europe (the Pannonian plain), and Southeastern Europe (the Balkan peninsula). This boundary splits Serbia roughly in a ratio of 1:3 alongside the Danube and Sava rivers. The northern parts of the republic are Central-European lowlands while the southern and central parts are mostly mountainous. There are more than 15 mountain peaks rising to over 2,000 metres above sea level. The navigable rivers are the Danube, Sava and Tisa. A moderate continental climate predominates, with a more Mediterranean climate in the south.

The variety of scenery and cultural and historical monuments, curative spas, hunting grounds and fishing areas give the basis for Serbia's tourism. International roads and railway lines link Western/Central Europe with Greece, Turkey, the Near East, Asia and Africa. The main air transport routes between West and East and North and South cross this country, too.

The Serbian lands were the crossroads of various civilizations in the past, with different spiritual, architectural, artistic and cultural influences. Serbian culture and its historical heritage is diverse because of mixture of various influences. Numerous prehistoric and classical monuments represent some unique examples of the changing times (Vinca culture, Starcevo culture, Lepenski Vir, etc.) Serbia is a land of natural, historic, cultural and ethnic contrasts. The northern lowlands (the province of Vojvodina) form the Central European part of the country. The Fruška Gora hills are the only mountains in that part of Central Europe. Central Serbia is characterised by fields, hedges, orchards and meadows. Southern Serbia has bigger mountain ranges with wide river valleys and hollows. The altitude of some of the mountains is over 2,500 m, the highest peak being in Kosovo province--Djeravica, 2,656 m above sea level. However, Kosovo's status is disputed; the government of Serbia refuses to recognise the territory's independence.

Eastern Serbia is covered with mountains which belong to the Carpathian mountains but also to the Balkan mountain system. Here, the Danube river cuts the Kazan, the longest and narrowest part of the Djerdap Gorge. Western Serbia is another mountainous region, with many picturesque canyons, forests and great natural and climatic advantages. Waters in Serbia-rivers, lakes, artificial lakes and mineral springs, represent an important natural resource for tourism. The Danube, the largest and the most important waterway in Europe flows through Serbia, covering some 591 km inside its borders. The river Sava was formerly the largest national river in Yugoslavia, connecting Slovenia, Croatia, Bosnia and Herzegovina and Serbia in length of about 900 km; the river's mouth is located north of Ljubljana and the river's end is in Belgrade, where it flows into the Danube by an ancient fortress of Kalemegdan.

Flora and fauna are especially attractive. Throughout Serbia there are numerous animal species and game stock, which is a very favourable precondition for the hunting tourism. Many tourist resorts have sprung up with accommodation facilities, ideal for rest and recreation, situated in this diverse combination of natural and human mightiness. As a tourist area, Serbia has a very long tradition. For more than 150 years, guests have been coming to Serbian spas--Palic and Vrnjacka Banja being the best-known among tourists. The current receptive basis of tourism and catering industry consists of 125,000 beds in basic and supplementary accommodation facilities. There are nearly 40,000 hotel beds in various classes.

Belgrade, the capital of modern Serbia, is situated at the confluence of the Sava and the Danube. In the course of its long history it has been captured 60 times, and razed to the ground at least 38 times; however every time it got leveled to the ground the city had arisen from its ashes, like a phoenix- which is a legend connected to the city. Today, it is a modern city of about 2 million inhabitants. To visitors Belgrade offers its rich programme of cultural, artistic and sports events, many museums, cultural and historic monuments. With the Sava Congress Centre and numerous hotels, Belgrade has become one of the major congress and convention centres in Europe.

The convention facilities offer the other large towns: Novi Sad (the "Serbian Athens"), Priština, Niš, Subotica, Kragujevac, Leskovac, Kruševac, Uzice, Valjevo, Vršac, Sombor, Pristina Sremska Mitrovica as well as the mountain centres: Kopaonik, Tara, Zlatibor, Divcibare, Brezovica, and the spas: Vrnjacka Banja, Niska Banja, Bukovicka Banja, Soko Banja and many others tourists resorts.

TOURISM IN MOLDOVA

Moldova attracts tourists from neighbouring countries and all the world. From January 2007, Moldova established a visa-free regime for the US, Canada, Japan, Switzerland, and EU countries, which should facilitate more trips by foreign tourists. Hotels in Moldova also charge high prices, while the quality of service on average is quite low.

Moldova is well-known for its rich traditions in wine making. Wine tours are offered to tourists in Chi?in?u and other towns across the country. Vineyards/cellars include Cricova, Purcari, Ciumai, Romanesti, Coju?na, Milestii Mici and others.

TOURISM IN FRANCE

France attracted 78.95 million foreign tourists in 2010, making it the most popular tourist destination in the world. France offers mountain ranges, coastlines such as in Brittany or along the Mediterranean Sea, cities with a rich cultural heritage, châteaux (castles) like Versailles, and vineyards. Tourism is accountable for 6% of the country's income (4% from French tourists travelling inside France and 2% from foreign tourists), and contributes significantly to the balance of payments.

Paris, the capital city, is the most visited city in the world. Paris attracts tourists with museums such as the Louvre and Musée d'Orsay, and attractions like the Eiffel Tower, Arc de Triomphe, the cathedral of Notre-Dame, and Disneyland Paris.

In the eastern parts of France there are skiing resorts in the Alps. Notable French cities are Avignon with the Popes' palace, Arles, Aix-en-Provence, Bordeaux, Lyon, Marseille, Nice, Saint-Benoît-du-Sault on the Loire River, Toulouse on the Garonne, Strasbourg on the border with Germany, and the beautiful city of Nantes.

All over France rental accommodations and hotels are available. For example, the English like to spend their summers in the Dordogne valley, the Spanish vacation in Biarritz and St Jean de Luz on the Basque coast, and the Irish often visit Lourdes. Tourists also travel to see the annual cycle race, the Tour de France.

France's Mediterranean beaches on the French Riviera, in Languedoc-Roussillon, or in Corsica, are famous. Away from the mainland tourists are French Polynesia (especially Tahiti), the Caribbean islands Martinique, Guadeloupe and others.

CHAPTER-6

EASTERN REGIONAL TOURISM

The Eastern Region of Ghana is home to one of the friendliest and excessively polite people in the country. Split into unequal halves by the vast Volta Lake and one of its tributaries, the Afram River, the region conjures up lots of fantasy in the minds of many a Ghanaian: cute ladies, aka, Koforidua Flowers.

But the Eastern Region sandwiched between five of the remaining nine regions of the country, a feat comparable to only the Brong Ahafo region is more than just charming ladies.

Squeezed in the lower abdomen of the country, the region is a rich blend of dramatic landscape, historic relics and traditional cultures. Indeed, the ancient impressively blends with the 21st century in this region so close to but with such a striking contrast with Accra.

The huge Volta Lake dominates the Eastern region sandwiched between the Ashanti, Brong Ahafo, Central, Greater Accra and Volta regions.

Two of the monuments Ghana's first President, Osagyefo Dr. Kwame Nkrumah built on assumption of office after independence are here. These are the Akosombo Dam, the largest supplier of electricity to the country and the Senchi Bridge.

The Dam is built on a gorge created by the River Volta in the region at Akosombo town. The famous Senchi Bridge at Atimpoku links the rest of the country to the Volta Region in the middle.

The Akwapim Ridge, the Krobo Mountains, the Kwahu scarp, and the rolling hills overlook striking landscapes of gently flowing rivers and untouched forest and fauna.

The Eastern Region famous for its large areas of lush tropical forest, cascading falls and endangered birds and insects species is home to the biggest tree in the entire West African sub-region.

The region has more than its fair share of the unique history Ghana is international acclaimed for. Slave market, colourful festivals, waterfalls, research institutions, shrines and virgin forests.

If there is anything that has so revolutionalised the Ghanaian economy in the last two centuries, then it is cocoa. The first cocoa seed ever planted in the Gold Coast now Ghana was buried at Mampong in the Eastern region. The home of Tetteh Quarshie who brought the cocoa seed from Fernando Po remains an attraction to many visitors.

There are remarkable traces of the 17th and 18th century slave market at Abonse an important town crossroads on the Slave Route.

Eastern Region contains Ghana's only commercial diamonds mine at Akwatia. Despite loosing some brightness following the general economic mess, the diamond industry remains an important part of the region's economy.

The region, one of the smallest but heavily populated has four of the ten major traditional authorities and some of the glamorous festivals in the country. These are the New Juabenhene, Okyehehe, Okwapehene and the Akwamuhene.

Some of the festivals are Akantukese of the people of New Juaben, Odwira by the Akwapims and the Akyems.

Traditional and historic villages and towns are part of the richness of the region. Rituals surrounding the initiation of young girls into the adulthood called Dipo is an important part of the people in the region particularly the Krobos. Many have talked against the ritual during which the luscious flesh of young girls are exposed. Only a tiny piece of cloth and beads cover their womanhood.

Despite public outcry against the ritual Dipo continues to attract lots of people from all parts of the country and foreign tourists.

But any cruise to the region of many rivers, cascading falls, unspoiled forest and raw wealth cannot be complete without a visit to Aburi Gardens.

Open in 1890, Aburi Botanical Gardens is home to many endangered plant species in the world. It is an important research garden for many scientist and budding scientists. Its unique architectural design is breathtaking. You find something fresh and beautiful each time you set foot the well-manicured tropical gardens.

UPPER EAST REGION TOURISM

The Upper East Region is the smallest of 10 administrative regions in Ghana, occupying a total land surface of 8,842 square kilometers or 2.7 per cent of the total land area of Ghana. In terms of population, it is the ninth most populated region with a population of 920,089 in 2000, accounting for 4.9 per cent of Ghana's total population. The regional capital is Bolgatanga, sometimes referred to as Bolga. Other major cities are Bawku and Navrongo.

Location and Size

The Upper East region is located in the north-eastern corner of Ghana and bordered by Burkina Faso to the north and Togo to the east. It lies between longitude 00 and 10 West, and latitudes 100 30"N and 110N. The region shares boundaries with Burkina Faso to the north, Togo to the east,

Upper West Region to the west, and the Northern Region to the south. The region is divided into 9 districts, each headed by a district chief executive.

Tourism

Parks

Paga crocodile pond

Gbelle game reserve

Sombo Bat Sanctuary

Jafiiri Sacred Royal Python Sanctuary

Recreation Areas

Tongo rocks

Historic Sites

Naa Gbewaa's shrine

Navrongo's mud-built church

Festivals

The region plays host to many festivals throughout the year, most of which are either to bring a good planting season or celebrate the harvest.

Gologo Festival

Fao Festival

Paragbiele Festival

Willa Festival

Zumbenti Festival

Kobina Festival

Kakube Festival

Other Tourist Attractions

Bolga market

Demographics

Population

The center of population of the Upper East Region is located in its capital city of Bolgatanga. According to the 2000 census, the region had a population of 920, 089 making it the ninth most populous region.

The population is primarily rural (84.3%) and scattered in dispersed settlements. There are generally no distinct boundaries between communities as compounds in contiguous villages over lap. The rural population in 1984 was 87.1 percent. There was, thus, a 2.8 percentage point reduction in the rural share of the population between 1984 and 2000 .

With only 15.7 per cent of the population living in urban areas, the region is the least urbanized in the country. In fact, together with Upper West, they are the two regions with a less than 20 per cent urban population.

Ghanaians by birth or parenthood constitute 92.5 per cent of the population of the region. Naturalized Ghanaians constitute 5.3 per cent and the rest are non-Ghanaians. The main ethnic groups in the region are the Nabdam (30.5%), Kusasi (22.6%), Nankani & Kassena (15.7%), Builsa (7.6%), Busanga (6%) and Mamprusi (1.8%) .

Religion

The religious affiliations of the people of the Upper East region are:

- Traditional - 46.4%
- Islam - 22.6%
- Christian - 28.3%

Transportation

Three National highways - N2, N10, and N11 - and a few Regional highways such as the R113, R114, R116 and R181, serve the region.

The N10 originates from Yemoransa in the Central Region and connects through Kumasi in the Ashanti Region and terminates at Paga in the Upper East Region. The national capital of [[Accra] is also connected to the region by the N2 which terminates in Kulungugu in the Upper East Region. Both these national routes are connected by the N11 which links the regional capital of Bolgatanga to Bimpiela, also in the region.

REGIONAL TOURISM IN AUTRALIA

Tourism Victoria

Tourism Victoria is a vibrant and dynamic State Government statutory authority actively marketing Victoria as a premier tourism destination both domestically and internationally.

Mission Statement

Together with Victoria's tourism industry, Tourism Victoria is working to maximise employment and the long-term economy of tourism to Victoria by developing and marketing the State as a competitive tourism destination.

The Tourism Victoria Board, comprising 10 experienced private sector representatives, provides the strategic direction for Tourism Victoria based on four broad goals:

* Marketing: Increase visitor numbers, length of stay and visitor expenditure by implementing innovative and effective marketing strategies to position Victoria as a distinct and competitive tourist destination.
* Leadership: Take a leadership role in the tourism industry, encourage professional standards and the development of cooperative arrangements which maximise industry effectiveness.
* Infrastructure: Improve the tourism assets of Victoria by identifying infrastructure opportunities and facilitating development projects.

* Management: Maximise the effective use of resources by conducting the business of Tourism Victoria in accordance with professional commercial management principles.

Australian Federation of Travel Agents

To be truly representative of the travel agents of Australia.

To enhance the professionalism and profitability of its members through effective representation in industry and government affairs, education and training, and by identifying and satisfying the needs of the travelling public.

To promote travel and domestic tourism.

AFTA encourages all members to embrace the AFTA Code of Ethics as shown below, in the interests of good business practice, however, it is acknowledged that this is not legally binding or enforceable by law.

ATEC Australian Tourism Export Council

ATEC is the peak industry body representing Australia's $26 billion tourism export sector. Our mission is to build better business relationships for our members and to represent the inbound tourism industry before government and business leaders.

We are the largest membership-based organisation representing Australia's tourism export sector. Our 1100+ members come from across the country and across the industry - including inbound tour operators, tourism product suppliers and service providers. The members of our ATEC family have one major thing in common - a commitment to growing Australia's international tourism market.

Backpackers Operators Association NSW

BOA NSW is the industry association for professionals and businesses in the backpacker sector of the tourism industry.

We are a not-for-profit organisation, directed by a membership elected executive committee. Committee members come from all sector of the industry, which ensures broad representation.

Our members are accepted into one of the three membership categories: Hostel Business (sub-divided according to number of beds), Other Backpacker Businesses (sub-divided according to number of employees) and Associate/Non-Voting (for industry suppliers and other stakeholders). All members are required to comply with the Code of Conduct and Objects and Rules.

Bed & Breakfast and Farmstay Association of NSW & ACT Australia

Accommodation seekers can fast track their way to high quality accommodation alternatives in NSW, Australia with the Bed and Breakfast Directory web site. A free copy of the Bed and Breakfast Guide print publication - Australian B&Bs throughout Sydney, NSW regions and Canberra ACT is also available.

Business Events Sydney

Business Events Sydney (BESydney) is the official organisation responsible for promoting Sydney and New South Wales (NSW) as an international business meeting and conference destination.

Bus NSW

It was on January 12, 1942 that bus operator Roy Corrigan was provided with a desk in what was then the premises of Reo Motors in William Street, Sydney and he was handed a list of 50 names of people to be contacted. His brief was to get the newly formed NSW Omnibus Proprietors' Association up and running. He had just been appointed Association Secretary. Six years previously, Roy had established a service car and taxi operation between Berowra and Berowra Waters; he later acquired the Hornsby-Galston-Arcadia bus service.

For the ten years prior to that January day in 1942 the interests of private bus operators had been catered for by the Feeder Bus Owner's Association. But membership had begun to decline due to the difficulties being experienced by operators as World War 11 tightened its grip. It was decided to revitalize the association, change its name from the Feeder Bus Owners Association to the NSW Omnibus Proprietors' Association and expand its membership throughout the State. The State was to be divided into districts, with branches at Newcastle, Gosford, Katoomba and Wollongong. Metropolitan branches were to be established at Parramatta, Liverpool, Hurstville and North Sydney. Later other branches were to be formed at Lismore, Grafton, Broken Hill, Wagga Wagga, Cowra and Nowra. Brian LeQuesne was elected president, and Roy Corrigan was chosen to look after the administrative side.

Hotel Motel and Accommodation Association of Australia

The Hotel Motel & Accommodation Association is the peak body for the Australian accommodation industry. It is a specialist organisation working for employers in the accommodation industry.

HMAA represents a range of accommodation establishments including 5 Star Hotels, Resorts, Motels, Motor Inns, Bed & Breakfasts, Boarding Houses, Backpackers and Time Share Establishments in metropolitan and regional Australia adding up to a membership base of over1500 properties and some 60,000 guest rooms. HMAA offers a range of services and opportunities which will assist accommodation properties and corporate businesses in their day-to-day activities.

The Association was formed to represent the interests of registered accommodation operators within the Tourism and

Hospitality Industry and is registered as an Industrial Organisation of Employers.

Tourism Queensland

Tourism is one of Queensland's key sectors, directly employing almost 119,000 people or 5.7 per cent of all persons employed. The sector directly contributes $8.8 billion to the Queensland economy and accounts for 4.5 per cent of Queensland's Gross State Product.

Tourism is the state's second largest export earner, generating around $4.0 billion annually. As one of the key drivers of Queensland's economy, the relative importance of the industry will continue to grow into the foreseeable future.

The benefits of tourism are enjoyed across the state. The industry is made up of thousands of small businesses and is an important contributor in regional areas. A range of government agencies support the industry's needs.

South Australia Tourism

The South Australian Tourism Commission (SATC) is committed to growing the State's tourism industry. Tourism is big business in South Australia, creating work for South Australians and offering strong prospects for long-term growth. The industry contributes to the State's economic activity, generating jobs and export dollars by attracting interstate and international tourists. It also enhances the State's cultural attributes and offers sustainable development for the environment.

Tourism NT

Tourism NT markets and influences the development of the Northern Territory as a competitive and compelling travel destination for the continuing benefit of all Territorians.

Tourism NT works with three main partners and stakeholders to achieve these outcomes:

1. Tourism industry partners who work with Tourism NT to market the destination interstate and overseas
2. The travel industry that provides the necessary coordination for working with wholesalers, retail agents and airlines to facilitate the distribution of Territory travel products
3. Tourism NT provides the Northern Territory Government, through the Minister for Tourism, with policy and service delivery advice

Australian Travel and Tourism Network

Australia Travel & Tourism Guide for Australia. For accommodation, hotels in australia, travel insurance, travel agents, tours, last minute travel, reservations, places to go, attractions, sightseeing, tours, hotel specials, road maps, car hire, transport, discount travel vouchers, travel tips and more

Sydney and Regional NSW

Tourism NSW - Official tourism site for Sydney and New South Wales accommodation, attractions, tours and events.New South Wales lies on the east coast of Australia, between Queensland and Victoria. Sydney is Australia's premier gateway, the State capital and Australia's largest city, and is easily reached by frequent flights from Asia, Europe, North America and Oceania. NSW is also well serviced by a network of regional airlines, trains, buses and coach services.

Sunshine Coast

Miles of pristine coastline and lush hinterland, superb cuisine, action and adventure or just the perfect piece of sand on which to sit and ponder? The Sunshine Coast is one of Queensland's premier holiday destinations.

Tourism Wollongong

Tourism Wollongong represents product in the Local Government Area of Wollongong in New South Wales, Australia. Bordering the southern suburbs of Sydney and stretching south along the coast, the city is showcased to the east by the Pacific Ocean, with the magnificent Illawarra Escarpment as a picturesque backdrop.

Tourism Department

The Strategy will assist the Government in achieving its overarching policy goal, which is to maximise the net economic benefit of the tourism industry to the Australian economy. The Strategy will provide a long-term vision for the tourism industry and establish the basis for consistent long-term policy engagement with the tourism industry by successive governments. The Government has signalled that the development of the Strategy will be based on the application of a rigorous economic and industry policy framework.

Melbourne Victoria Australia

The official travel website for Melbourne, Victoria, Australia. Find out about destinations, accommodation, festivals and events, attractions and touring routes in Melbourne, Victoria, Australia. This site also provides accommodation information and booking services.

Tourism Victoria

Welcome to Tourism Victoria's corporate website. This site features the latest Tourism Victoria news and media information plus tourism and travel industry resources, development advice and assistance., Tourism Victoria.

Melbourne Victoria Australia

The official travel website for Melbourne, Victoria, Australia. Find out about destinations, accommodation, festivals and events, attractions and touring routes in Melbourne, Victoria, Australia. This site also provides accommodation information and booking services.

Backpackers to Melbourne, Victoria, Australia

The official backpacker site for Melbourne, Victoria, Australia. Find work, info out about destinations, places to stay, nightlife, festivals and events, attractions, and work and study in Melbourne, Victoria, Australia.

Tourism Western Australia

Tourism Western Australia is responsible for promoting Western Australia as an attractive holiday, event, convention and incentive travel destination, nationally and overseas and enhancing the tourism industry, infrastructure and product base.

Queensland Holidays

Where the rainforest meets the reef you'll find a land rich in unforgettable holiday experiences. Tropical North Queensland is a finely tuned blend of natural beauty and man-made comfort.Two World Heritage listed areas, the Daintree and Great Barrier Reef compete for your attention in this warm and welcoming wonderland.

Maroochy Tourism Queensland Australia

It is the heart of the Sunshine Coast, and has a wealth of attractions, both man-made and natural, golden beaches, rivers, beautiful rainforests and breathtaking vistas from the Blackall Range.

Sustainable Tourism CRC

Sustainable Tourism Cooperative Research Centre (STCRC) was established under the Australian Government's Cooperative Research Centres program in 1997, and has grown to be the largest dedicated tourism research organisation in the world.

STCRC was formed to underpin the development of a dynamic, internationally competitive, and sustainable Australian tourism industry.

Gold Coast Tourism QLD Australia

Australia's Gold Coast is a fun and diverse city, offering an explosion of action packed days and fun filled nights enjoyed by more than 10.5 million visitors every year.Families, couples, business delegates and solo travellers will all find an experience to suit their needs at a price to suit their budget, as the Gold Coast offers more attractions and venues than any other destination in the southern hemisphere.

Tourism Research Australia

Tourism Research Australia collects research and intelligence across domestic and international markets and the tourism industry and undertakes respected, reliable research and analysis.Tourism Research Australia manages tourism surveys that cover the inbound, domestic and outbound markets. Key information collected from travellers includes expenditure, places visited, activities, accommodation, transportation and demographics.

Eurobodalla Coast Tourism

Eurobodalla is neither old world nor old fashioned, it's not off the beaten track nor is it backward. Like the mountains, rivers, lakes and ocean that come together here, socialising with each other in a gently beautiful fashion, Eurobodalla has a timeless feeling about it, both in how it greets the eye and in the way people live here.

This is rare in a world that's always in a hurry to be somewhere else, be something different, be bigger and be the latest. It's this collective refusal to give into change for change's sake, that puts such great personal distance between this pretty, quiet corner of Australia and much of the rest.

Canberra Tourism

Canberra became the site for the newly federated nation of Australia in 1908 by a ballot in Parliament after extensive searching. The Indigenous peoples of this area have lived here for over 20,000 years. Since then the city has grown to become the proud home of the Australian story.Canberra is a fantastic base from which to explore the many treasures of the surrounding region. Explore historic townships, natural wonders, beautiful coastlines and the famous Snowy Mountains. So allow enough time to linger longer and enjoy all the nation's capital has to offer.

Noosa Accommodation

Discover Noosa's natural environment. Watch whales, enjoy pristine beaches, explore the dramatic hinterland landscape, and visit the world's largest sand island.Have an outdoor adventure - walk, dive, paddle, ride or cycle through Noosa's coastal and hinterland landscapes.

Sample the extraordinary breadth of the Noosa gourmet scene. Attend a cooking course, experience local produce at farmers' markets or book a table with a view at a Noosa restaurant.

AAA Tourism

Accommodation STAR Ratings are recognised worldwide with around 70 countries operating rating schemes. These can vary from compulsory government run schemes to voluntary schemes such as ours in Australia.

The Australian STAR Rating Scheme is one of the world's leading quality certification

Gippsland Tourism

Welcome to the Gippsland Region. Gippsland is one of the few unique and diverse regions in Australia. It comprises of snow fields, wilderness, rainforests, beaches, industrialised areas, farm land and much much more. With Australia's number one highway running through the centre of Gippsland, access to the country has never been easier. From a central location day trips can lead to an abundance of different events and activities that can be tried, or spend some time to bask in the glories of what the area has to offer. Explore the Gippsland Lakes and soak up the sun on the beautiful Ninety Mile Beach. Visit the largest concentration of Open Cut Mining & Power Generation activity in Australia. Or Journey to Phillip Island and catch a glimpse of the unique penguin parade.schemes and its Standards are periodically reviewed to ensure it keeps inline with world's best practice.

Christmas Island Tourism Association

Christmas Island is one of natures most impressive feats, an island full of natural wonders: from the unique annual red crab migration to rare and unusual birds and glorious deserted beaches where the only footprints in the sand are those made by nesting turtles.

With so many endemic species, the island is often referred to as the Galapagos of the Indian Ocean. Yet it also displays a curious amalgam of cultures, history and industry, emerging as a place where all these elements create a truly unusual travel experience.

Capricorn Tourism

Capricorn Tourism is one of the fourteen Regional Tourism Organisations in Queensland, recognised by Tourism Queensland and Tourism Australia.

The region incorporates the local authority areas of Rockhampton Regional Council & Central Highlands Regional Council, stretching from the Capricorn Coast and Great Keppel Island in the east, west through Rockhampton, Mount Morgan and Gracemere, then travelling out to Emerald, the Sapphire Gemfields and Carnarvon Gorge.

Wildlife Tourism Australia

Wildlife Tourism Australia Inc. is the peak non-profit body in Australia for wildlife tourism. Whether you are traveling within Australia and want to experience our unique fauna and flora, own or manage a tourism business, conduct research or simply have a keen interest in wildlife, Wildlife Tourism Australia is the place for you. You can: Between 1998 and 2004, a pioneering research program studying Wildlife Tourism in Australia was conducted at the Co-operative Research Centre for Sustainable Tourism, based at Griffith University, Queensland. This program led to a joint initiative between the CRC and Tourism Tasmania to jointly host a Sustainable Wildlife Tourism Convention in Hobart in October 2001. From that Conference, planning was soon underway to create a national organisation to represent zoos, sanctuaries, wildlife parks and other wildlife operators around Australia. The Organisation's intension was to further the recommendations of the Conference. * Customise a wildlife trail and accommodation for your trip * Promote your business or product * Keep up to date with research, news and events * Find tips on delivering best practice tourism experiences * Learn how to present quality interpretation * Catch up on past conferences and workshops * Learn how to tread softly in our environment * Learn about our unique wildlife * Take advantage of special member benefits * Subscribe to our e-newsletter

Prom Country Tourism

Wilsons Promontory National Park was first reserved as a national park back in 1898. It covers 50,512 hectares including offshore islands and the Light Station. You will find fantastic beaches, cool fern gullies, great views, spectacular rock formations and abundant wildlife.

Wilsons Promontory is home to more than 700 native plant species, 30 kinds of mammal--from tiny antechinuses to kangaroos, wallabies, wombats, koalas, seals & bats--and approximately 180 species of birds. Reptiles, amphibians, insects & other invertebrates are also numerous & diverse.

Murrindindi Regional Tourism

Murrindindi is located North East of Melbourne, Victoria. It encompasses townships and villages such as Alexandra, Buxton, Eildon, Flowerdale, Highlands, Kinglake, Lake Mountain, Marysville, Narbethong, Strath Creek, Taggerty, Thornton, Toolangi, Yea and Yarck.You will find spectacular water features, lakes, rivers, National Parks, State Parks and an abundance of wildlife.

AAA Tourism

Accommodation STAR Ratings are recognised worldwide with around 70 countries operating rating schemes. These can vary from compulsory government run schemes to voluntary schemes such as ours in Australia.

The Australian STAR Rating Scheme is one of the world's leading quality certification schemes and its Standards are periodically reviewed to ensure it keeps inline with world's best practice.

Wollondilly Tourism

Wollondilly is a popular destination for visitors, yet the name is often unfamiliar until memories stir with the mention of more prominent features such as Razorback Range and Burragorang Valley or towns like Picton, Appin and Warragamba.

Wollondilly, on the south western outskirts of Sydney and at the foothills of the Southern Highlands, is surrounded by spectacular, natural beauty and rural pastures. It's 2,560 square kilometres stretch from Bargo in the south, Appin and Menangle in the east, Warragamba in the north with the Nattai wilderness, Yerranderie Ghost Town and Burragorang Valley to the west.

Barossa Tourism Wine Region

The Barossa is located in South Australia, approximately 1.25 hours drive, north-east of Adelaide the states capital city. The region is geographically compact (approximately 40 km by 30 km) and it is only a short drive between towns.

Travellers from Adelaide can take the main north road through Gawler and Lyndoch, or the Sturt Highway to Nuriootpa from the city and be in the Barossa in just over 60 minutes. Visitors can also travel through the Adelaide Hills to Angaston or through Williamstown and Eden Valley.

Adelaide is well serviced by regular domestic and international flights with hire cars available at the airport. For private charters there is a light-plane airport at Parafield, just 45 minutes south of the Barossa in metropolitan Adelaide

Ipswich Visitors and Tourism Association

Ipswich, Queensland's oldest provincial city, is an alluring blend of heritage charm, metropolitan sophistication and expansive green spaces. Early colonial buildings stand proud in the city centre, lovingly restored Queenslanders perch on hills and quaint townships dot the surrounding countryside.

Just 40 minutes west of Brisbane and an hour from the Gold Coast, Ipswich combines rich heritage with the energy of being the hub of today's growth region in South East Queensland. Whether you're looking for family friendly fun, outdoor adventure, adrenalin action, pure indulgence or a glimpse back to bygone days ... come and This quaint village earned its special place in Queensland history when, in 1865, the first section of railway built in the Colony was completed between Ipswich and Grandchester, then known as Bigge's Camp. The railway would eventually link the rich Darling Downs to Brisbane and, as it expanded, settlers soon followed. Townships sprang up around the new stations all along the track as railway workers, farmers and shopkeepers and their families settled throughout the region. Much of Grandchester's railway heritage is preserved for today's visitors to enjoy. Its charming railway station building is the oldest surviving example in Queensland, and its square water tank is a reminder of the days when thirsty steam engines were frequent callers. Visitors can also experience the days of the steam engine at Grandchester's Model Steam Railway (open the first Sunday of each month from 10.00am to 3.00pm) by riding scale models of steam (and diesel) locomotives. The Grandchester Sawmill was established in 1940 and powered by an old C17 locomotive steam engine. Other notable attractions include the railway gatekeeper's cottage, the railway dam, Bigge's Camp Park and the town's historic cemetery.

Northern Territory

The Northern Territory is the quintessential Australian experience and a geographer's dream. The journey from north to south begins with the tropical shores of vibrant Darwin and ends in the dramatic deserts of the Red Center, taking in the cattle stations and sweeping savannahs of the Barkly Tablelands along the way.

The Northern Territory is home to World Heritage-listed Uluru-Kata Tjuta and Kakadu National Parks, which preserve and perpetuate both natural and cultural treasures.

In fact, the Red Center is home to the world's oldest river system, the Finke River, and Arnhem Land is home to the world's oldest living culture.

Queensland Tourism Industry Council

Queensland Tourism Industry Council (QTIC) is the State peak body for tourism. We are a not for profit membership organisation representing members' interests - both large and small. Queensland Tourism Industry Council (QTIC) is the State peak body for tourism. We are a not for profit membership organisation representing members' interests -

both large and small. QTIC provides a broad range of membership services and maintains strong industry representation in all relevant forums. QTIC is owned and governed by our members through member based Councils, Boards and Committees, QTIC truly reflects the views of the industry at all levels throughout Queensland.

Murrindindi Regional Tourism

Murrindindi is located North East of Melbourne, Victoria. It encompasses townships and villages such as Alexandra, Buxton, Eildon, Flowerdale, Highlands, Kinglake, Lake Mountain, Marysville, Narbethong, Strath Creek, Taggerty, Thornton, Toolangi, Yea and Yarck.You will find spectacular water features, lakes, rivers, National Parks, State Parks and an abundance of wildlife.

Tourism Department

The Strategy will assist the Government in achieving its overarching policy goal, which is to maximise the net economic benefit of the tourism industry to the Australian economy. The Strategy will provide a long-term vision for the tourism industry and establish the basis for consistent long-term policy engagement with the tourism industry by successive governments. The Government has signalled that the development of the Strategy will be based on the application of a rigorous economic and industry policy framework.

Tourism Gippsland Australia

Yarram is at the heart of the most beautiful country in Gippsland. From the splendour of Ninety Mile Beach to the delicious cool atmosphere of Tarra Valley National Park, from the historic excellence of Port Albert to the natural wonder of Wilsons Promontory, there is somewhere here to please everyone. The town of Yarram itself offers the visitor a wide range of varied options. There is a lovely eighteen hole Golf Course, frequented by many kangaroos at one end of the town and the superbly cared for Bowling Greens at the other. In between there are tennis courts, a swimming pool, extensive shopping facilities, hotels and the recently restored Regent Theatre.

Lithgow Tourism

The City of Lithgow is situated on the western slopes of the Blue Mountains about 2 hours drive from Sydney, NSW, Australia. Lithgow is at an altitude of 900 metres and enjoys warm summer days and occasional snowfalls in Winter.

There are many historical, natural and scenic attractions in the Lithgow district. Please enjoy exploring these pages. You will find comprehensive information on accommodation, attractions, tour operators, events, arts and galleries and services in the area.

Lithgow Visitor Information Centre

The Lithgow region is located on the traditional lands of the Dharruk, Gundungurra and Wiradjuri Nations. Lithgow is situated 140 km west of Sydney, on the western edge of the Blue Mountains.

Tourism In The North Eastern Region

The eight States of the North Eastern Region form part of the East Himalayan region, which extends from Sikkim eastwards and embraces the Darjeeling Hills of West Bengal. The rich natural beauty, serenity and exotic flora and fauna of the area are invaluable resources for the development of eco-tourism. The Region is endowed with diverse tourist attractions and each State has its own distinct features. The attractions are scattered over the entire region and are largely located in remote areas within highly fragile environments. These attractions and the people of the Region constitute the tourism resources at large. The facilities for stay, food, shopping and entertainment are improving tremendously.

Development Of Tourism In North Eastern Region

Government attaches great importance to the development of tourist infrastructure in the North Eastern Region in view of immense tourist potential of the region. Despite abundance of natural beauty, snow peaked mountains and white water rivers, the flow of incoming tourists has been marginal due to lack of infrastructure. Accordingly, there has been a continued thrust on development and upgradation of various tourist facilities namely Tourist Accommodation, Wayside Amenities, Budget Accommodation, Beautification and Refurbishment of Historical Monuments/Monasteries etc. Under Adventure Sports, River Rafting equipment, Water Sports equipment, Adventure Tourism equipment

Ujjayanta Place (Tripura) have also been provided under the Central Financial Assistance. In order to develop and promote tourism in the region, the Ministry of Tourism has taken following steps : -

a. In pursuance of PM's initiative for North East, a full-fledged Institute of Hotel Management and Catering Technology has been set up at Shillong.

b. A chapter of Indian Institute of Tourism and Travel Management has been opened at Guwahati.

c. The Food Craft Institute at Guwahati has been upgraded to the level of Institute of Hotel Management, Catering Technology and Applied Nutrition and the existing infrastructure is being expanded.

d. The Department of Tourism has upgraded the Government of India Tourist Office, Guwahati from Director to Regional Director level. This will facilitate in speeding up the work of classification/re-classification of 1-3 star function hotels located in the North Eastern States which were earlier covered by the Regional Director, Government of India Tourist Office, Kolkata.

e. A video film on tourist attractions for North East has been produced by Ministry of Tourism in order to give wide publicity to the region. This is being screened by Air India in their flights
f. North Eastern States are given a free booth in the world's largest Tourism Fair, International Tourism Mart, Berlin
g. Financial Assistance for promotion of fairs and festivals is also being provided to North Eastern States every year on continuing basis
h. North Eastern States are given a special focus in the Marketing Conferences of Overseas Offices of the Ministry of Tourism. All these overseas offices are giving due publicity to the North Eastern States for the promotion of tourism in the region.

During the year 2000-2001, Ministry of Tourism sanctioned an amount of Rs.24.52 crores for new projects relating to development and promotion of tourism, out of which Rs.7.79 crores were released to North Eastern States and Sikkim. In addition, an amount of Rs.4.96 crores was also released for ongoing projects. For the year 2001-2002, 121 projects relating to development and promotion of tourism amounting to Rs.32.57 crores were prioritised for the North Eastern States including Sikkim

Interest Subsidy is available to 1-3 Star/Heritage category hotels on loans sanctioned by Tourism Finance Corporation of India, Industrial Development Bank of India, Industrial Credit and Investment Corporation of India, Small Industries Development Bank of India, Industrial Finance Corporation of India and the State Finance and Industrial Corporations @ 5% if they are located in the Guwahati-Kaziranga-Shillong-Tawang Travel Circuits identified for intensive development in the National Action Plan for Tourism.

As per section 4 of the Expenditure Tax Act, expenditure tax has been waived off in respect of hotels located in hilly areas or rural areas or places of pilgrimage or a specified place of tourist importance with effect from 1st April, 1998 and until 31st March, 2008. For all other areas it is applicable only to hotels with a single room rent of Rs.2000/- and above. Once the hotel comes under the expenditure tax, then it is applicable to room charges as well as all other products and services sold through the hotel.

EASTERN REGIONAL TOURISM DISTRICT

The Eastern Regional Tourism District is publicly funded and made up of 42 towns in Eastern Connecticut, marketing the region as Mystic Country. The organization's mission is to contribute, through tourism, to the economic prosperity of these towns. This is accomplished by marketing the region, to domestic and international travelers, as an attractive destination for vacations, group tours, and meetings, and by assisting the businesses making up the tourism industry of the region in successfully promoting their products and services to these visitors.

EASTERN REGIONAL TOURISM DEVELOPMENT

The unique characteristics of tourism offer employment and cultural benefits to the community and regional economy. In 2007/08 tourism accounted for the employment in one in twelve people across a broad range of sectors in Australia, and contributed over $40 billion to Australia's gross domestic product (National Long Term Tourism Strategy, 2009).

Tourism contributes through the development of infrastructure that benefits residents (e.g. trails) and the appreciation of cultures through the exchange between visitors and residents.

Perth's Eastern Region offers visitors the opportunity to experience food and wine; arts, heritage and culture and interact with nature.

Perth's Eastern Region is grouped into three precincts:

- Swan River, comprised of the Town of Bassendean, and Cities of Bayswater and Belmont;
- Swan Valley, consisting of the City of Swan; and
- Perth Hills, comprised of the Shires of Kalamunda and Mundaring.

The EMRC supports member Councils in the management, development and promotion of the precincts.

Providing a welcoming face to the region are the three visitor centres, based in Guildford, Mundaring and Kalamunda. These visitor centres are supported by tourism industry associations and Councils, providing strategic and on ground services to visitors.

Eastern Regional Tourism Strategy 2010 - 2015

The EMRC has facilitated regional tourism development activities through collaboration with member Councils and industry since 1998. In performing this function the EMRC has previously been guided by various strategies, including the Regional Tourism Development Plan (2004).

In 2009 the need to develop a new tourism strategy document was identified due to changes in the tourism industry environment; development of economic and tourism strategies by member Councils; and revisions to local tourism industry management structures.

The new Regional Tourism Strategy (RTS) will guide the EMRC in the delivery of agreed regional tourism activities for the period 2010 to 2015. The RTS will ensure that tourism activities delivered by the EMRC at the regional level continue to complement those of member Councils at the local and precinct levels.

CHAPTER-7

WESTERN REGIONAL TOURISM

A tourism region is a geographical region that has been designated by a governmental organization or tourism bureau as having common cultural or environmental characteristics. These regions are often named after historical or current administrative and geographical regions. Others have names created specifically for tourism purposes. The names often evoke certain positive qualities of the area and suggest a coherent tourism experience to visitors. Countries, states, provinces, and other administrative regions are often carved up into tourism regions. In addition to drawing the attention of potential tourists, these tourism regions often provide tourists who are otherwise unfamiliar with an area with a manageable number of attractive options.

Some of the more famous tourism regions based on historical or current administrative regions include Tuscany in Italy and Yucatán in Mexico. Famous examples of regions created by a government or tourism bureau include the United Kingdom's Lake District and California's Wine Country.

DEVELOPMENT OF TOURISM REGIONS

Tourism scholar Jaarko Saarinen has identified a "discourse of region" in which a region's social and geographical qualities are combined with familiar and traditional representations of the region. The resulting discourse is "produced and reproduced" in the form of advertisements, travelogues, and regional literature, as well as in the larger media. Most tourism regions belong to a larger economic and administrative unit which takes on the role of developing the discourse of the tourism region into a marketable product. According to Saarinen, once the discourse of a tourism region has been established, the parent region helps shape further development of the area as a tourism region. This earlier period is characterized by rapid development, construction, investment in greater advertising, and increasing tourism. Eventually, if the region becomes successful as a tourism region, a mature stage in the development of a tourism region is reached where the "meaning and history of the destination are continually produced anew" in cycles of decline, reinvention, growth, and stability.

History of Tourism Regions

18th and 19th Centuries

Historically, tourism regions often developed in areas widely considered to a of historical, cultural, or natural importance such as the Niagara Falls region of New York and Canada, the Lake District of England, the French Riviera and the Italian Riviera. Others developed around specific attractions such as a major city, i.e. Paris, or a monument such as the Pyramids of Giza. Tourist regions have existed for thousands of years for relaxation and leisure as well as for religious expression. The ancient Romans visited the hot springs of Bath in Roman Britain while Santiago de Compostela was a site of mass Christian pilgrimage supported by a major medieval tourism industry that provided travelers with accommodations along their pilgrimage route.

The modern tourism region emerged out of the Industrial Revolution as cities grew in size, pollution increased, and an expanding middle class possessed greater amounts of disposable income. From the Enlightenment through the nineteenth century, the fashionable Grand Tour of continental Europe for wealthy young men popularized the idea of leisure travel. The popularity of the Grand Tour, combined with the stresses and benefits of the Industrial Revolution, encouraged wealthy and middle-class European and American families to explore leisure travel, though on a more local scale. These families began frequenting seaside resorts known for their health benefits such as the Roman resort town of Bath, particularly during hotter months that left industrializing cities extremely unpleasant.

The development of faster methods of transportation during the nineteenth century allowed tourists to travel greater distances in smaller periods of time. This period also saw the "seaside" developed as a "spatial area for 'mass tourism,'" a phenomenon that resulted in the development of specific coastal areas as tourist regions. Among elite groups in the nineteenth century, "the mountains" also became increasingly popular in the winter months; the most popular of these regions was the Tyröl region of Austria. Tourism regions were often subject to downward mobility as areas frequented by the upper class such as the Catskill Mountains of New York and Bath in England were abandoned by wealthier visitors when they became too popular with the middle class.

The romantic movement of the 19th century encouraged the appreciation of the natural world, leading to the explosion in popularity of scenic tourism regions such as the English Lake District and the Niagara Falls region. According to Peter Murphy, "increased competition" encouraged private development of hotels, resorts, and entertainment facilities as well as "municipal investment in parades, parks, piers, and baths." These trends marked an important intervention of the state into the evolution of tourism regions.

20th Century

In the late 19th and early 20th centuries, governments increasingly took a role in encouraging the development of tourism regions. Federal and state governments in the United States, with the encouragement of conservation groups, and European countries and their colonies began setting aside areas as parks, monuments, and trails for preservation and future enjoyment. Some of these, such as Niagara Falls, were existing tourism regions while parks such as Yellowstone National Park were areas selected by these organizations as future tourism regions.

At the same time, regions became an increasingly important aspects of nationalism. It is also during this period that the English phrase "tourist region" came into use. Eric Storm has argued that in the later decades of the nineteenth century "the stress was put on the region in order to underline the intimate bond between everyone's own community and the nation." According to Strom, many people believed that "only by being faithful to its own character could the region contribute to the welfare of the whole." The idea of the region as part of a whole nation gained further ground in the first years of the twentieth century, particularly after World War I, as an argument was advanced that "every region had its own 'soul'...an organic part of the nation." During this period, regional officials and businesses began promoting regions as tourist destination. Through this process, "tourism promoters strove to balance the demands of multiple identities: local, regional, state, national...They instructed their audiences that the regions' political, social, and economic fates were inextricably bound to their landscapes and geography." Tourists were portrayed "as important historical actors whose engagement...played a vital role in shaping the outcome of that bond."

Although local and regional governments took the larger role in promoting regional tourism in the late nineteenth and early twentieth centuries, during the Great Depression of the 1930s, national governments in Europe and the United States began aggressively promoting travel within their own borders. In doing so, they drew upon nationalist sentiment to imbue tourism regions within the state with greater cultural and historical meaning. Travel became a patriotic gesture as citizens and subjects were encouraged to explore their nation's tourism regions. Nazi Germany's Strength through Joy program subsidized travel for working-class Germans. One of the major projects of the program included "assert[ing] that Germans everywhere should be interested in the various regions" of Germany and that "part of preserving German culture...was to get to know it in all its variants." According to D. Medina Lasansky, in Italy, one piece of tourism literature argued that "'every region of Italy represents a page in the great book of shining national glories from which each one of us could learn to be proud of being Italian.'"

In the United States, "regional diversity" gave strength to a national whole in the United States' tourist guidebooks produced by the New Deal's Federal Writers' Project. As Andrew Gross argued, the guidebooks "transform[ed] local culture into a tourist attraction, and the tourist attraction into a symbol of national loyalty, in order to reproduce patriotism as a form of brand-name identification." In these WPA guides, the region became an object of nostalgia, a victim of the national identity that flourished through celebration of the regionalism it was helping to weaken.

Recent Developments

Continuing earlier trends, governments have attempted to maximize tourism potential by reverse engineering tourism regions. This process consists of dividing their territories into discrete tourism regions in such a way that every inch of that country, state, or region is given an attractive name, provided with advertising, and basic tourism infrastructure such as signage. Some traditionally heavily touristed countries such as France have implemented this strategy to encourage tourists who would normally only spend time in more famous areas such as Paris and the French Riviera to venture out into designated tourism regions such as the Western Loire Valley and Franche-Comté. The first of these is a more recently constructed region, while Franche-Comté has been a distinct political and cultural region since the Middle Ages.

Other governments, such as that of the American state of Nebraska, have attempted to use the creation of tourism regions to help produce a tourism industry in a state not frequently considered by potential tourists. The state's "Lewis and Clark" region in northeast Nebraska and the "Frontier Trails" region of south-central Nebraska attempt to deemphasize the state's reputation as a place people cross on their way somewhere else by capitalizing the role the state's territory played in the United States' often romanticized project of westward expansion.

TOURISM IN DENMARK

Tourists in Denmark consist mainly of people from neighboring countries, especially Germany, followed by Sweden, Norway, and the Netherlands. With 4.7 million visitor arrivals in 2007, Denmark ranked 43rd in the UNWTO's World Tourism rankings. Statistics show, however, that the total annual number of overnight stays in Denmark is currently declining.

Denmark has many sandy beaches which attract mainly German tourists. Swedish and Norwegian tourists often come to visit the relatively lively city of Copenhagen while many young Scandinavians come for Denmark's cheap and readily accessible beer, wines and spirits.

As Europe's oldest kingdom and the home of Hans Christian Andersen, Denmark is often marketed as a "fairytale country". The term is so ingrained that it is still used in international news reports, especially when the news is of a nature contradicting the image such as the Copenhagen riots or the Jyllands-Posten Muhammad cartoons controversy.

The Capital

In 2004 Copenhagen Region had 136 hotels with a total of 4.9 million nights spent. There were 250 cruise liners calling at Copenhagen Port with more than 350,000 passengers.

Among the major tourist attractions are Tivoli Gardens, the Freetown Christiania and The Little Mermaid, all located in Copenhagen. A survey conducted by the newspaper Berlingske Tidende in July 2008 listed The Little Mermaid as the most popular tourist attraction in Copenhagen.

Surrounding Area

The old road north from Copenhagen to Helsingør follows the scenic coastline passing through Klampenborg with its vast Dyrehave Park and the Bakken amusement fair, Rungsted with the Karen Blixen Museum and Humlebaek with the Louisiana Museum of Modern Art. The most impressive sight is however Kronborg Castle in Helsingør, famous for its associations with Shakespeare's Hamlet.

Southern Sealand, Lolland, Falster and Møn

In view of its proximity to Germany, one of the most popular areas of Denmark for visitors is the South of Sealand and the neighbouring islands. Møn, with its magnificent chalk cliffs, Liselund Park and its sandy beaches is one of the main destinations. Falster has a number of sandy beaches including those at Marielyst. The area also has several tourist attractions including Knuthenborg Safari Park on Lolland, BonBon-Land near Næstved and the GeoCenter at Møns Klint.

Bornholm

The island of Bornholm in the Baltic Sea to the south of Sweden offers tourists a variety of attractions including rocky seascapes, picturesque fishing villages and sandy beaches. Among the quaint towns worth visiting are Gudhjem, Sandvig, Svaneke and Rønne. The magnificent ruin of Europe's largest castle, Hammershus, is the island's most famous monument. There are ferry services to Bornholm from Køge near Copenhagen, from Ystad in the south of Sweden and from Rügen in the north east of Germany. There is also an airport at Rønne.

Funen

Funen, linked to Sealand by the Great Belt Bridge, has strong associations with Hans Christian Andersen who was born in Odense. The small coastal towns of Fåborg and Svendborg are popular with tourists both as attractions in their own right and as centres for visiting the surroundings, particularly the castles of Egeskov and Hvedholm and the unspoiled islands of Thurø, Tåsinge and Ærø with their narrow streets and thatched cottages.

Jutland

Major Cities

The cities of Aalborg, in the north, and Aarhus, in the east, attract a considerable number of visitors, whether for business or pleasure. Aalborg's 14th century Budolfi Church, 17th century Aalborghus Castle and the Jomfru Ane Gade (a lively old street close to the city centre) are major attractions. In Aarhus, Den Gamle By (the Old Town) is in fact a museum village in which old houses from various parts of Denmark have been brought together.

Regional Attractions

Among Jutland's regional attractions are Legoland close to Billund Airport, the easterly village of Ebeltoft with its cobbled streets and half-timbered houses, Skagen in the far north famous for its seascapes and artist community and the north-west beach resorts of Løkken and Lønstrup. Finally the island of Mors, famous for its natural beauty, attracts tourists to its Jesperhus Flower Park and to the cliff at Hanklit which overlooks the sea.

Jelling, near Vejle in the south-eastern part of Jutland, is a World Heritage Site, famous for its two great tumulus mounds erected in the late 10th century and its runic stones erected by King Harold.

Near Esbjerg on the west coast stands Svend Wiig Hansen's enormous sculpture of four chalky white figures gazing out at the sea. Known as Mennesket ved havet or Men at the Sea and standing 79 m high, it can be seen for miles around.

Cuisine

The most typically Danish meal of the day is the traditional lunch or smørrebrød consisting of open sandwiches, usually on thinly sliced rye bread. Traditionally, the meal begins with fish such as marinated herring, smoked eel, crab, or breaded plaice filets with remoulade and moves on with slices of roast pork or beef, frikadeller (meat balls), hams and liver paté. The sandwiches are richly garnished with onion rings, radish slices, cucumbers, tomato slices, parsely, remoulade and mayonnaise. The meal is often accompanied by beer, sometimes also by shots of ice-cold snaps or akvavit.

In the evening, hot meals are usually served. Traditional dishes include fried fish, roast pork with red cabbage (the national dish), pot-roasted chicken, or pork chops. Game is sometimes served in the autumn. Steaks are now becoming increasingly popular.

Transport

Air

Copenhagen Airport is the largest airport in Scandinavia. The airport is located at Kastrup, 8 km from central Copenhagen. It is connected by train to Copenhagen Central Station and beyond as well as to Malmö and other towns in Sweden.

For the west of the country, the major airport is Billund although both Aarhus and Aalborg have smaller airports with regular connections to Copenhagen.

Rail

Denmark has a good national railway network. There are also frequent train services to Malmö and other parts of Sweden. Germany is connected both by rail services using the ferries from Puttgarden to Rødby and by services across the Flensburg-Padborg land border in the south of Jutland.

Road

Motorways are well developed across the country, the only tolls being on the major bridges (over the Great Belt and to Malmö).

Bicycles

Outside of the towns and cities there are often bicycle tracks parallel to, but separated from, the roads between towns. During the summer months, there are free "city bikes" stationed at various spots in the downtown area of Copenhagen. The idea is that anyone can take a bike from one of the spots and ride it to one of the other spots and leave it there for the next person. There are numerous national and regional bicycle routes throughout Denmark. They are all marked and include rest areas with benches and other necessities.

TOURISM IN BELGIUM

Tourism in Belgium is one of Belgium's industries, and its accessibility from elsewhere in Europe still makes it a popular tourist destination. The tourist industry generates 2.8% of Belgium's Gross Domestic Product and employs 3.3% of the working population (142,000 people). 6.7 million people travelled to Belgium in 2005. Two thirds of them come from the larger nearby countries - France, The Netherlands, the United Kingdom and Germany.

In 1993, 2% of the total workforce was employed in tourism, less than in many neighbouring countries. Much of the tourism industry is located either at the heavily developed coastline or in the Ardennes. Brussels and the Flemish cities of Bruges, Ghent and Antwerp attract many cultural tourists.

Belgium ranked 21st on the World Economic Forum's 2007 Travel and Tourism Competitiveness Index, lower than all the neighbouring countries. Although the country scored highly for 'natural and cultural resources', it was ranked only 114th in the world for both 'price competitiveness' and 'availability of qualified labor'. In recent years the number of international tourists has stayed relatively stable, but the income they generate has increased to 9.863 billion US Dollars in 2005.

TOURISM IN BOSNIA AND HERZEGOVINA

Tourism in Bosnia and Herzegovina offers a favourable tourist business investment environment with an increasingly active tourism promotional system.

Bosnia and Herzegovina has been a top performer in recent years in terms of tourism development; tourist arrivals have grown by an average of 24% annually from 1995 to 2000 (360,758 in 2002).

According to an estimation of the World Tourism Organization, Bosnia and Herzegovina will have the third highest tourism growth rate in the world between 1995 and 2020.

The major sending countries in 2002 have been Serbia and Montenegro, Croatia, Slovenia, Germany, Italy, USA, Australia, Poland, Great Britain, Austria, China, and Spain.

In 2006, Lonely Planet named Sarajevo, the national capital, the 43rd Best City in the World, in its Best Cities Book.

With its #43 spot Sarajevo has come ahead of Dubrovnik, #59, Ljubljana at #84, Bled at #90, Zagreb at #125 and Belgrade at #143, making Sarajevo the best ranking city on the Balkan peninsula behind Athens, Greece.

Tourism in Sarajevo is chiefly focused on historical, religious, and cultural aspects. (see also: Sites of interest in Sarajevo)

Sarajevo, the national capital, hosted the 1984 Winter Olympics, which, at the time, were the largest Winter Games ever (in terms of athletes and media).

The country lost its reputation as an excellent ski destination during the war-torn period between 1992 and 1995.

TOURISM IN BULGARIA

Bulgaria is a country with a historical and cultural heritage, and attractive natural landscapes, one of the most visited tourist destinations in Southeast Europe. Tourism, as an industry, has been an important source of economic growth. In 2008 Bulgaria was visited by 8.9 million tourists, measured as outlined by the World Tourism Organization. Tourists from three countries - Greece, Romania and Germany - account for 40% of visitors. The country has historical cities and towns, summer beaches, and mountain ski resorts. New types of tourism, including cultural, architectural and historic tours, eco-tourism, and adventure tours, are expanding the range of visitor experiences.

TOURISM IN THE CZECH REPUBLIC

The Czech Republic, and in particular the capital Prague, has become one of the major tourist destinations in Europe. Other highly-visited destinations include Karlštejn Castle, Kutná Hora, ?eský Krumlov, and Lednice.

Tourist Attractions

Nightlife-Prague attracts large amounts of foreign (mostly German and Russian) tourists because of low costs associated with nightlife. The large number of bars and clubs, located close together and often open late, serve as additional incentives for tourists from Western Europe.

Hiking and skiing-The Czech countryside offers protected areas such as Bohemian Paradise (?eský ráj), Bohemian Karst (?eský kras) and Šumava National Park. The countryside features castles, caves and other landmarks. In Southern Bohemia, the Šumava Mountains contain many hiking and cross-country skiing possibilities. The nature reserve Rejvíz is a popular destination in the Jeseníky Mountains.

Skiing resorts are located from Northern East to Northern West Czech Republic. The most famous and popular resorts lies in the Krkonoše Mountains. Krkonoše includes the tourist centre of Harrachov.

Vineyards-Moravia is famous for its wine.

Traffic-Prague is served by Ruzyn? International Airport. For travelling within the Czech Republic it is common to use InterCity-trains or overland buses. Roads are in good condition and include a highway network. There is good tourism infrastructure in every big city and most tourist resorts.

TOURISM IN FINLAND

Finland attracted over 4 million tourists in 2005, with most coming from Sweden. The value added by tourism is about 2.4% of the Finnish GDP, and provides around 60,000 jobs. The Finnish tourism brand is stated by the Finland Promotion Board. The brand has four main dimensions beginning with letter C: Cool, Contrasts, Credible, Creative.

The Nature and the Finnish Summer

The summer is marked by long days in Finland, especially in the far north where the sun does not set at all. Tourists can go fishing and canoeing. There are several large lakes, including lakes Saimaa, Inari, and Päijänne. Walking is quite a popular activity in the summer. There are no high mountains in Finland, so climbing is somewhat limited. The highest mountain is Halti near Enontekiö. It rises 1328 metres above sea level.

Attractions

Finland is famous for its many lakes, nearly 200,000 of them (larger than 500 m^2/0.12 acres). Finland is also known to have excellent water quality, and green deep woods and forests around the sea, rivers, and the waterways. In Finland, tourists can sit on the shore of a lake, fishing, watching reindeer or moose and enjoying silence.

Alcoholic drinks form an important part of the Finnish culture. When travelling through Finland it is imperative to try national favorites like: the national vodka Finlandia vodka, Koskenkorva, the liquorice flavored Salmiakki Koskenkorva and drinks including cloudberry liqueur. In wintertime Finland provides excellent opportunities for cross-country skiing and some for alpine skiing too. Many of the popular ski resorts are situated north of the Arctic Circle in Lapland, but there are exceptions like Kuusamo in the northeastern part of Oulu Province.

Santa Claus is commonly known to live on Korvatunturi in Finland. In the town of Rovaniemi there is the Santa Claus Village for tourists to visit.

Northern Finland and Winter Sports

In the winter there is a large snowcastle with an Ice hotel built every year in the northern town of Kemi. Rovaniemi is a place from which to see the Aurora Borealis or Northern lights. Tourists in the north of the country in winter often enjoy trips in reindeer sleighs with Sami drivers, or in dog sleighs.

It is also possible to ski, with downhill resorts at Saariselkä and Levi, and many cross country ski tracks throughout the northern part of the country. Ice hockey is a popular sport in winter, and it is possible to go ice yachting, or ice skating on the ice. Most lakes are also frozen, so ice fishing (pilkkiminen) is quite popular.

The Cities

Helsinki, Finland's capital and largest city, receives many visitors year-round. During the summertime thousands of tourists approach Helsinki by cruising boats travelling across the Baltic Sea. Helsinki is known as a clean, modern and safe meeting point between the east and west. Helsinki has a reputation as the coolest party city in the Nordic countries. Other popular tourist destinations within Finland include Tampere, Turku, Oulu, Rovaniemi and Porvoo.

Transportation

The Finnish rail system is called VR. It offers InterCity and express trains throughout the country, and the faster Pendolino trains connecting the major cities. There are very large discounts (usually 50%) available for children (7-16 yr), students, senior citizens, and conscripts. There are international trains to St. Petersburg (Finnish and Russian day-time trains) and Moscow (Russian over-night train) in

Russia. Connections to Sweden are by bus due to rail gauge differences. It's possible to take the Silja and Viking Line ferries from Helsinki to Mariehamn in the Åland archipelago, Stockholm (Sweden), Rostock and Travemünde in Germany, and to Tallinn, (Estonia).

There are about 25 airports in Finland with scheduled passenger services. Finnair, Blue1 and Finncomm Airlines provide air services both domestically and internationally. Helsinki-Vantaa airport is Finland's global gateway with scheduled non-stop flights to such places as Bangkok, Beijing, Guangzhou, Nagoya, New Delhi, New York, Osaka, Shanghai, Hong Kong and Tokyo. Helsinki has an optimal location for great circle airline traffic routes between Western Europe and the Far East. Hence, many foreign tourists visit Helsinki on a stop-over while flying from Asia to Europe or vice versa. The Helsinki-Vantaa Airport has been ranked as one of the best airports in the world.

TOURISM IN GERMANY

According to Travel and Tourism Competitiveness Reports, Germany is rated as one of the safest travel destinations worldwide. Germany is also the third most visited country in Europe, with a total of 369.6 million overnights during 2010. This number includes 56.5 million nights by foreign visitors, the majority of foreign tourists in 2009 coming from the Netherlands, the United States and Switzerland (see table).

The official body for tourism in Germany is the German National Tourist Board (GNTB), represented worldwide by National Tourist Offices in 29 countries. Surveys by the GNTB include perceptions and reasons for holidaying in Germany, which are as follows: culture (75%), outdoors/ countryside (59%), cities (59%), cleanliness (47%), security (41%), modernity (36%), good hotels (35%), good gastronomy/cuisine (34%), good accessibility (30%), cosmopolitanism/hospitality (27%), good shopping opportunities (21%), exciting nightlife (17%) and good price/performance ratio (10%) (multiple answers were possible).

More than 30% of Germans spend their holiday in their own country. With more than 133 million foreign visitors (2008) Germany is ranked as the 7th most visited travel destination worldwide. A total of 27.2 billion Euros is spent on travel and tourism: this is equivalent to 3.2% of Germany's GNP.

TOURISM IN GREECE

Greece attracts more than 16 million tourists each year, contributing 15% to the nation's Gross Domestic Product. Greece has been an attraction for international visitors since antiquity for its rich and long history, Mediterranean coastline and beaches. In 2005, 6,088,287 tourists alone visited the city of Athens, the capital city.

TOURISM IN SAN MARINO

Tourism in San Marino contributes over 2.2% of San Marino's GDP, with approximately 2 million tourists visiting in 2009. Most tourists who visit San Marino are Italian, usually consisting of people who come to spend holidays in the Romagna riviera and decide to spend a half-day or at most a night in the country. Even though there are only a small amount of actual non-Italian foreigners who visit the country, they still are vital to the Sammarinese economy.

TOURISM IN SWEDEN

Sweden is mostly visited by tourists from its neighbouring countries Denmark, Norway and Finland. Thereafter follow tourists from Germany and the United Kingdom. A popular route for German tourists is to go by train from southern Sweden, through the European routes, up to Sweden's northern parts. Attractions along the way are historical, natural and cultural. According to the CIA World Factbook, Sweden is the 21st most visited country in the world, with 7,627,000 arrivals in 2006.

Most Swedish cities are small compared to other European cities such as those in the United Kingdom and Germany. The largest city is Stockholm, with approx. 802,000 inhabitants, followed by Gothenburg with 493,000 and Malmö with 270,000.

Stockholm has been Sweden's capital since at least the 14th century. It is Sweden's metropolis, the centre of the parliament, government and media. Not only is its waterfront and adjacent Stockholm Archipelago one of a kind, but the old parts of Stockholm with its history and culture are spectacular in their own kind.

Gothenburg is a relatively recently built city dating from the 17th century, and is visited for its beauty, attractions, friendliness and shopping opportunities. According to a recent survey of Swedish media, Gothenburg was voted the most popular major city in Sweden. More than 60% of all Swedes would like to live in Gothenburg, which has a reputation of being even friendlier and more welcoming than the Swedish capital.

Malmö has recently emerged as the eastern part of the Oresund region, tied together with Copenhagen, Denmark, through the impressive Oresund Bridge. During the last 15 years, Malmö has been focusing more on culture, as it previously had a solid reputation as a working class city. The twisted skyscraper Turning Torso has become the new landmark, replacing the ship-crane at Kockums. Both Malmo and Gothenburg are hosting the Uefa U21 European Championships this summer

Other cities have solid places in Sweden's history:

- Uppsala became the seat of the Archbishop of Sweden in 1167, with Sweden's and Scandinavia's largest church building Uppsala Cathedral inaugurated in the 1440s. Uppsala also became the center of education in Sweden with the Uppsala University founded in 1477.

- Lund was among the cities belonging to Denmark until 1658. Previously, it had been the seat of Denmark's archbishop, in the city of Lund. In 1666, Lund was granted Sweden's second university, the Lund University, Scandinavia's largest.

The Swedish rail system is called SJ offering slower-speed trains throughout the country and the faster X2000 trains connecting the major cities. Connection by rail is possible to Norway, Denmark and to Finland by bus, due to rail gauge differences. It's possible to take the Silja and Viking Line boats from Stockholm to Helsinki, Finland, Rostock, Germany or Mariehamn island. Scandinavian Airlines System and other airlines provides access by air for longer trips.

TOURISM IN MALTA

Tourism in Malta is an important sector of the country's economy, contributing about 15 per cent of the nation's gross domestic product (GDP). It is overseen by the Malta Tourism Authority, which in turn falls under the responsibility of the Parliamentary Secretariat for Tourism, the Environment and Culture. Malta features a number of tourism attractions encompassing elements of the island's rich history and culture, as well as aquatic activities associated with the Mediterranean Sea. In addition, medical tourism has become popular in Malta in recent years, especially since government efforts to market the practice to medical tourists in the United Kingdom.

The number of people who visited Malta in 2009 dropped considerably compared to the figures for 2008 - overall, the country's tourism industry suffered an 8 per cent drop from 2008. Visits from non-European Union countries dropped more considerably than visits from European Union countries (and even more so than visits from Eurozone countries), while the average stay length remained the same for both 2008 and 2009. Visitors from most countries require a visa to visit Malta. The nationalities requiring a visa are standardised as per European Union rules. Visitors already holding a valid Schengen Area visa most likely will not need to complete any more formalities to enter Malta (so long as they are already inside the Schengen Area). Visitors holding citizenship of the European Union do not require a visa to enter Malta as they hold the right to free movement within the European Union. In recent years, the country's tourism industry has been faced with a number of issues relating to the nation's small size, both in terms of area and population. These issues include stretched resources and infrastructure (such as water, waste management, beaches and roads), especially during the summer months of July and August.

Malta has a long and rich history, and this is reflected in the island's cultural attractions. The Phoenicians, the Carthaginians, the Romans and the Byzantines have all occupied Malta at some point in history, leaving a mix of many different architectural styles and artifacts to explore. The sovereignty of the Knights Hospitaller over Malta from 1530 to 1798 resulted in a legacy of elaborate artistry and architecture throughout Malta. The country's modern museums and art galleries feature relics from Malta's history for tourists and Maltese residents alike to enjoy.

There are also a number of aquatic activities to enjoy on Malta as well as Gozo and Comino. Northern Malta is home to the country's beach resorts and holiday areas, with the beaches most popular with holiday-makers being Mellieha Bay, Ghajn Tuffieha and Golden Bay. These beaches are large enough to be able to house cafes, restaurants and kiosks, but small enough to be crowded rarely. Malta's northwest is home to the island's quietest beaches, and it is on these that the main island's neighbouring two are nearest. Gozo and Comino are also popular beach spots for holiday-makers, although these are much more likely to be quieter, rockier and more suitable for snorkelling. The Mediterranean Sea surrounding Malta is popular for diving - while shallow dips may be attractive to beginning divers, more experienced divers may be able to dive deeper to find historical artifacts from World War Two or earlier.

TOURISM IN NORWAY

The main tourist attractions of Norway are the fjord-indented coastline and its mountains, the unspoiled nature of the inner parts of the country, and the cities and smaller towns. The main attraction of Norway are the varied landscapes that extend across the Arctic Circle. It is famous for its fjord-indented coastline and its mountains, ski resorts, lakes and woods. The main tourist cities in Norway are Oslo, Bergen, Stavanger, Trondheim and Tromsø. Much of the nature of Norway remains unspoiled, and thus attracts numerous hikers and skiers. The fjords, mountains and waterfalls in Western and North Norway attract several hundred thousand foreign tourists each year. In the cities, cultural idiosyncrasies such as the Holmenkollen ski jump attract many visitors, as well as historic and cultural buildings and areas such as Bryggen in Bergen and the Vigeland Sculpture Park in Oslo.

The culture of Norway evolved as a result of its sparse population, harsh climate, and relative isolation from the rest of Europe. It is therefore distinct from other countries in Europe in that it has fewer opulent palaces and castles, smaller agricultural areas, and longer travel distances. Regionally distinct architecture, crafts, and art are presented in the various folk museums, typically based on an ethnological perspective. Norsk Folkemuseum at Bygdøy in Oslo is the largest of these.

The Norwegian highway system covers more than 90,000 kilometres, of which about 67,000 are paved. The highway system includes ferry transit across waterways, numerous bridges and tunnels, and several mountain passes. Some of these mountain passes are closed during the winter months, and some may close during winter storms. With the opening of the Oresund Bridge and the Great Belt Fixed Link, Norway is connected to the European continent by a continuous highway connection through Sweden and Denmark.

The 4,058 kilometres long rail network connects most of the major cities south of Bodø. The Norwegian rail network is also connected to the Swedish network. Oslo Airport, Gardermoen is the most important airport in Norway, with 19 million passengers in 2007. Most cities and towns have nearby airports, and some of the largest also have international flights. The cruise ferry Hurtigruten connects the cities on the coast between Bergen and Kirkenes. In the summer, the coastal cities are visited by numerous foreign cruise ships, Bergen being the main cruise port.

TOURISM IN BRAZIL

Tourism in Brazil is a growing sector and key to the economy of several regions of the country. The country had 4.8 million visitors in 2009, the main destination in South America, and second in Latin America after Mexico, in terms of the international tourist arrivals. Revenues from international tourists reached US$5.3 billion in 2009. Both arrivals and revenues fell in 2009 as compared to the previous year due to the effects of the 2008-2009 economic crisis.

Brazil offers for both domestic and international tourists, an ample gamut of options, with natural areas being its most popular tourism product, a combination of ecotourism with leisure and recreation, mainly sun and beach, and adventure travel, as well as historic and cultural tourism. Among the most popular destinations are the Amazon Rainforest, beaches and dunes in the Northeast Region, the Pantanal in the Center-West Region, beaches at Rio de Janeiro and Santa Catarina, cultural and historic tourism in Minas Gerais and business trips to São Paulo city.

In terms of 2008 Travel and Tourism Competitiveness Index (TTCI), which is a measurement of the factors that make it attractive to develop business in the travel and tourism industry of individual countries, Brazil reached the 49th place in the world's ranking, second among Latin American countries, and sixth in the Americas. Brazil main competitive advantages are shown by the subindex measuring human, cultural, and natural resources, where Brazil ranks sixth at the worldwide level, and third when only the natural resources criteria is considered. The TTCI report also notes Brazil's main weaknesses, information and communications technology infrastructure (ranked 58th), ground transport infrastructure (ranked 95th), and safety and security (ranked 128th).

CHAPTER-8

DEVELOPMENT OF REGIONAL TOURISM

Policy makers often see tourism as a tool for the achievement of sustainable regional development. It could become a vehicle for the attainment of economic growth by some of the Russian regions, one of which is Saratov oblast'. Occupying a vast territory along the Volga River in the South-West of Russia, it possesses a substantial tourism potential, but lacks the essential economic development and infrastructure.

REGIONAL TOURISM PLANS

The Tourism NSW Regional Tourism Action Plans aim to provide a consumer driven focus with clear, individual marketing and development paths.

Central to this is an agreement between Tourism NSW and the Regional Tourism Organisations (RTOs) to produce and implement a strategic plan for each region. The plans guide is as follows:

1) 'In region' development of tourism initiatives specifically in the areas of:

- new infrastructure development
- transport Access information and service
- product development / enhancement

- industry development

2) 'In region' and external marketing strategies and activities that:

- identify the region's competitive advantage
- identify activities that build on the development initiatives as well as existing product strengths
- identify key products
- include a market demand analysis and a review of visitation trends and forecasts
- address distribution and marketing channel considerations
- outline promotional activities, for example campaigns and public relations, etc
- develop regional alliances and integrated destination marketing

Each RTO is currently developing their strategic plan. The most current plans can be viewed below:

Building Australia's premier tourism region: A vision for tourism developed in th Hunter Region 2005 - 2008

Blue Mountains Regional Tourism Plan 2004 - 2007

Outback NSW Tourism Development Plan 2004 - 2008

Central NSW Regional Tourism Plan 2004 - 2007

North Coast NSW Regional Tourism Plan 2004 - 2007

Capital Country Regional Tourism Plan 2003 - 2006

Riverina Regional Tourism Strategy 2003 - 2006

South Coast Regional Tourism Plan 2003 - 2006

Northern Rivers Tourism Strategic Plan 2009 - 2011

New England/North West NSW Regional Tourism Plan 2001 - 2005

Snowy Mountains Regional Tourism Plan 2001 - 2004

Regional Development & Sustainable Tourism

Tourism development and tourism marketing (at the destination level) are fundamentally tied to local economic, civic & environmental wellbeing. Each influences the other ... and together they all warrant a more closely integrated planning & management approach by community leaders.

Achieving excellence in tourism planning & development, at its best, involves enhancing & protecting local quality of life (sustainable community development). This results in a more sustainable tourism vision, based on shared community values, needs, dreams and opportunities.

For example, community-based town improvements and conservation measures can serve to create benefits for visitors ... and vice versa (i.e. sustainable visitor-based improvements that benefit local communities in various ways).

The world's most significant industry

Adopting the view that tourism is only about low paying jobs is not only erroneous, but a serious strategic mistake - specially in the regional context. Tourism is now the world's largest & most economically significant industry.

For many non metropolitan regions - particularly those that have suffered major declines in their more traditional local industries - tourism (and its many economic multipliers) may be one of the only serious economic options left.*

[*Assuming sufficient visitor drawcards and amenities exist or can be created ... and that other key influences like proximity & accessibility to markets are reasonably favorable, and genuine community support for tourism exists.]

Planning for a managed & sustainable approach

By way of example, in many coastal areas (particularly those experiencing significant residential growth), sustainable tourism now lies at the heart of their economic futures.* Tourism will strongly affect each community's prospects for creating more jobs and keeping local businesses viable - let alone more profitable.

A further dilemma is that, given visitors' fundamental attraction to 'the ocean' ... and water in general (for its relaxation and other pleasurable properties) ... rapid growth in tourist numbers will most likely occur - whether desired locally, or not.

Consequently, how well tourism is managed and planned for, will also help determine the kinds of impacts it will have on the locally desired way of life, its ecology and life support systems, and any special 'sense of place' that has been attracting people to both live in, and visit, a particular area.

As a consequence of its extensive state and regional tourism planning experience, TCDS can readily assist newly emerging destinations with their tourism-based, civic, economic & business development needs.

We are also able to offer services at affordable rates to smaller communities, counties & regions, and newly emerging destinations (state, regional, local) - including drive tourism audits, development policies and plans, branding strategies, visitor center assessments and visitor communication reviews (brochure, website, maps, signage). These will help determine if the approaches in use are achieving their true potential and impact.

Tourism Development and Regional Integration in Central America (ARI)

Central American integration has been a contested and complex process throughout its many different stages. At present, the Central American Integration System (SICA) comprises the seven Central American countries (Belize, Guatemala, El Salvador, Honduras, Nicaragua, Costa Rica and Panama) plus the Caribbean Dominican Republic.

Through a number of regional agreements, these governments are committed to a series of integration processes. At the same time as the revived regional integration project which has been underway since the early 1990s, changes in the political economy of the region have restructured the productive economies of Central American countries away from traditional agriculture to predominantly service-based economies in less than 20 years. One of the most significant features of the new service economy has been the phenomenal rise of tourism. Through its contribution to foreign exchange earnings and the generation of direct and indirect employment, tourism has emerged as a primary development strategy for the region and the countries within it.

This ARI argues that there is a convergence between the current model of Central American integration and the specific characteristics of tourism development. As such, tourism has become one of the driving forces of the contemporary integration process, even while other issues such as internal migration have remained more contentious. I begin with an overview of Central American integration in its historical context, then trace how tourism has emerged as a primary development strategy for the region. The paper then explores the contemporary relationship between tourism development and regional integration.

Historical Perspective

The model of Central American integration has always been explicitly tied to the region's political economy. As across much of Latin America, in the 1970s the region developed an import substitution industrialisation (ISI) model based on intra-regional integration and state-led development, a fundamental component of which was the establishment of the Central American Common Market. The extensive trade liberalisation of the 1980s set the stage for the deeper 'Washington Consensus' reforms of the next decade and further oriented Central American economies towards the market-led export economy and away from the preceding state-led inward-oriented model of development. The 1990s saw a revitalisation of the integration project started by the CACM. The Tegucigalpa Protocol of 1991 - which established the major institutions of Central American integration- stated that the best model for Central American development would be one based on the concept of 'dual growth': inward growth through regional economic union and outward growth through the export-led, free-trade model.

The further embedding of 'trade-led growth' is being facilitated by increasing outward-oriented integration, exemplified by trade agreements such as the Dominican Republic-Central America Free Trade Agreement (DR-CAFTA) and the EU-Central America Association agreement currently being negotiated. While these are not integration agreements in their own right, nevertheless they continue to shape Central American political economy and define the contours of regional integration. The renewed regional integration project sets the context for the growth of the importance of tourism to Central American development due to the industry's potential for enhancing competitiveness and advancing the new trade agenda.

Developmental Strategy

Tourism has been a significant development strategy for many of Central America's island neighbours in the Caribbean. The 'mass tourism' model pursued by Caribbean countries has been extensively criticised for its developmental outcomes, as the economic benefits of the industry have tended to accrue to large international hotel chains and travel companies at the expense of the local economies. The rejection of the Caribbean model can also be accounted for in part due to the changing tastes of consumers, with a growing dismissal of the mass tourism model for a more 'authentic' or 'adventurous' style of tourism. As such, the strategy adopted by Central American tourism institutions has been to create a niche for the Central America 'product' within the global tourist market based on Mayan archaeology, biodiversity and beaches.

The tourism industry has been established and promoted predominantly through private-sector investment by transnational corporations, expatriates and local people. Large-scale foreign investment projects have been a significant feature of tourism in Central America. The first example of this kind of tourism was through the Papagayo Project in Costa Rica, where the Fiscal Incentives Law of 1986 was created to lure investment from large hotel chains such as the Four Seasons and others along the Pacific coast during the 1980s and 1990s. In Belize, the 'boutique' nature of foreign investment is being considerably undermined by the growth of cruise-ship tourism, predominantly controlled by Carnival Cruises. Between 1996 and 2004, Belize saw a 4,000% increase in visitor numbers, from 14,000 to 850,000. The growth of this industry has generated significant political opposition from the country's small-scale tourism sector. In interviews, representatives of the Belize Tourism Industry Association expressed concern that the growth of cruise-ship tourism may lead to the destruction of the local tourism industry.

In Honduras, attracting large-scale foreign investment is a key feature of the National Tourism Development Plan. The most significant of such projects is the 'Tela Bay' project, jointly funded by the private sector (principally the US company Resorts of the World) and the Inter-American Development Bank. The project's aim project is to create a series of four- and five-star resorts, the first of which will be 'Los Micos Golf and Beach Resort'. Despite resistance by local communities, the project is being pursued and justified with the argument that it will bring economic development and job creation to a deprived area. In an interview, the project director argued that Los Micos will have a multiplier effect of 2.5 direct jobs, with a further 40,000 indirect jobs being created.

Large-scale investment by multinational tourism corporations is undoubtedly a key feature of tourism development strategies in Central America. Spanish companies in particular have invested widely across the region, with a large presence for Barceló and Sol Meliá hotels. However, the tourism sector of each country is still predominantly comprised of small- and medium-sized enterprises, usually owned by local people and expatriate residents. According to the Director of the Central American Tourism Integration system, small-scale enterprises make up a total of 70% of all tourism in Central America. However, despite the prevalence of small-scale enterprises in the regional tourism industry, when interviewed, representatives of the small- and medium-sized enterprise sector were critical of the vision of foreign investment-led development endorsed by the regional tourism integration project. As such, there is a clear tension over which model of tourism development should be encouraged and much debate over whether the pursuit of foreign direct investment is compatible with the more small-scale, locally-owned tourism that is part of Central America's 'niche' appeal.

Along with a dynamic and influential private sector, tourism development is being extensively promoted and funded by bilateral and multilateral donors. Tourism is endorsed by donors as a key tool for achieving commitments to poverty reduction. Two aspects of contemporary development policy in particular are presented as compatible with tourism: (1) the integration of previously marginalised populations into productive activity (Millennium Development Goal 1); and (2) the promotion of gender equality and women's empowerment (Millennium Development Goal 3). This understanding of the relationship between tourism and poverty reduction was echoed by tourism policy-makers interviewed across Central America.

In practice, this has led to a wealth of funding for tourism development projects, many of which have an explicit focus on integrating indigenous people and/or women into the benefits of tourism.

One such example is the World Bank's 'Regional Development in the Copán Valley' Project (RDCP) which disbursed US$2.96 million in seed capital for tourism-based microenterprises with the aim of targeting indigenous people and indigenous women in particular. Another example is an IADB project in Costa Rica entitled 'Rural Community Tourism in Costa Rica and Replication in Central America'. The project is a pilot study which will start initially in three communities in Costa Rica, but aims to develop a model for tourism-based poverty reduction across the whole of Central America. As with earlier projects in Honduras and Belize, the project's objectives include strengthening entrepreneurialism and integrating the rural poor into the productive sector through tourism-related economic activity. Poverty-reduction projects funded by the World Bank and IADB are thus becoming a significant dimension of tourism development in Central America.

Tourism Development and Regional Integration

Tourism has emerged as a primary Central American development strategy due to the influence of the local and international tourism private sector and the promotion of tourism by bilateral and multilateral donors. However, the embedding and institutionalisation of tourism development have taken place through a concurrent process of regional tourism integration. I now set out the ways in which tourism has become a foundational aspect of the contemporary regional integration project. The 1996 'Declaration of Montelimar' signed by representatives of the seven tourism integration countries (incorporating Belize and Panama) recognises tourism as a force for enhancing Central American global competitiveness, and increasing the diversification of economies. The over-arching institution for political and economic integration in Central America is the Central American Integration System (SICA), of which there are ten Specialist Technical Secretariats.

Of the various dimensions of regional integration, tourism integration has arguably made the most rapid progress, with a plethora of institutions and organisations springing up to facilitate policy-making in this key development area. The Central American Tourism Integration Secretariat (SITCA) is the key institution responsible for tourism policy-making. SITCA, responsible for the overall regional management of tourism policy, works closely with the Central American Integration Body and the Central American Development and Competitiveness Body, thus coordinating tourism policy with other aspects of the regional integration project. More specific to tourism is the Central American Tourism Council (CCT), comprising an Executive Committee made up of the seven Tourism Ministers, whose aim is to:

'Facilitate and promote the development of tourism in the whole Central American region in order to integrate the industry as a strategic sector in each country with the aim of contributing to sustainable tourism development in the region. In addition, it aims to facilitate and stimulate the development of tourism across Central America, eliminating any obstacle and impediments to the free movement of people in the region and integrating tourism promotion -as a role of the state- into all activities of the different branches of government'.

Private sector interests have been entrenched within the Central American tourism integration project from the start. Indeed, it could be argued that the project originated primarily as a response to the pressure of tourism industry actors wanting to invest or expand in the area. A key element of SITCA's policy strategy is the incorporation of the private sector into public sector decision-making, agreed by all governments in the 2002 'Declaration of San José'. As such, the formation of tourism development policy is heavily influenced by the objectives of the tourism industry -both regional and international- and the interests of such actors are strongly represented in the policy process. A particularly influential institution over policy-making is the Federation of Central American Tourism Chambers (FEDECATUR), representing the key tourism enterprises of each country and promoting policies such as investment incentives and tax breaks. Also representing the private sector, the Central American Federation of Tour Operators (FACOT) liaises with governmental institutions on policy matters. In addition to the inclusion of the local private sector in policy-making, the interest of large-scale tourism enterprises are further entrenched within the tourism development project. The Tourism Action Plan commits governments to carrying out an analysis of the levels of competitiveness of each country's investment laws and a reorientation of these laws towards promoting greater tourism capital flow into the region. As argued above, such strategies may in fact conflict with the interests of smaller producers represented by FECECATUR and FACOT, who continue to pressure the tourism institutions to focus on small-scale, community-based tourism.

In addition to regional institutions, a number of donors (both bilateral and multilateral) are funding different aspects of regional tourism integration. The most prominent donor here is the Spanish Agency for International Cooperation and Development (AECID). AECID funds one of the key institutions of tourism integration, the Central American Tourism Promotion Agency (CATA), based in Madrid and allowing direct access to the European tourist market and potential European investors. According to CATA's Director of Marking, the aim of the institution is to court investment from EU companies and attract European tour operators in order to contribute to the development of the tourism industry in Central America. AECID also funds tourism activities within its Regional Cooperation with Central America Programme (PCRC). This aims to strengthen tourism as a productive activity as a fundamental component of regional integration. A second phase of AECID funding - the Fondo España-SICA 2010-2013- has most recently funded the establishment of a tourism route based around volcanoes and colonial cities, which will act as a 'multi-destination tourism itinerary'.

A further example of bilateral funding is the Regional Collaboration to Develop a Sustainable Tourism Sector (FODESTUR). Funded by the German overseas development agency, the FODESTUR project has generated initiatives such as the 'Sustainable Tourism Certificate' (CST) and the 'Central American Green Initiative' (ICV) that form a key part of the sustainability dimension of the regional project. These projects, under the guidance of FODESTUR, are expressed primarily in market terms. The ICV, for example, offers affiliation to private-sector organisations oriented towards market segments interested in contact with nature. This ties in with the regional policy commitment to 'reinforcing programmes oriented towards elevating the competitiveness, quality and excellence of the region's tourist services', as agreed in the San José Declaration. Other such regional tourism integration initiatives include the Swiss Agency for Development and Cooperation's funding of the Government-Private Sector Network, which links Central America into the Global Clearinghouse, established by the Monterrey Consensus on Financing for Development to facilitate private sector investment in developing countries.

As argued in this ARI, the particular political economic juncture in contemporary Central America has created the conditions in which tourism development and regional integration can be seen as mutually reinforcing processes. The interplay between the structural changes taking place through private sector activity and the increasing institutionalisation of tourism development at all levels of policy-making help to explain the prominence of tourism in the new political economy of Central America. Tourism development policy in Central America is highly consistent across tourism institutions at the national, regional and international level. Key features of this consensus include the role of the private sector in the consultation and implementation of policy, the role of tourism as a vehicle for poverty reduction through generating employment and offering microenterprise opportunities, and the commitment to enhancing competitiveness through the continued liberalisation of the tourism sector.

The high level of coordination between regional and national institutions in the tourism policy-making process helps to embed the particular model of tourism development outlined above. Moreover, these institutional changes driven by tourism development further embed a particular vision of regional integration, and contribute to developing consensus (at least at the policy level) over the current development model across the region. The coherence of the goals of tourism development institutions operating at different levels means that this consensus is able to be maintained despite conflict between different tiers of the tourism industry and ongoing resistance to large-scale tourism projects such as luxury resorts and cruise-ship tourism. The convergence between the particular characteristics of tourism development and the current trajectory of regional integration means that for the time being tourism is likely to continue to be a driver of Central American integration. It is important to note the role of the Spanish government and Spanish companies in supporting tourism integration -both at the level of the private sector and political institutions-. The high levels of private investment and developing funding detailed here suggest a growing commitment to tourism as a pillar of Spanish development cooperation.

Chapter-9

National and Regional Tourism Structures

The publication of the British Tourism Framework Review is the latest change to tourism's national decision-making and delivery structures, an area that seems to have been in almost constant flux for the last 10 years. Having to operate in an environment where the imposition of organisational change, with its accompanying uncertainty prior to conclusions being reached and inertia as changes are implemented, significantly hampers operation and long-term planning. It is hard enough keeping pace with changes in consumer demand and behaviour.

If the new national structure is to work it has to be underpinned by a strong, confident regional and sub-regional destination network that can deliver quality products and data to the VisitBritain and VisitEngland marketing platforms and respond effectively to objectives set in a new national strategy.

But, to borrow Donald Rumsfeld's unique take on scenario planning, there are some "known unknowns" that call into question the effective establishment of that network - primarily around the future of England's Regional Development Agencies (RDAs) and the capacity of local authorities to maintain viable destination management services.

In both cases the organisation of tourism as a sector at sub-national level is bound up in wider debates about the role of regional agencies, the balance of power between Westminster and town halls, and the merits of elected representation against government appointed agencies.

Tourism is a large and important sector in its own right. An effective sub-national structure free from excessive disruption from wider policy decisions - one that is able to establish and maintain a clear role and strong links to private sector and local authority interests - should be the subject of separate consideration and discussion.

As the change spotlight turns on these areas, it is worth raising the debate about what sub-national structure for tourism the sector wants to see to best complement the new national set-up.

VARIOUS FORMS OF REGIONAL TOURIST TRAVELS

There are various forms of regional tourist travels. The most common among them are the following:

1) Tourist triangle, when within one trip tourists visit three countries. For example, most travels to Central Asian region include the combined tours: Uzbekistan-Turkmenistan- Tajikistan, including a visit to Penjikent, or Uzbekistan-Kazakhstan- Kyrgyzstan, including the visit to Lake Issyk-Kul.
2) Ring travels, when tourists are offered to visit several neighbouring countries of the region starting and finishing the tour in the same country. For example, while travelling to Central Asian region the Taiwan tourists chose mainly Uzbekistan-Tajikistan-Turkmenistan-Kyrgyzstan-Kazakhsatn-Uzbekistan route.
3) Transnational tours, when travel starts in one country and finishes in the third, fourth or fifth country, after

crossing the territories of these countries. Thus among such tours we can reckon the itinerary which starts in Armenia, continues in Georgia and completes in Azerbaijan. A grand transnational tour along the Silk Road is the travel which starts in Armenia, proceeds through the territory of Georgia, Azerbaijan, Turkmenistan, Uzbekistan, Tajikistan, Kyrgyzstan, and Kazakhstan and completes in China.

4) Radial tours, when foreign tourists stay in one country and make one-, two- or three-day trips to the neighbouring countries.

The process of region-building in tourism industry has particularly intensified in the Age of Globalization. This is connected in the first place with the new modern means of communication and transportation. Though in all cases the end-product - tourist region - is the same, the mode and procedures of its formation (creation) vary: from tourist associations to different kinds of economic and political treaties. It is generally agreed that creation of tourist regions is particularly beneficial for small countries which cannot compete with more developed tourist countries. The countries with poorly developed tourist infrastructure benefit by such integration most.

Concept of a region in tourist context is much broader than a traditional geographical one. From the standpoint of tourism there exist three main types of region:

1) Functional region, which consolidates the localities on the principle of community of geographical, historical or cultural realities. The concept of such a region is based on tourist practice of regional tourist product creation and joint activities aimed at attracting foreign tourists to the region. For instance, within the framework of functional tourist region there are several countries around Uzbekistan: Turkmenistan, Kyrgyzstan, Kazakhstan, Tajikistan and Xinjiang-Uygur Autonomous Region of China.

2) Formal region, which consolidates the states that pursuing certain aims and tasks, at their own choosing, consolidate on certain basis. Formal regions can be represented by geopolitical regions where tourist collaboration is conditioned by geopolitical interests of the states and external political situation.

3) Imaginary region, which is formed for certain purpose. Such a region typically does not have exact boundary and can vary depending on specific marketing goals.

Rich historic and cultural heritage of the region's countries reflect the century-old history of the region, which first of all is connected with the history of the Great Silk Road, stretching from antique Rome to the ancient Japanese capital - Nary. Therefore this vast area is offered to potential tourists as Silk Road region. Since late 1980s - early 1990s the brand of the Great Silk road is actively employed both in political rhetoric of the region's countries, and in advertising and commercial activity of tourist companies. By now it has become a global brand exploited in political as well as commercial purposes.

A vivid example of the brand utilization in creation of imaginary region is "The Great Silk Road" tourist project initiated by WTOON (United Nations World Tourist Organisation) in 1993. Special logo of "The Great Silk Road" WTOON tourist project is actively used by both state organizations and private companies of tourism industry of the region's countries. A number of joint marketing initiatives of the region's tourist companies and countries have been actualized in this respect so far. Among these initiatives we can mention the project of consolidation of tourist companies' efforts - Silk Road Destinations.

"The Great Silk Road" tourist project is a transcontinental concept of creation of the region's tourist image which demands cooperation and active collaboration between the countries of this region. Image of the tourist region is one of the most important elements which are attractive to tourists, which impel visits and thus activate the entire tourist system.

As is well known, today in the world's tourist market not only tourist companies but tourists countries and even regions compete with each other. The Great Silk Road as a tourist product competes today with the travels to Africa, Latin America, countries of the Asian-Pacific region, and some others. Under tough competitive activity the counties and their tourist companies have to seek for new ways of effective promotion of their tourist product. From experience it is known that one of the operative ways in this respect is consolidation of the efforts of several companies or several countries. Under joint regional projects the tour operating companies set such goals as intensification of promotion in the markets of developed countries of region's tourist product, expansion of scope of services by means of maximizing the efficiency of marketing activities along with concurrent marketing costs reduction, development of joint promotional printed materials and enhancing their effectiveness, reduction of expenditures on participation in international travel fairs and more active involvement in international tourist events, mutual promotion of each other to potential partners. But the main objective of joint activities is to create and develop a purely new tourist product - multinational tours throughout the region.

These are the evident benefits that tour operating companies of the Silk Road countries are guided by when they participate in regional tourist projects and when they organize various joint stands at the international travel fairs. Such joint stands have been organized since 2001 and they arouse great interest of the tourist industry professionals from different countries

The Future of RDAs

The future of RDAs seems to hinge entirely on the next election. Current Conservative policy is to abolish the RDAs if elected. Tourism organisation at regional and sub-regional level would be caught up in this.

With the polls continuing to show the Tories in the lead, scenario planning would make this event highly likely with a high impact in the medium term, the consequences of which would be extremely disruptive unless a coherent replacement structure can be established quickly. The Conservatives' current "Task Force on Tourism" has yet to report, but the manner in which it accommodates tourism organisation within the Party's wider regional manifesto will be of significant interest.

Local Authority Support for Tourism

There is little sign that the continued squeeze on local authorities budgets is going to go away. Increasing government debt and strong commitments to core policy areas (health, education, defence, social policy, etc) suggests that irrespective of who is in power, local authority settlements are not going to get bigger in the short term.

Conservative and Liberal Democrat plans to put regional funding in the control of local authorities suggests that extra resources for tourism may be available at county, unitary and district level. But this comes with the promise of loosening central government control on that spending and giving local councillors the power to decide where spending goes. With no statutory duty on local councils to deliver tourism services there is no guarantee that the level of investment in tourism currently provided by the RDAs would be sustained. Consistent local authority funding for tourism across the whole country at current levels is by no means assured.

But is there consensus within the industry about the sort of regional structure it would like to see? Currently, the debate seems to centre around whether or not the 1969

Tourism Act should be updated. That may well be the way to achieve the ultimate end of a strong, securely funded sub-national tourism network, but it does not answer the key questions about what the make-up, scale, and business models for those structures might be.

Options for a Future Tourism Structure

In thinking about the model for a sub-national structure, there are five objectives that, this article suggests, need to be built into its design.

- Strong private sector involvement in decision making and investment in programmes.
- Maintaining the current level of funding into sub-national structures.
- Continued rationalisation of sub-regional destination management into industry and consumer-recognised organisations.
- Retaining strong local authority involvement - the concept of place making will remain an essential ingredient in destination management .
- Creating organisations free from excessive influence of wider policy changes.

To start to get a focus on the debate one might consider four basic options and the likelihood of the above objectives being met under each system.

1. The Regional Tourist Board (RTB) model - a return to regional tourist boards linked to VisitEngland.
2. The direct funding model - independent regional tourism agencies funded directly from government.
3. The sub-regional model - the removal of regional tourism structures and devolution to sub-regional agencies.
4. The local authority model - devolution of powers and responsibilities to local authorities.

The RTB Model

The re-instatement of a network of standalone regional tourist boards, core-funded by VisitEngland (VE) from a grant provided by the government, would be a return to a period some consider as the "golden age" of tourism. Certainly, in contrast with the recent past it seems, in retrospect, a period of relative calm and consistency, with RTBs able to operate as discrete businesses free from the direct impact of wider external policy shifts.

Any external influence would come through the allocation of RTB funding from the government and VE. A future government may find it hard to resist the opportunity to cut the current levels of spending on tourism in the regions when it is aggregated together in one budget, and to attach policy objectives to the funding that is released.

There is also the added question of whether VE might seek to top-slice regional funds for national projects. This was a regular bone of contention between RTBs and the former English Tourist Board (ETB) and would require clear guidelines from government on the level of funding devolved to the regions, filtered no doubt through the electoral and policy perspectives of which region required the most resources.

Partnerships and Shared Working

Clearly defined and stable regional structures would help to engage both the private and public sector partners. Business models that built partner involvement into decision making and planning processes would further strengthen the links. Assured and adequate core funding from the public purse would also offer RTBs the option to operate without the membership schemes that were a feature of the original organisations. This would offer the opportunity to work with and support all businesses and local authorities regardless of whether or not they were subscribers, and in doing so presenting a more inclusive face to the industry.

This model also offers the potential for regional agencies, through co-ordination at national level, to exchange best practice, develop merged data collection models, and share marketing and IT platforms. One of the early criticisms of the RDAs was that they did not work together. This is being addressed through the Partners for England programme which would be a ready-made vehicle to take regional co-ordination further.

If regional agencies exist in whatever form, there will be the inevitable discussions about the best level for specific services to be delivered - at regional or local authority level. This argument is not restricted to tourism, but in the case of delivering tourism services a "tourism" solution, rather than a generic public service solution, is required to maximise partner involvement and consumer profile.

The establishment of confident, secure regional tourism agencies with inclusive models of governance can provide a stable platform to work through these issues, devolving responsibility when appropriate, and delivering regional programmes where there are economies of scale, strong links to other regional programmes, and clear business advantage. Positive, well-supported resolutions around these issues, particularly if local authorities are firmly on board, would help to continue the rationalisation of sub-regional tourism delivery; a subject which becomes more pertinent as local authority funding is squeezed.

Disadvantages

The decoupling of regional tourism agencies from other service programmes - particularly the skills, business advice, economic development, and sustainability agendas - could jeopardise the synergies between programmes and could lead to "silo thinking" in tourism delivery. The National Tourism Strategy will be influential in setting out clear objectives and identifying partnerships to deliver outcomes; partnerships that should be replicated at regional level. In a period of straitened financial circumstances, the aim to reduce spending duplication becomes paramount.

The Direct Funding Model

The essential difference between a RTB model and a direct funding approach would be for the Government to grant aid regional tourism agencies directly rather than through VE.

Advantages

The success of a regional agency, its capacity to work with partners, devolve responsibility where appropriate, support sub-regional rationalisation, and deliver what the industry wants, is to a large extent dependent on the agency's financial security and confidence in its own role. A confident, independent organisation can be more flexible in its decision making, more accommodating in its relationships with partners.

Notwithstanding the fact that they would still be vulnerable to annual budget setting by government, directly-funded agencies may feel more secure in their role and therefore more confident in delivering outcomes rather than protecting their position.

Disadvantages

However, breaking the direct link with VE and a close fit with the delivery of a national tourism strategy and programmes could threaten the coherence of the national structure and lead to the creation of regional "empires" seeking to work on their own. The opportunities to share best practice, and to co-ordinate data collection and marketing programmes may also be lost, although Partners for England should remain as a bulwark against that outcome. The quid pro quo for directly-funded regional agencies would most likely be targets and outputs attached to government funding in return for the security and independence of direct core funding.

Partnerships

The issues around private sector and local authority engagement are the same for the both the RTB and direct funding models. Clearly defined, well-established regional agencies will help to engage partners. The one difference may be in perception. Partners may see a directly-funded agency as having more authority and being better able to make its own decisions. As a consequence they may feel better disposed to working with the organisation and investing in its programmes.

Scale and Boundaries

In both regional models there is the interesting question about scale and boundaries. Should the current regional boundaries be retained? Should the old RTB boundaries be reinstated? Should new consumer/brand-led organisations be set up, possibly smaller in size that the current regions, but larger than county councils or local authority groupings?

There are invariably two issues pulling in different directions.

- Consumer/brand-led organisations lead towards smaller geographical areas often defined by administrative boundaries (eg counties, large urban areas) or landscape areas (eg the Lake District, the Cotswolds).
- Economies of scale, the potential synergies with other public programmes, and more effective liaison with the national body lead towards larger organisations closely aligned to other regional agencies.

The balanced solution has to date focussed on creating regional agencies with devolved sub-regional organisations (Destination Management Organisations (DMOs),

Destination Management Partnerships (DMPs), etc), well resourced and supported by the private and public sectors. This has been achieved to varying degrees of success in different regions, and the potential demise of RDAs is a threat to the progress that has been made so far.

Given the sense in creating and marketing destinations with consumer appeal, the increasing need to make the most of reduced local authority tourism budgets, and the fact that small and micro-businesses more readily identify and engage with sub-regional agencies that represent their locality, a sub-regional network linked to a regional agency that can run shared services at economies of scale, work closely with partner agencies and programmes, and liase with VE, seems the most effective delivery model.

There are, however, some who disagree and who would prefer to see all current regional funding devolved down to smaller sub-regional structures. These are the two options explored below.

The Sub-regional Model

If there are good reasons for establishing sub-regional organisations - that can deliver marketing, business engagement, local authority involvement, quality skills and development services in conjunction with VE, Partners for England, and shared local authority services - why have regional agencies?

The Argument in Favour

As local authority funding is squeezed, so the impetus to work with neighbouring authorities to build effective sub-regional structures gathers pace. This is driven also by growing awareness that many local authority areas do not figure as destination options on the public's radar and by the move in some areas towards unitary status for bigger areas. Despite budget cuts local authorities still outspend regional agencies in tourism provision and the opportunity to deploy that spending more effectively, with the addition of devolved RDA resources, is a good reason for strong sub-regional tourism organisations.

The resources required by VE to effectively work with a large number of sub-regional organisations, and the impact that may have on the delivery of national strategy targets are factors that need to be considered. Based on the current set-ups across the regions, something approaching 40 bodies could be established, assuming local authorities are able to agree on rational partnerships.

Concerns

It is the apparent inability of local authorities to work together despite being encouraged to do so for some time that casts some doubt on the effectiveness of this model. Arguably, the regions where there has been most success in setting up sub-regional bodies are those where the RDAs have been the most proactive in terms of both direction and financial support and without that involvement rationalisation would not have taken place. In many areas there still seems to be historic barriers between county and district councils working together - and that is without factoring in any political differences that are bound to arise and act as a drag factor on the establishment of rational sub-regional bodies.

The other strong concern about this model is that the devolution of RDA funds to sub-regional bodies may offer the opportunity for local authorities to pull out of tourism funding, citing the new resources from above as a good reason to do so. The total level of current funding across the spectrum of tourism service provision may go down.

The Local Authority Model

The strong vein of political thought that demands much more power and autonomy for local councils at the expense of national and regional organisations might drive the devolution of tourism services, caught up in a much wider political agenda, down to local authorities as the sole providers. It would then be up to the will of individual councils as to whether or not they were to pursue a tourism programme and at what level, what partnerships and associations they might form, and how far they engage with the industry and VE.

Pros

Positive reasons for exploring this option include:

- decision making in the hands of local people and the micro businesses that are grounded locally and make up such a large part of the sector
- a very close relationship between tourism service delivery and the place-making agenda
- the examples of local authorities who manage and deliver tourism services to the highest standard.

Cons

However, if consistent policy making and service provision across all the tourism sector is an ambition, this model is likely to work against that. Even if there was the introduction of a statutory duty on local authorities to consider and run tourism services there would still be differences in the level of service provided depending on local opinion, organisation and size of authority.

VE are unlikely to welcome the prospect of dealing with a large number of individual councils to deliver the national strategy and build marketing programmes as are national and regional agencies delivering partner programmes in skills and business advice.

NATIONAL TOURISM DEVELOPMENT PROGRAMME

The aims of the National Tourism Development Programme are as follows: to assess recent changes in the tourism sector; to elaborate a further tourism development policy and means for its implementation which would encourage development of the Lithuanian tourism sector; to establish priorities for state aids, investment promotion and investment priorities; to enhance the scope of local and foreign tourism; to promote the scope of Lithuanian export; to table means for forming Lithuanian image and popularising tourism.

The programme focuses on the service sector which forms gross tourism product of the country and determines the nature of its application. Local population and foreign visitors use tourism services. Tourism sector covers such activities as travel organisation, accommodation, catering, information, and entertainment, rent as well as any other services related to tourism.

A tourist is a person who, with the aim of educational, professional-businesslike, ethnical, cultural, recreational, religious or special purpose travels within or through the country and stays there at least for one night (no more than for one year) outside his/her permanent place of residence, and the goal of their trip is other than hired labour which is remunerated either in the country being visited or in the country of permanent residence.

Foreign tourism is an effective means of increasing export of domestic services and promoting the use of domestic products and goods and use of tourism resources, as well as preserving thereof. Foreign tourism is one of the most effective means of introducing Lithuania to the world community and creating the image of Lithuania abroad.

Local tourism also contributes to the development of tourism services. Trips by local Lithuanians have many values - they help to get acquainted with the homeland, to create own personality and teach how to cherish natural and cultural values. Local tourism is a means of recreation contributing significantly to the qualitative results of the local labour.

The variety and supply of the tourism services rendered have impact on the circus of the respective users; on the other hand, a user solvency influences the use and demand of various services. In economic terms, the market determines the relationship between the supplier and the user; therefore, a status of a local or foreign user is more a statistical and social concept.

While drafting the present programme, the results of the National Tourism Development Programme for 1993 have been taken into consideration. Quite a number of means established in the said programme have been already implemented. That is why a newly drafted programme emphasises further means for promotion of the tourism product and possibilities of disseminating information about tourism and services both in Lithuania and abroad. For the development of individual types of tourism (rural tourism, cultural tourism) target programmes are being elaborated; hence, National Tourism Development Programme focuses only on major aspects of these types of tourism.

CHAPTER-10

INTRA-REGIONAL TOURISM AND INCREASED EXCHANGES

The importance of tourism had been recognized since early days of SAARC. The Leaders during the Second Summit held at Bangalore in 1986 underlined that concrete steps should be taken to facilitate tourism in the region.A Technical Committee on Tourism was created in 1991. During the First Meeting of the Technical Committee on Tourism held in Colombo in October 1991, an Action Plan on Tourism was formulated.

First Meeting of the SAARC Tourism Ministers was held in Colombo in September 1997. It adopted Colombo Resolution and approved a number of important activities. In 1999, the task of promoting tourism was assigned to the SAARC Chamber of Commerce & Industry (SCCI) Tourism Council.

The Twenty-fourth Session of the Council of Ministers (Islamabad, 2-3 January 2004) approved establishment of the Working Group on Tourism. The First Meeting was held in Colombo in August 2004. The Working Group on Tourism prepared Plan of Activities which includes promotion of SAARC as a common tourist destination, to encourage private sector in promoting regional cooperation in tourism, human resource development, promotion of South Asia identity through tourism, cultural and eco-tourism development. The Working

Group was authorized to periodically review implementation of this Action Plan.

During the Thirteenth Summit (Dhaka, 12-13 November 2005), the Leaders stressed that continued efforts would be made by the Member States at all levels to promote people-to-people contact by facilitating travel among SAARC countries, promotion of youth exchanges in culture and sports, promotion of intra-SAARC tourism, establishment of linkages among professional bodies and through adoption of other concrete measures. They decided to launch 2006 as "South Asia Tourism Year." They directed their Ministers for Tourism to meet at an early date and elaborate a plan of activities to be undertaken during the year 2006.

The Tourism Ministers who met at Cox's Bazar (Bangladesh) in May 2006, adopted the Cox's Bazar SAARC Action Plan on Tourism.

Second Meeting of the Working Group on Tourism, held in Colombo on 3-4 July 2006, recommended that for promoting SAARC as common tourist destination (i) national airlines may use SAARC logo on aircrafts and other promotional brochures; (ii) national airlines may also use SAARC flag with their own flag as well as national flags at their offices and (iii) the Head of Mission representing the Chair of SAARC will organize special events in celebration of SAARC Charter Day on 8 December, with focus on promoting tourism.

In the Fourteenth Summit the Heads of State or Government while noting the cultural and social ties among the SAARC countries, based on common history and geography, reiterated that the future of peoples of South Asia is interlinked. They stressed the importance of people-to-people contact as a key constituent in regional connectivity. They acknowledged the importance of intra-regional tourism and increased exchanges, particularly among the youth, civil society, and parliamentarians. They agreed to take measures to charge nationals of SAARC Member States fees for entry into archeological and heritage sites as applicable to their own nationals.

The Heads of State or Government during the Fifteenth Summit underscored the vital contribution that tourism could afford to the economic development of the SAARC region. They agreed to make every effort to implement the comprehensive action plan adopted by the Second Ministerial Meeting held at Cox's Bazaar, Bangladesh. These efforts would include facilitating the movement of people through improved travel infrastructure and air, sea and land connectivity among the SAARC countries, collaboration in human resource development and the promotion of SAARC as a common destination through public-private partnerships and joint campaigns.

The Working Group in its Third Meeting held in Colombo in April 2009 reviewed the status of implementation of the Summit directives, SAARC Action Plan on tourism, and various decisions taken by the Ministerial and Working Group Meetings. It also finalized a list of activities to be undertaken during the year 2009-10 for tourism promotion among the SAARC countries.

INTRA-REGIONAL TRAVEL MARKET REPORT

Against a background of growing international competition in tourism, the Caribbean Tourism Organization (CTO) compiled this study with a view to identifying the size and scope of the intra-regional tourism market. Caribbean governments are committed to creating a network of interest among tourism personnel, travel agents, and other tourism suppliers within the Caribbean to sell the Caribbean product to Caribbean nationals, as an alternative to international destinations. CTO was mandated by member governments to develop and promote a Caribbean Market

Guide similar to those created for other markets, but adapted to suit the Caribbean situation.

The intra-regional market study was compiled by KPMG Management Consultants (KPMG), and drew from information, statistics, travel trends and other appropriate sources of primary and secondary data readily available in the industry. The information collected served to highlight the importance of intra-regional travel to the overall tourism performance of Caribbean destinations, and presented recommendations to facilitate the growth and the development of this market.

In defining the intra-regional market we consider only travel between distinct jurisdictions, excluding all cruise traffic to the countries and territories of the region. Travel by residents of a jurisdiction within that country or politically-linked islands is not addressed in the report. For example, although residents of St. Kitts may travel to Nevis to visit friends and relatives or to vacation at a resort, this movement would not be captured in the statistics as an intra-regional visit and intra-jurisdictional marketing is not specifically considered.

Unlike the single country market reports previously commissioned by CTO, the intra-regional report considers data from 33 countries and territories, which creates unique challenges for both data collection and marketing. Although quantitative baseline data is provided for each country and territory, we discuss trends and marketing approaches using logical groupings and specific examples.

One of the challenges in developing this report on intra-regional travel was the availability of comparable statistical data for each country and territory. Where possible we have filled in the gaps in quantitative data based on the professional judgement of the project team, and have flagged the data accordingly.

In developing the report tremendous effort was made to solicit both factual information and perspectives from each destination. National tourism organizations, Ministries of tourism, statistical departments, hotel and tourism associations, CTO chapters and airlines were contacted and their input sought. Despite many calls and follow up requests by many members of our project team, less than half (42%) of those who were asked to provide information responded. {See Appendices B, C, D, E, F & G.) In some instances this may reflect a lack of interest in intra-regional travel, but in most instances we believe it is but a symptom of one of the region's systemic weaknesses - the inability to develop and implement tourism related initiatives that transcend political boundaries.

The information presented in the report is current as of the date of publishing, however you are encouraged to consult original reference sources whenever up to date information is required. We have identified the original sources in the tables and graphs to assist you in accessing the credibility of these references and locating original sources of information.

SAARC to Promote Intra Regional Tourism

Sri Lanka's Deputy Minister of Economic Development Lakshman Yapa Abeywardena emphasized the importance of strengthening and promoting tourism within the South Asian Countries at the recently held SAARC Tourism Ministers Meeting held in Katmandu, Nepal.

The deputy minister speaking at the event said SAARC is the only region where inter regional travel is greater than Intra regional travel. The difference being south Asians travel to other regions in the world than travel in the South Asian region itself.

"Dependence on other regions for tourism should be done away with as increase in tax on long haul travel, and the economic set back in Europe will compel us to promote intra regional tourism in the future" he added.

Sri Lanka is a good example on how to promote intra regional travel. "For instance, our regional promotions have resulted in India becoming the largest market" the deputy minister remarked.

Furthermore he said the way forward to promote this segment of tourism is to develop a regional strategy for Cruise Tourism with a combined travel to two or more destinations within SAARC.

"We have already taken measures to re-commence the ferry service between Sri Lanka and South India that will naturally boost tourism." Intra regional tourism between SAARC countries are expected to grow in the future as the middle income group of south Asia is growing at a rapid pace, according to the UN World Tourism Organization and the Pacific Asia Travel Association (PATA).

ECONOMIC DEVELOPMENT

If ever there was a consumer decision with plentiful choices and beyond-appealing options, it would have to be in the travel and tourism industry.

With an estimated $740 billion annual spending in the U.S. alone, consumers' choices in destinations, transportation, lodging, attractions, and products and travel services have never been greater. The communications clutter is pervasive and everyone is ponying up for consumers' loyalty. At the end of the day, if your product or service is not on the itinerary or in the suitcase, it's waiting "standby," a consideration for the next trip. What's more, shifting trends, economic influences and word-of-mouth persuasion all impact the travel and tourism industry significantly more than others.

Ogilvy PR's Travel and Economic Development team knows the travel world from the front door to a destination and back. Our global team of travel professionals works with airlines, car rental, rail and cruise lines; destinations and attractions; lodging providers; online travel planning and ticketing resources; and countries, visitor services and trade boards to help each differentiate their product or service to important decision makers.

We are successful because of our insight into the travel mindset, our relationships with influencers and media who sway these decisions, and flexibility to keep our clients relevant within trends capturing travelers' attention. We also know the important backbone of the industry - travel agents, tour operators, corporate meeting planners and meetings and incentive providers - and work to address their unique needs. For trade development boards, we understand the investor and business landscape, the importance of promoting core industry areas and regularly demonstrate the ability to facilitate mutually beneficial business relationships for our clients.

True to Ogilvy PR's 360° communications perspective, we provide the full offering of services needed by travel and economic development clients: internal and external branding, consumer marketing, influencer engagement, media relations, event marketing, trade show support, economic development, business marketing, digital influence, public affairs, issues and crisis management. We are here to build, and protect, your travel brand. Going "standby" is no way to achieve success.

Tourism Industry Battered

As the U.S. dollar loses value, the colón has appreciated, hovering near the ?500 mark during the past three months. While the stronger colón has resulted in one of the smallest increases in consumer prices in the last decade (around 4 percent so far in 2010), economic sectors that are fueled by sales in U.S. dollars, but pay most expenses in colones, are taking a beating.

One of the most important of these sectors is tourism, an industry that accounts for around 7 percent of the nation's gross domestic product (GDP) and generates annual revenues of around $2 billion.

Last Thursday, the Costa Rican National Tourism Chamber (Canatur) hosted a presentation to highlight just how severe the damage to the industry caused by the exchange rate has been. Amid the torrent of data and statistics put forth to demonstrate the financial strain placed on the sector in 2010, one fact stood out: in a Canatur survey, 66 percent of hotels and other tourism-related businesses reported being negatively affected by this year's fluctuations in the exchange rate.

And that might be an underestimation.

"It's changed the entire chain of the tourism industry from one end to the other," said Boris Marchegiani, president of the Gaia Hotel and Reserve in Manuel Antonio, on the central Pacific coast. "It's not just the hotel part of it. It's affected the food that we provide, which we have to pay for in colones converted from dollars, it has affected the tour operators, because they charge in dollars and have to pay employees in colones, as well as the costs of amenities and all other operating costs. Just think of any element of the tourism industry, and the exchange rate is destroying it."

A similar sentiment was shared by representatives of the sector in all corners of the country contacted by The Tico Times this week. Given that most revenues generated by the tourism industry are in U.S. dollars, the roughly ?70 colón decrease in the value of each dollar over the past year has resulted in often traumatic losses. For example, if a family spends a few nights at a hotel and racks up a $1,500 tab, in 2009 that translated to around ?862,500, whereas one year later, that same amount translates to ?757,500, or about $200 less.

Increased operating costs, which are paid in colones, have brought further financial anguish to the industry. According to Canatur, in the past four years, average operating costs have increased 11 percent, cost has risen 31 percent and minimum salary is up 46 percent. Employee salaries, for example, are paid in colones. If an employee makes ?500,000 per month, in 2009 that salary was worth $870. In 2010, the same wage has a value of $990.

"The Costa Rican Electric Institute (ICE) raised the price of commercial electricity 30 percent across the board," said Dan Wise, the owner of the Río Colorado Lodge in Barra del Colorado. "Now, with the colón increasing about 15 percent, our electric bill went up 45 percent. There was the 30 percent increase plus an additional 15 percent increase because of the colón adjustment. My power bill is now up 45 percent compared to where it was a year ago."

Wise said that the minimum wage for his employees had also increased significantly despite his not granting any raises.

"Let's say a salary has gone up $50 per month for a minimum wage employee," Wise said. "If you have 50 employees making $50 more a month, that's an additional $2,500 in expenses per month that you weren't paying last year. And that's without even giving a raise. It's brutal."

At the conclusion of Canatur's presentation last week, Juan Carlos Ramos, the organization's president, was asked what he thought the future would hold for the tourism sector should the value of the U.S. dollar continue to depreciate.

After a slight pause, Ramos responded:

"There could be hotel closures. There are a lot of hotels having tremendous difficulties with the exchange rate fluctuations this year. If the value of the dollar doesn't improve soon or there is no government or bank intervention, more hotels could close by the end of the year."

According to Carlos Lachner, president of the Costa Rican Hotel Chamber (CCH), there have already been several hotel closures in 2010, including "three or four" in the La Fortuna area near Arenal Volcano in north-central Costa Rica. Lachner indicated that many other hotels are struggling to pay debts and could also go under if the dollar fails to recuperate.

Ramos said that various tourism industry associations - including the Costa Rican Tourism Board (ICT), the Costa Rican Tourism Professionals Association (Acoprot), the Costa Rican Restaurant and Hospitality Chamber (CACORE), CCH and Canatur - have held meetings with the Central Bank of Costa Rica (BCCR) and President Laura Chinchilla to discuss strategies to reduce the impact of the exchange rate's volatility on the industry.

According to Ramos, the discussions hinged on the idea of reevaluating the system of exchange rate bands, whereby the value of the colón is allowed to fluctuate freely between established maximum and minimum values. Fluctuations generally occur in response to the supplies of colones and dollars in the Costa Rican market, as well as other factors, such as the value of the dollar against other currencies.

The bands system, which was installed in 2006, replaced the system of mini-devaluations, which assured a daily depreciation of the colón versus the dollar in small, predictable increments. When the mini-devaluations system was installed in 1984, a U.S. dollar was worth around ?50.

In 2010, the bands system has fallen under intense scrutiny, as dollar-based economic sectors, such as tourism and exports, have been punished by the devalued dollar and the unpredictability of the exchange rate.

"The mini-devaluations made it much easier to plan your finances," said Jean Waller, the owner of Casa Viva cabinas in Punta Uva, on the southern Caribbean coast. "You could budget ahead of time because you knew what the value of the dollar would be. With the current system, that just isn't possible."

A Casa Presidencial spokesman told The Tico Times that no official decision had been made on whether the government would take action to influence the exchange rate, which is a responsibility of the BCCR (the president and board of directors of the bank are appointed by the Executive Branch).

In an interview with The Tico Times in August, BCCR President Rodrigo Bolanos said that "the Central Bank is going to keep [upper and lower] limits that have been established where they are with the hope that the exchange rate continues to remain within those bands.

"Whenever the Central Bank has to intervene to control the fluctuation of the exchange rate, it weakens the natural activity of the monetary system," he said. "I would say that my objective is to look for a way to monitor the exchange rate in case of external economic shocks and to attempt to limit the Central Bank's intervention in adjusting the value of colones to dollars (TT, Aug. 13)."

While economic conditions are often cyclical, the pains of the tourism sector caused by the exchange rate arrive at a time when the industry is already limping. In 2009, the ICT reported that the number of tourists who visited Costa Rica fell 8 percent from 2008. While the ICT reports a 9 percent increase in the number of tourists in 2010, the drop in the exchange rate has worked to counteract any positive impact of the increase in visitors.

"The devaluing of the dollar came at the worst possible time for this industry," Marchegiani said. "We have been warning the government that the exchange rate could break tourism for years now, and they haven't reacted. But it's not only the present, it's the future as well. If someone is considering investing in Costa Rica or building a new hotel here, who would want to invest in a country with an unstable currency? I wouldn't recommend it to anyone."

As the dollar continues to lose strength, vital pieces of the Costa Rican economy are weakening, even as other sectors - such as consumer prices - benefit. But if the dollar doesn't recover soon, the tourism industry, one of Costa Rica's biggest economic muscles, might lose quite a bit of its punch.

TOURISM EXCHANGE AUSTRALIA

ATDW and V3 have formed an alliance to provide the Australian tourism industry with a combination of the current services offered by the ATDW and V3. This alliance will deliver a national, inclusive booking exchange called Tourism Exchange Australia (TXA).

The ATDW collects tourism content from all Australian States and Territories and publishes it on multiple websites while V3 enables consumers to book the product immediately. The TXA will connect both the ATDW and V3Travel systems and services to deliver a comprehensive suite of online, bookable Australian tourism products to consumers via ATDW's licensed distributors.

TXA is an inclusive booking exchange that incorporates inventory and pricing from multiple booking systems and then distributes it widely to various websites. TXA offers distributors and operators the opportunity to increase their sales and provides consumers with the ability to source high quality tourism content and book it securely online.

Key Points

- ATDW will continue in its current role in providing high quality content and images for publishing on licensed distributor websites
- V3 offers a complementary technology that enables the consumer access to inventory from the tourism industry including accommodation, tours, events and attractions

- TXA brings all tourism industry parties together on an integrated platform to provide consumers with a seamless booking experience as well as high quality tourism information and images
- TXA will integrate inventory and pricing held in other systems and make it available for use by distributors
- ATDW distributors that integrate TXA services will start coming online in the first quarter of 2008

Benefits to Operators

Tourism operators who use TXA will be provided with many benefits. Please see the list below for a sample of the benefits operators can receive:

- Ability to select the distributors you wish to book your product
- View the Terms and Conditions and Commercial Terms before agreeing to the contract (opting in)
- Stop participating (opt out) at any time
- Customise your rates for different distributors
- Increase the exposure of your products in new markets
- Receive money immediately upon booking into your nominated bank account
- Always remain in control of your own inventory

Benefits to Distributors

TXA provides distributors with many benefits including:

- Consumers will be guided from "look" to "book" in a seamless process
- Current consumer experience will be enhanced by facilitating end-to-end transactions
- Includes tours, attractions and events, not just accommodation

- Access to the depth and breadth of Australian product with bookability
- Ability to set your Terms and Conditions and commissions. Operators have the option to accept or decline your offer
- Potential to generate additional revenue source from your website
- Commissions will be automatically deposited into your nominated bank account.

TOURISM PRODUCT DEVELOPMENT

Tourism product development is mainly undertaken to facilitate product diversification, development or improvement of tourism products with the help of knowledgeable and qualified staff. It aims at enhancing visitor experience by building consensus and strategic alliances with business stakeholders in order to bring about socio-economic growth. Tourism product development seeks to support in the maintenance, development and enhancement of the tourism product.

A large number of companies offer training programs and advice on tourism product development. The services include sustainable tourism product planning and development, presentations, seminars, campaigns and strategies for destination marketing organizations, individual operators and agencies. These companies make use of a community and stakeholder-based approach to assist businesses and destinations to plan for successful tourism in the long-term from cost-effective, environmental and communally sustainable perspectives. These companies provide an extensive range of specialized services designed to help individual tourism operators, associations and product clubs, educational institutions and government agencies effectively attain their short and long-term goals. Some of these companies are designed to assist government and quasi-government agencies in the development of the tourism industry, principally by coordinating and aiding timely action between public and private sector interests.

Tourism product development aims at long-term sustainable development by the execution of a number of strategies. These strategies bring into focus a generic idea to increase competitiveness, build an inclusive industry by promoting closer integration of people and develop and maintain the environment. Tourism product development is designed to increase the income in the sector. Tourism product development involves implementation of a comprehensive plan of action that will guide towards dealing with estimated increase in business over the short, medium and long-terms.

Tourism product development helps in improving product quality by complying with the standards set by international benchmarks. It helps in product improvement by tourism training. It helps in product diversification by acting as a channel, facilitator and controller for development through sports and community based development with stress on culture, heritage and eco-tourism.

CHAPTER-11

REGIONAL TOURISM MARKETING & TRAVEL SERVICES

Marketing is a human activity. All the activities of tourism marketing bear a glaring testimony to this fact. In tourism marketing, we deal with mobile, enthusiastic and pleasure-seeking humans. They are on travel sprees. They want to enjoy the nice places of the world! They are efficient (at least during the courses of their journeys), conscious of the environs they visit, always careful about the money they spend, keen to explore and receptive to every phenomenon/ product/service that makes comfortable or ecstatic.

We have defined Marketing in this chapter. Let us now define the term Tourism Marketing. According to Krippendorf, "Marketing in tourism is to be understood as the, systematic and co-ordinated execution of business policy by a tourist undertaking, whether private_ or State, owned at local, regional, national and international levels, to achieve the optimal satisfaction of the needs of identifiable consumer groups and in doing so, achieves an appropriate return."

According to Burkart and Medlick, "Tourism marketing activities are systematic and coordinated efforts extended by the National Tourist Organisation and/or tourists at local levels to optimise the satisfaction of tourist groups and individuals in view of sustained tourism growth."

According to A Kumar, "Tourism marketing is the delineation and execution of activities related to tourism their professional planning and execution and finally, ensuring the satisfaction of customers (tourists) in such a manner that the marketing objectives of the tourism organisation are achieved within the framework of social, economic, political and environmental components of the place/region/country of origin as well as that of the place/region/country of tour destination."

Thus, we can arrive at some conclusions regarding tourism marketing, as follows :-

1. Tourism marketing is the process of delivering satisfaction to tourists and in this process, the tourism marketer achieve his personal goals or the goals of the firm he works for.
2. Tourism marketing is a service-based activity. Some parts of its realm are products, some of them (like food beverages etc.) being very important.
3. Just like other types of marketing, tourism marketing also involves:

Strategic Planning (which includes definition of business mission, corporate strategic planning, business strategic planning, goal formulation definition of a marketing plan, finalization of marketing programmes, implementation of marketing programmes and finally, receipt of feedback and control);

Analysis of Marketing Opportunities (which includes marketing research, study of marketing environment, study of consumer behaviour and finally, study of competition);

Selection of Targeted Markets (which includes forecasting market demand, defining market segments, making plans for market targeting and finally, product positioning);

Design of Appropriate Marketing Strategies (which includes definition and identification of market leaders, challengers, followers and niches, defining the PLC of the product and using this knowledge to create market niches for the product/service and finally, understanding the intricacies of import and export management);

Planning Marketing Programmes (which includes definition and management of product lines and brands, development and testing of new products, brand management, marketing of services, pricing policies and discounts, definition and consolidation of marketing channels, study and consolidation of physical distribution channels, making effective promotion strategies, defining sales promotion and public relations programmes and finally, management of the sales force);

Implementing Marketing Programmes (which includes study/creation of a marketing organisation and implementation of marketing programmes in targeted market niches); and.

Controlling (which includes various types of control systems in the parlance of marketing).

(1) It is a process of transforming potential customers (tourists) into actual customers.

(2) It is a fine technique for generating and consolidating tourism demand.

(3) It can be used to increase market share of the tourism marketer.

(4) It essentially uses the tenets of communication, business management and psychology to win the markets in the parlance of tourism administration.

(5) It deals with human beings most of the times; they are the customers with very special and weird needs. Most of them indulge in activities related to tourism due to the fact that they want to enjoy. This peculiar feature of tourism marketing makes it special. It also demands different marketing strategies to woo the customers towards the products and services that are offered to them.

(6) Tourism packages, Group inclusive Tours, economy package deals and luxury packages area part of the gamut of tourism marketing.

(7) It involves many services or products of the infrastructure of a region or country. This makes it a Herculean effort; without making right types of teams, a tourism marketer cannot succeed in this effort.

(8) Tourism marketing starts from implementation of local or regional programmes but eventually, all the marketers try (or dream) to win international market hitches which were hitherto beyond their reach.

Tourism is predominantly a service. It involves many people (tourists, tour operators, transporters, hotel staff, guides, restaurant staff, disk jockeys etc.). It is of perishable nature.

The unique features of tourism demand are as follows :-

(a) It is perishable by nature.

(b) The demand is more during peak seasons and very low during off seasons.

(c) Tourists demand products and services of different kinds from the producers of the same set of tourism services or products. But they have to produce all such types of these services or product to remain competitive in the markets.

(d) Demand for luxury products and services is low. Demand for low-end services and product is very high.

(e) Some tourists, who may be belonging to middle-income strata of the society, may try to touch, albeit occasionally, the luxury norms of the strata that are above their strata.

(f) For some tourist spots, the demand is more or less inelastic. But for others, it is elastic.

As already stated, tourism is a service. It comprises some products as well. These include food, liquor, beverages, gifts, souvenirs, items, of daily use etc. But basically, the tourist (customer) buys services while he takes up a tour or itinerary. Example: One cannot expect a tourist to go to Mauritius to buy a few items that are typical to that country. He travels to that country to enjoy her environs, swim in the blue waters of the ocean, stay at exotic places and have a glimpse of the coral reefs that are under the waters of the ocean. He may or may not buy gifts or souvenirs, though he would certainly eat the cuisine of Mauritius.

Now that we are clear about the tenet that tourism is a service, we would have to weave a strategy set to bring customers to our fold. Service marketing is different from product marketing. It is intangible; the tourist cannot consume a tourist spot can only enjoy its environs. When he goes back to his native place, he takes sweet memories along with him. The tourism product is, therefore, essentially associated with 3 features, as follows: -

(A) Perceptions in the mind of the tourist-to-be about the tourist spot, including his expectations and a portrayal of what is in store for him.

(B) The actual experiences (good or bad) of the tourist at the spot.

(C) Sweet memories (even bitter ones) that he takes back along with him to his native place.

If a customer tries a product and does not like it, he discards it. But if a tourist tries a tourist spot and does not like it, he cannot cancel his tour. This feature differentiates tourism (as a service) from other services and products. He cannot call it a day in the middle of the journey because he was offered beef and pork by the hotel! He has to drag on somehow. Our advice to the tourism marketer is-do not let the tourist have the feeling of dragging on; eliminate this feeling as soon as it develops in his mind. If you don't, he would not give a good word-of-mouth about your tourist spot or service to others. You would lose him as well as scores of other tourists who could have become your customers, had he been treated nicely to kill that feeling of dragging on.

Further, tourism, as a service, is given only when political stability of the region is ensured.

Instance: Kashmir is a paradise on the earth but not a hot spot for tourists because of the supremacy of terrorists in that valley. A tourist does not like the hullabaloo of crowd, rallies, riots, arson and instability. He wants to enjoy and relax at the tourist spot; he may have spent the savings of his return to undertake the trip. Every tourism organisation must understand this fact.

NATURAL TOURISM RESOURCES

Forests, lakes, rivers, the Baltic Sea, interesting geo-morphological structures and aesthetic landscapes suitable for tourism make around one third of the total area of the country. General attendance of areas intended for tourism is estimated at more than 60 million people per annum. Lithuania has 5 national parks and 30 regional parks (8.5% of the total land area of the country) which enjoy most favourable conditions for tourism. Natural complex of the Lithuanian seaside has best available conditions for tourism in the whole Baltic Sea region. One third of woods is suitable both for recreation and hunting. The network of rivers and lakes can be applied for water tourism. 194 parks, 353 natural monuments and 130 reservoirs under the state protection can also be of educational tourism value. Those natural resources should not be only a subject to natural protection; they should serve as resources used for educational tourism and recreation. Those resources are impeded from being used for tourism by the following factors: not readiness, shortage of recreation and accommodation basis or its non-compliance with the current hygienic requirements, lack of information, not readiness of local public authorities and the status of the so-called 'dependant'. The use of resources not prepared for visitors is harmful to their protection and lessens their attraction to tourists.

CULTURAL TOURISM RESOURCES

The abundance of cultural heritage (over 10 thousand objects enjoying the status of a monument) create preconditions for the development of cultural tourism. However, only 350 objects are currently attractive to foreign tourists, a number of those used is even smaller. Lithuania is an active member of European project Way of Baroque, it also participates in Amber Way and Hanza Way projects. Castles, old towns, manors, cloisters may become separate products for cultural tourism. Other important resources of cultural tourism resources are such as museums, exhibition and art centres, theatres, handicraft and ethnical culture. Areas significant to the Lithuanian independence, old towns and sacred architecture and fine arts, ethnical architecture, local museums and folk art, cultural centres and thematic events - all these are unused opportunities for working out new tourism routes. Major problem is a not readiness of these objects for foreign tourists' visits, lack of information and popularisation, undeveloped marketing activities, lack of enterprise, little attention to local tourism. Use of cultural heritage for tourism is widely covered under National Tourism Development Programme which distinguishes three uses of the said heritage: expositional, infrastructure and miscellaneous. Limited state financial funds make it impossible to prepare many objects of natural heritage for cultural and tourism purpose. Therefore, a mechanism should be elaborated defining the way in which private financial funds should be used as an alternative means of cultural financing policy and as an alternative to the deterioration of natural heritage. Legal and economic conditions as well as the procedure of rent and privatisation of cultural heritage should be established which should be adjusted to render tourism services. Organisation of museum work should be market oriented; the base and expositions of museums of national importance should be extended. In general, the marketing measures should be applied in the field of culture; activities should be consumer oriented and co-ordinated with tourism companies. Cultural tourism and active development is an alternative to deterioration of heritage, an effective means of building general public awareness and acquaintance with the homeland, an effective means of introducing Lithuania to the world and creating its image.

HUMAN RESOURCES

Quite a number of places of employment in Lithuania are in the field of foreign tourism. A number of employment in tourism sector, i.e. servicing foreign tourists, accounts for no less than 4-5% of the total number of the labour force of Lithuania (73 thousand). Accommodation sector (hotels, in particular) is susceptible to employment. Non-obligingness to customers, however, is a second nature of the employees of the service industry.

ACCOMMODATION SERVICES

The quality of a Lithuanian tourism product is mostly determined by accommodation companies and sanatoriums that had 37.7 thousand places available in 1997. Total number of accommodation places covering interdepartmental dwellings and private households accounts for approximately 60 thousand (in 1992 there were 62.4 thousand places). A number of places in hotels has dropped from 10.854 in 1992 to 9.098 in 1997. General level of accommodation services remains to be low, since without investments major hotels have done little to improve the service quality, while a majority of recreation dwellings and sanatoriums have shown little signs of improvement. Despite the fact that only 32% of the total capacity of domestic hotels was used (for small hotels the respective figure stands at 80%) in 1997, major cities suffer from the shortage of hotels offering high quality services and suitable for hosting international events or of large tourism-oriented hotels. In the province, the problem with hotels is both qualitative and quantitative which can not be solved due to a decreased number of travellers. General level of hotel management and marketing remains to be low. Due to decreasing tourist flows from the closed eastern market and no noticeable growth of tourist flows from the West, the quality of other accommodation services is given no incentive for improvement and attracts no many major foreign investments. Individual tourists from western countries underline the shortage of campings which impedes the development of car tourism. Hotels for recreation and recreation dwellings suffer from their seasonal nature, whereas our tax system is not adapted to such a problem.

TRANSPORT SERVICES

In Lithuania tourists can use services of air, land and sea transport. Foreign tourists are not satisfied with the local railway network offering low quality services. For inland travelling foreign tourists use car transport only. Quality of transport services directly depends on the fact if the vehicle base is from time to time renovated, if the quality and service culture is improved, if stations are renovated and modernised.

CATERING SERVICES

Catering services is one of most rapidly growing tourism services since the majority of users of catering services is made of local population requiring any major investments. The core of highest quality catering companies is focused in major cities and health-resorts. In the light of the decline in needs for public catering and in the course of the privatisation process, a number of catering companies in province has decreased. However, the situation has begun to change over the past few years de to a growing demand for this kind of services. There is still some room for improvement in the field of meals quality and service culture.

LEISURE AND ENTERTAINMENT ACTIVITIES

One of the reasons why people travel is to do something special for their free time and take excitement in various sorts of entertainment, which in Lithuania's case, is quite a big problem. So far, major tourist attractions in Lithuania have been natural and cultural means. Nothing has been made for the establishment of entertainment potential, local initiatives are not encouraged; investment environment is not favourable for entertainment business. Therefore, municipalities should develop investment projects for leisure and entertainment centres as well as come with the means for their implementation. Entertainment centres operating in resorts could help to prolong a tourism season and solve the accommodation problem. The development of certain kinds of entertainment is impeded by non-differentiated limitations under the Law on Protected Areas (e.g. as regards seaside facilities), ban to provide casino services. Little use is made of important musical or theatrical potential of Lithuania, since neither separate creative institutions, nor the Ministry of Culture provide tourism companies and other institutions with the schedules of the forthcoming musical and cultural events.

TOURISM INFORMATION SERVICES

Tourist guides, Tourism Information Centres and other individual entities provide tourism information services. The provision of those services is regulated under the Law on Tourism. There are 16 Tourism Information Centres operating in Lithuania. The services of those centres are used both by foreign tourists and local citizens. The principal function of those centres is to enhance the volumes of foreign tourism coming to the country or its certain regions and to disseminate exhaustive information to coming visitors. In Lithuania Tourism Information Centres are established by local municipalities or local administrative bodies using the experience of western countries. Problems most acutely felt are insufficient awareness about and attention given to this activity on site, lack of experience, shortage of co-ordination, no existing tourism information system or its network.

FOREIGN TOURISM SERVICES

A number of foreign tourists coming to Lithuania had been decreasing till 1995; since 1996 the opposite trend has developed - tourist flows have been increasing each year by 19% in 1996 (excluding tourists who came by train) and by 6% in 1997. The forecast for 1998 is over 15%. A number of foreign tourists (visitors staying for a night in Lithuania) in 1996 accounted for 829 thousand, in 1997 - 1012 thousand (an increase by 22%). In 1997, a number of foreign tourists staying for a night in accommodation companies increased by 13% in comparison with 1996. Major tourist flows in 1996 divided by countries in 1997 distributed as follows: CIS - 51% of the total number of tourists who actually visited Lithuania, 34% - from Latvia and Estonia, 7% - from Poland, 2.1% from Germany. 71% of all travellers came by roads and 23% came by train. Foreign tourists accounted for 27% of all visitors who came to Lithuania (in 1996 this figure stood at 23%). In 1997 Lithuanian resorts and recreation dwellings accommodated 245 thousand people, out of which only 15% were made of foreigners. The majority of those foreigners came from Poland - 41%, from Belarus - 26%, from Russia - 13% and from Germany - 8%. No polls were carried out with local tourists.

EXPORT OF TOURISM SERVICES

The percentage of tourists who came to Lithuania in 1997 can be divided up by the purpose of their visit as follows: 46% came for business activities, 29% - came to visit friends / relatives, 15% came for recreation and the remaining 10% - for any other purpose. There were 58 thousand foreign tourists who used services of travel agencies. Average expenditure per capita stood at 1.200 Litas (in 1996 the respective figure was 1.130 Litas), average expenditure per day - 158 litas (126 litas), average duration of stay - 8 days (9). The above figures signify that Lithuanian tourism is not developed yet and that it is obvious that the more developed tourism is, the more tourists tend to spend. If developed, export of tourism services would increase which in 1997 reached barely 300 USD (covering services sold and goods available per each tourist). Gross tourism product of Lithuania in 1997 stood at over 300 million USD.

OTHER SERVICES

Tourist services include such daily services as trade, financial brokerage, rental, medicinal and hygienic services. Foreign tourists emphasise repeatedly a low quality of those services, whereas the level of hygienic services does not satisfy even local needs.

Income and Prospects of Tourism

According to the data of Lithuanian Bank, in 1997 foreign tourism generated 1.438 milliard Litas of income, this figure including tourist expenditures on goods and services; in addition, Lithuanian carriers received 157 million Litas of income for the carriage of non-residents by international routes. In 1996, accordingly, foreign tourism generated 1262.2 million Litas of income and Lithuanian carriers received 117.5 million Litas from the carriage of non-residents. Average annual growth of foreign tourism income (carriage included) stood at 15.7%. Estimated revenues from foreign tourism in 1997 totalled around 408 million Litas (collected in the form of five various taxes and social security contributions). VAT alone yielded 222 million Litas (nearly 10% of national VAT).

The forecasted growth of foreign tourism in respect of the total GDP in the period of 1998-2002 is expected to reach an increase of 6 percentage points from 4.2% to 4.8%; such forecasts are based on existing trends in tourist numbers and actual changes in GDP. General income from foreign tourism shall increase from 1.6 milliard Litas in 1998 to 1.89 milliard Litas in 2002; revenues shall reach 500 million Litas. Such estimates can be reached if tourist flows would grow from 1.2 million in 1998 to 1.7 million in 2002. A respective increase in a number of places of employment is to grow from 76 thousand to 90 thousand. Employment in the existing places of employment and creation of new places will be determined by an increase (decrease) in a number of tourists, i.e. opportunities to entry, growth of investments in tourism sector, etc. Seasonal nature of this particular sphere of services will remain unchanged and so will fluctuation in a number of labour engaged in rendering those services.

Institutional Structure And Management Of Tourism Sector

Institutional structure of tourism sector is comprised of State Tourism Department at the Ministry of Public Administration Reforms and Local Authorities, regional and municipal units; Tourism Board; associations of business people. State tourism sector is managed by State Tourism Department subordinate to the Ministry of Pubic Administration Reforms and Local Authorities as well as to regional and municipal administrative bodies. The Department works on and implements tourism development programmes under the Law on Tourism, co-ordinates tourism related activities of public administrative, regional and municipal bodies, activities of national parks. It also adjusts and submits conclusions on documents regulating territorial planning of tourism and the development of recreation infrastructures, as well as carries any other functions prescribed to it by the Law.

Regional administrative bodies and municipalities carrying out tourism management can encourage development of tourism services through adjustment and planning of mutual interests. Since various tourism services is a small and medium size business, municipalities could adopt that kind of approach in their respect and apply such target measures which would create more or less favourable conditions and, at the same time, would enhance the regional potential and attractiveness. At present many tourism units are in the process of formation in a majority of regions and municipalities.

The Law on Tourism defines Action areas of Tourism Board. Principal function is to represent interests of tourism business while implementing state tourism policy. Tourism Board together with tourism business associations jointly participate in elaboration of tourism draft laws and marketing measures. Tourism Board will be a new positive element in the development of tourism sector.

Changes In Ownership Relations In Tourism Business

During the first period of privatisation (1991-1995) 50 tourism companies were privatised partly or in full, including 35 hotels and 82% of trade and public catering entities planned for privatisation. A number of private hotels in 1997 accounted for 70% of the total number of accommodation companies. A speedier privatisation is needed in respect of state-owned (municipal) hotels. In order to speed up privatisation of accommodation and public catering companies, particularly in old towns, national and regional parks, legal and bureaucratic barriers should be eliminated which slow down the privatisation process as well as jointly decide on the issue of land ownership. Limitations to tourism (leisure) activities prescribed by the Law on Tourism should be revised, differentiated and explicitly defined; the state should establish target compensations for limitations on the ownership rights.

Tourism Specialist Training And Improvement Of Professional Skills

Tourism specialist training is directly affected by the growth of tourism service sector. Tourism specialists are trained in Vilnius, Kaunas, Klaipeda, Siauliai, and Utena higher schools. A couple of new schools have been opened which train tourism specialists: Klaipeda tourism school and Silute school of tourism and domestic services. New curricula have been introduced in Panevezys Light Industry School and labour market centres. The training covers the following curricula of the tourism sector: hotel administration, tourism administration, and hotel and tourism administration. A course on hospitality and reception of guests is offered in rural schools of agriculture. However, the issue of primary importance is improvement of skills of tourism specialists and training of tourism enterprise.

No methods have been worked out so far which would analyse and forecast the needs of tourism specialists. Short-term forecasts are provided by Lithuanian Labour Exchange and by training institutions themselves. In order to determine specialists' needs a co-ordination group should be established comprised of representatives of Ministries of Education and Science, Social Security and Labour, Land and Forestry, Tourism Department and any other tourism related institutions. Specialist training and training curricula should be standardised. All related social parties, including employees, should be involved in the process of drafting the said standards and requirements. To achieve this end, a specialist group is to be formed at the Specialist Training Centre at the Ministry of Education and Science which will define training priorities, organise the standardisation process, constant revision and monitor the execution of the same. High schools should be participating more actively in specialist training by introducing new courses on specialist training and special master studies.

Regulation And Control Of Tourism Services

Before September 1998, the Company Law regulated supply of tourism services. Pursuant to the established procedure, State Tourism Department issued licenses to entities providing tourism services at that time reaching a number of 360. Regulation of tourism activities largely depends on its international character due to its relation to foreign consumers; it also depends on maintaining high quality services and consumer protection. Thus, having taken into account the experience of foreign countries and having harmonised it with EU directives there have been determined minimum requirements for the supply of tourism services and conditions necessary for consumer protection. In order to implement the law appropriate rules will have to be worked out regulating supply of tourism services and business entities will have to be issued special certificates registered in Register of Tourism Services. Norms and requirements stipulated in the Law on Tourism form a legal basis for preparation of specific tourism standards and classification systems to be used then by business entities for the planning and organising supply of tourism services. Main point of all requirements is to create conditions satisfying consumer needs and ensuring fire-prevention and common safety, hygienic norms and qualified service. These standards will form a legal basis for a consumer to lodge any complaints against suppliers of services, monitor the compliance of those norms and classify services as a means necessary for tourist information. The law stipulates that legal acts when adopted should be assessed by appropriate tourism structures and be implemented.

International Aspects Of Tourism Development

State Tourism Department is a member of BTC (Baltic Sea Tourism Commission) as well as an affiliated member of WTO (World Tourism Organisation). Ever since 1993 WTO has been publishing statistical data on Lithuanian tourism provided by State Tourism Department. Lithuania has entered into international co-operation agreements in the field of tourism with such states as Greece, Turkey, Uzbekistan and Poland and is planning to conclude the same with Russia, Italy, Spain, Portugal and Bulgaria. In the process of EU integration and on the basis of EU directives, Lithuania will have to ensure free supply of goods, competitiveness, qualified services, correct information and consumer protection within EU internal market as well as will have to create possibilities for free movement of people. Owing to the shortage of financing, representation of Lithuania on the worldwide scale is not satisfactory and calls for improvement.

CHAPTER-12

REGIONAL TOURISM MARKETING

When making the choice to take a vacation, it is nice to have information available about the location. People often look to chambers of commerce or a city Web site for this information. These are highly useful tools for what is known as tourism marketing. As cities and regions want to attract more visitors, they look for creative and effective ways to let travelers know what attractions and amenities they offer. This is tourism marketing. For tourism marketing to be successful and effective, it needs to serve the needs of the visitor it is trying to attract and the organization producing the material. The point of these marketing resources is to promote what the resort, city, state or region has to offer in an appealing, yet honest manner. It is important to highlight the desirable aspects of a location without making too lofty promises or painting an unrealistic picture for the tourist. This will lead to less tourism in the long run. Ultimately, a successful tourism marketing campaign is able to provide economic benefits for those who live in the area while attracting visitors, new citizens and businesses.

TOURISM INFORMATION AND ADVERTISING

In Lithuania tourism marketing activities are made of tourism products and trade market research as well as supply of tourism products and advertising at home and abroad. Currently, the latter function is thoroughly implemented.

13 Lithuania-based Tourism Information Centres provide tourism information and 3 Tourism Information Centres are located abroad: Baltic Tourism Information Centre in Helsinki and Hussum (Germany) co-financed by all three Baltic States, Vytis Tours in New York supported by State Tourism Department. However, the efficiency of those three Centres is not very high since they are not true representatives of Lithuanian tourism image abroad. Hence, the state should establish and finance tourism information centres in strategic markets of Lithuanian tourism, namely in Germany, Russia, Poland, Sweden and Finland. Advertising-information tourism publications creating the tourism image of the country are prepared and distributed by State Tourism Department. The majority of those publications have been financed from PHARE funds (around ECU 25 thousand per annum). Those publications are distributed in tourism fairs and through Lithuanian Embassies, information centres, Lithuanian Airlines, public institutions. Demand for this type of publications is only partly satisfied, thus, it is necessary to ensure that an edition reaches 30-40 thousand publications; it would also be expedient to publish thematic tourism publications. When foreign aid will have been exhausted, the state shall continue the work of forming country's image and allocate funds necessary to this end. Advertising information activities should be maintained in regions and municipalities as a supportive means for foreign and local tourists. This activity is an important 'investment' into the development of tourism and an effective aid to business.

PARTICIPATION IN INTERNATIONAL TOURISM FAIRS

Participation in international tourism fairs is an important part of forming general country's image and introducing Lithuanian tourism product. State Tourism Department installs stands on Lithuania and organises participation of Lithuanian tourism companies in most famous tourism fairs in London, Berlin, Milan, Goteborg, Moscow, St Petersburg and 5-7 regional tourism fairs. Those activities are supported mainly from PHARE funds. In 1998 after the exhaustion of PHARE funds, the state should continue the work already started from state and private funds and allocate appropriate means for the installation of the said advertising stands in fairs.

CONTACTS WITH FOREIGN MASS MEDIA

Contacts with foreign mass media and tourism agencies shall become a permanent means of marketing of State Tourism Department and popularisation of Lithuania, which so far has been utilised very scarily. Private formations are not yet capable of organising any distinct Lithuanian advertising campaigns, whereas no means are earmarked to public institutions for the purpose of advertising Lithuanian tourism product. No consideration is given in drafting tourism budget to foreign practice popularising tourism, forming image and disseminating information (e.g. Finland's annual tourism budget is Litas 80 million, in Ireland - Litas 120 million, in Lithuania - Litas 2 million). This is why Lithuania clearly loses on the international tourism market. In order to raise efficiency of Lithuanian tourism marketing a Cupertino of public, municipal and commercial establishments is necessary, the allocation of funds and reasonable utilisation of the same, and selection of best measures and consideration of target researches of foreign markets.

TOURISM INFORMATION SYSTEM

Tourism Service and Resources Register elaborated following the prescriptions of the Tourism Law will serve as an incentive towards a more efficient work with and dissemination of tourism information. This database will make it possible an efficient supply of qualitative information on tourism services and facilities offered in Lithuania both for local and foreign users and will help to assess more accurately the tourism product. In addition, a solution will be sought regarding the exchange of information among municipalities, business representatives and users.

INVESTMENTS INTO THE SERVICE SECTOR

A majority of investments into tourism sector come from the private sector. State participation is necessary in raising indirect investments into tourism sector, in developing country's infrastructure and drafting tourism plans, in forming country's tourism information system, in implementing marketing and training activities. Material investments into hotel and restaurant sector in 1996 stood at Litas 23 million and made only 0.5% of the total material investments into Lithuanian economy. In October 1997 loans extended to hotel and restaurant sector accounted for only 1,1% of the total amount of loans granted to business sector. In total, the said sector has been extended Litas 30.7 million long-term and Litas 10 million short-term loans. At the beginning of 1997, there were 31 entities in the hotel and restaurant sector operating foreign capital; total amount of foreign investments of the said entities amounted to LTL 33.4 million.

FORMATION OF INVESTMENT ENVIRONMENT

Principal role of public institutions is to form legal framework favourable to tourism development and activities of tourism economic entities. A weighty factor is travel services rendered to foreign tourists by Lithuania-based companies and defined in the Tourism Law as export services. Success of tourism business and volumes of investments largely depend on measures applied by the state in respect of visas, i.e. whether or not the conditions related to supply of tourism services to foreign tourists are favourable. Another decisive factor would be the elimination of limitations and bureaucratic barriers applied in respect of this activity as well as on the success of tourism development issues solved by municipalities and regions.

AIRLINES AND ITS MARKETING

The basic task of an airline is the physical transportation of the client (tourist) to a tourist spot or a place that is closer to such a spot. The product/service mix of an airline should be such as to achieve synchronisation of core and peripheral services. While providing core services, central transport of passengers and goods/cargo is done. While providing peripheral services, decent dealings of air hostesses, timely arrivals, timely departures, nice food aboard the aircraft On-flight catering), permission to consume liquor, hospitality of the airline etc are the factors to be pondered over.

The strategy for defining a marketing mix for the airlines industry should also include:

(a) banking;

(b) insurance;

(c) foreign ,exchange regulations;

(d) customs rules;

(e) declaration forms;

(f) various methods of airline promotion;

(g) various tools for promotion of air packages; and

(h) aviation safety issues.

Sophistication of technology (which involves aircraft maintenance, use of modern jet aircraft and supersonic craft), efficiency of passenger/cargo management (which involves fully automatic baggage handling systems) and an empathetic attitude for customers (which is a part of hospitality) are the factors for succeeding in the air travel business. But it is no' easy to integrate these three factors to deliver concrete results. That is why, some airlines do not find customers for their aircraft services while some others remain booked throughout the year. Brand image also plays an important role in selling tickets air passengers. Airline transport business is vital for the country's economy; it also affects world economy.

Ideas of Product Mix

The following features are prominent :-

(a) It is an intangible product.

(b) Three major core services form a part of the product mix-passenger transport, cargo transport and mail transport.

(c) Expectations of customers must be matched with high quality of services. If this is not done, the airline can lose its vital market niches.

(d) Airlines operate in specific areas, called Sectors. Such sectors are created and covered according to the rules of the IATA, PATA, ICAO and other international organisations.

(e) Normally, the passenger service is of three types-Royal First Class, Royal Executive Class and Economy Class. These classes may be defined in a different manner by different airlines.

(f) Cargo management must go along with passenger transport. That is became the baggage of passengers must accompany them in the same aircraft. It must be loaded in the cargo much before the aircraft takes off.

(g) The USP of an airline is has 3 sub-USPs-transport by air at minimum costs, essential services to be given to the aircraft while the aircraft is airborne and movement of passengers to and from the aircraft. Flight data display is also a part of core services.

(h) Peripheral services are pleasant mannerisms (courtesy) of the aircrew, luxury levels inside the aircraft, music system, movies onboard the aircraft and above all, in-flight catering services. We can also include disaster management in the category of peripheral services.

Clearly, many persons are involved in giving services of various types to air passengers. Airport staff check documents of passengers. Airlines or their travel agents 'arrange tickets for them. Immigration officials check visas when the passengers arrive at least 2 hours before the departure of the aircraft. Transport officials (at the airport) receive the luggage and check it for the presence of any explosive/contraband items in the same. This procedure is carried out with the help of special machines. These machines scan each and every suitcase and bag. Then, these bags and suitcases are transferred to the luggage bay through an automatic conveyor belt. From that bay, transport vehicles (four wheelers) carry the luggage to the aircraft. The passengers move to departure terminals after they dear all the immigration formalities. They may have to pay airport taxes if the same have not been added to the ticket prices. Aboard the aircraft, passengers are welcomed by the airhostesses and shown their respective seats. These seats are mentioned on the boarding passes that are issued to passengers at the airport. Passengers are given fruit juice, light drinks, white wine, red wine or liquors when the aircraft becomes stable in the air. Beer is also served (in cans). Then, lunch or dinner is served by air hostesses. Information is displayed on the screen to give details of flight data. When the aircraft lands, passengers get up and leave the aircraft. The crew thank the passengers. At the destination airport, passengers get their passports and visas checked. Then, they proceed to collect their luggage, which arrives in the departure lounge through automatic conveyor belts. Every passenger is supposed to identify his or her luggage and pick it up from the conveyor belt as and when it arrives.

Passengers put their luggage on wheeled trolleys and leave the airport. If the passenger has a tie-up with a travel agency, resort or hotel, the passenger is whisked away by a coach or taxi that represents that travel agency, resort or hotel.'

Ideas of Price Mix : The price of an air ticket comprises a basic fate and airport taxes, In addition, some airlines also impose a surcharge that is to be taken from passengers because of the rules and policies of a country. Sales tax is also a part of the bill. Nowadays, aviation turbine fuel costs, airport maintenance costs, aircraft costs and vacant seats have forced airlines to increase airfares of all the categories. This change varies from 5 to 15 per cent of the basic ticket cost. If a passenger or customer wishes to send cargo by air, he would have to get the goods booked at the airport. He would be issued an airway receipt, called Airway Bill. It is similar to a Railway Receipt (RR) in the case of rail transport or a Goods Receipt (GR) in the case of surface transport. The goods would be taken by air to the destination. The original document (airway bill) would have to be presented by the receiver at the destination airport so that he could get the delivery of goods. Obviously, the sender would send this receipt by courier, air or other method so that the receiver' is able to collect these goods. He would also be required to pay customs duty (if it is applicable) and other taxes that may be applicable from time to time for providing such services.

During off seasons and also during holiday seasons (May to July), airlines woo their customers by reducing airfares. This is a common practice followed by all the airlines of the world. Similarly, special incidents like the attacks on the WTC towers on September 11 ,2001 also force many airlines to cut down their prices. That is because the number of passengers falls rapidly in the wake of threats to passengers. They prefer to travel by sea or road due to these incidents. Thus, airlines reduce their fares so that passengers may continue to extend their patronage to them.

In order from the prices to be competitive, airlines must ensure that their seats do not go vacant when the aircraft is airborne. More the number of vacant seats, more would be the cost to passengers. If operational costs and landing charges at airports increase, airfares are bound to increase. Wars (like Iraq-US war in 2003), national calamities (like SARS in China, Hong Kong and Taiwan) and bad weather (like dust storms or fog at the IGI Airport) adversely affect smooth flow of air traffic. Rising price of Air Turbine Fuel (ATF) is also a deterrent in this context.

Air India and Indian Airlines have offered some lucrative schemes in the past to attract customers. Example: The IA had offered a ticket for Rs 15,000 and allowed unlimited travel to any destination of India till March 31, 2003. The IA-Taj offer allows passengers to stay in any of the hotels of the Taj Group at an additional cost of Rs 2,000. Many other schemes are in vogue that persuade passengers to travel (at low costs).

Ideas of Promotion Mix

An airline can use the following components in rational combinations to define its promotion mix :-

Advertising : It can advertise through magazine, newspapers, local newspapers and on Internet to promote its products/services. Normally, travel agents do this job for the airlines. Airlines normally issue advertisements for image building in reputed magazines like India Today, Trav Talk, Go Now etc. Travel agents issue advertisements (without giving names of airlines) in newspapers.

Separate Business Class Fares : Austrian Airlines now flies you from Delhi to Vienna 4 times a week. Via the hub, Vienna International Airport, you have perfect connections to North America, Canada and more than 70 destinations in Western and Eastern Europe. And at Vienna Airport your ongoing flight will be only a few steps away.

Booking and Reservations : www.aua.com and at your travel agency.

Finally, brochures and catalogues are also printed (in four colours) to effect more sales.

Publicity : Travel agents, media persons and customers (medium and heavy uses) purchase the services of airlines. These may be given incentives to promote the services of the airline. PROs, executives, ticketing executives, marketing staff and sales staff of a travel agency do these jobs with great enthusiasm because they are in touch with existing and prospectus customers at all the times. Further, if the airline participates in air transport shows, tourism fairs, exhibitions and seminars, it displays its brand name, logo, life-size cut-outs etc to publicise its products and services. But it does not sell these at such occasions but only indulges in an awareness drive.

Sales Promotion: Free air packages for infants, discounted airfares for children of 2-10 years of age and special discounts for chartered flights are a part of this campaign. Passengers may be given free air bags, gifts or bottles of wine when they enter into the aircraft. They may be given discounts for their next air journeys (though the same airline). Frequent flyers are given heavy discounts. Passengers, who are supposed to take connecting flights, are not charged extra. Passengers can also move from the station of origin to the destination station and choose another station (in the sector) to come back to their station of origin. They can travel to that station of the sector travelled in by taxi, coach or rail. The airline can pick up the customer from a station that may be different firm the one, which is a part of the total itinerary. Example: DEL-BKK by Thai; BKK-SING by Thai; SING-KL by coach (Nice Travels); KL-BKK by a connected flight (MAS); BKK-DEL by Thai.

Personal Selling: These efforts are made by the staff of travel agencies Receptionists, sales girls at reception counters and booking executives undertake personal selling efforts on behalf of airlines that they represent. Tour operators and owners of resorts/hotels also indulge in personal selling exercises and promote those airlines with which, they are associated.

World-or-Mouth Promotion: Satisfied passengers tell their relatives and friends about the quality of services of airlines they had used for the purpose of domestic or international travel. So, those relatives and friends also prefer those very airlines. So much so, they also undertake those tours to domestic or foreign destinations that were undertaken by the actual customers.

Telemarketing Exercises: Travel agencies and tour operators appoint tele-marketers who sell airline packages and/or comprehensive tour packages to customers.

Distribution: Physical Based : It is synonymous with Place in the context of marketing management. Travel agencies, executives of tour operators, travel agents and producers of various services set up their offers at offices such places where tourists-to-be could approach them. Alternatively, these operators send their executives to homes/offices of these customers and deliver air tickets or documents related to packages, namely, passports with stamps of visas, transfer vouchers, tickets of night shows, tickets for entry to forts and museums etc.

Further, airlines are also able to provide excellent catering services to customers aboard the aircraft. Documents of customers are checked at airports by the airport authorities and customs officials. Customs duties are imposed on passengers who buy goods of values that are more than the value of free goods (i.e, those goods, which do not attract any customs duty). Hence, executives of travel agencies, tour operators, resorts, airport facilities and aircraft are a part of Place in the parlance of physical distribution efforts of airlines. The idea is to give two types of services to the customers core arid peripheral. At some times, the customer approaches the airline and at some others, the travel agency/ airline/tour operator/hotel owner/spot owner sends his representative or sales staff to the office or home of the customer.

Diverse Equipments : All the aircraft, cargo, handling equipment (like cranes, trolleys, container movers, lifts, maintenance equipment etc) aircraft maintenance machines, electrical utilities, mechanical utilities etc are a part of the technology that makes an airline operational.

Well-Trained Staff : The gargantuan tasks related to air travel cannot be executed without motivation and support of well-trained staff. Cabin crew, transporters to/from airport, truck operators, lift operators, maintenance staff, engineering staff etc are of part of the vital human resource that makes an airline transport system a success. Nowadays, there is emphasis on efficiency, performance and innovation and not just on a nine-to-five job. Airports have to be managed round-the-clock. International aircraft fly only after 10:00 pm from major airports. Airhostesses must remain on their toes at all the times. And our readers can understand fully well that managing an airborne vehicle carrying 300-400 passengers demands dexterity and perseverance of the caption of the aircraft. That is why, proper education and training in various streams of airline transport has become important nowadays.

Demands for Hotels : Under this concept, the basic idea is to convert light users (guests) of a hotel into medium users and medium users into heavy users. Competition is increasing in the hotel industry. So, poorly managed and: non-graded hotels may not survive in the times to come though they may remain favourites of the lower-end markets.

Demand for hotels increases if airline, cruise and coach bookings increase in terms of number of seats. If the tourist destination is a peaceful one (or located in a tourist country like Switzerland), these hotel bookings are regular. In some countries, demand is seasonal. Example: Hotel bookings in Shimla are full during the days of snowfall. During summer months, the hotels are booked to a large extent. But July, August and September are the lean months so far as hotel bookings are concerned. In southern India, snowfall is not the USP. But people visit popular tourist destinations throughout the year. In Goa, July and August are lean months. But December, January, February and May-June are the golden months.

Wars, ecological disasters and force majeure' affect hotel bookings in an adverse manner. Example: Hotel bookings in the gulf region were adversely affected in March-April, 2003 because of the Iraq--Us war. Tourists preferred not to visit the Gulf due to fierce fighting going on in Iraq. Although, the aircraft of the IA continued to fly to and from Kuwait city, yet people and tourists were generally not keen to move to that region due to fears related to this war.

Hotel's Product : The product of a hotel has a tangible component and an intangible component. The intangible component is equally important, just like the tangible one. Hotel professionals must design an overall package-that should make the customer realise that his money was well spent. Hotel rooms restaurant, cafe, shopping, entertainment and basic amenities like water, electricity, ventilation, air conditioning etc., are a part of the hotel product.

Prices of Hotel Rooms : The price of a hotel room is associated with its grade or classification. Non-graded hotels do not have any pricing policies. But these are the ones that engage in bargaining with customers. Finally, the customer arrives at a decent price. In graded hotels, the question of bargaining on the price front does not arise. However, some hotels do offer price discounts, free bottles of wine, chocolates for children or free hotel-to city transfers. Local sight seeing is to be paid for if the guest has not planned it (with his travel agency).

The hotel product is also perishable. So, if a room remains vacant, the hotel loses money. This problem is being faced by graded hotels that cannot give discounts beyond certain limits. Guests also cannot force them to reduce prices. So, price reduction is voluntary according to the norms decided by the FHAII or other hotel organisations. Because of lean business cycles in 2002, the hotel owners of five-star hotels had to reduce the prices of luxury suites and economy suits by as much as 40 per cent. Hence, sales had picked up during 2002. The government slaps heavy tax rates on five--star hotels. Seven-star hotels and intercontinental hotel are much more costlier than their five-tar cousins. Thus, the pricing policy of a hotel is controlled by the rules of the government. If they give discounts, they burn holes in their own pockets.

CHAPTER-13

ECONOMIC IMPACT OF REGIONAL TOURISM

International and domestic tourism are sensitive to disastrous events which make areas inaccessible to visitors, less attractive or more dangerous. One form of tourism disaster is the outbreak of an exotic disease, of which Foot and Mouth Disease (FMD) is a prime case. It is now well documented that the 2001 FMD outbreak in the UK had a greater impact on tourism than on agriculture. It has been estimated than an FMD outbreak in Australia would impose a cost of about $13 million. The impact on tourism would be highly dependent on the extent and duration of an FMD outbreak, as well as on any management and containment restrictions imposed by the authorities in their attempt to control and eventually eradicate the disease. Public perception and thus the provision of accurate information and the way in which the media report disasters will also play an important role in determining the impact on the tourism industry. The economy of Tropical North Queensland relies heavily on international visitors, and an FMD outbreak in the region would impose a large cost to the regional economy, conservatively estimated here to be of the order of $200 million per year.

TOURISM DEVELOPMENT OPPORTUNITY

It is estimated that by 2020, three times as many people will travel as do today. Developing countries are recognizing the tourism sector's potential contribution to national development goals, particularly by creating employment opportunities, stimulating small businesses and reducing poverty.

With the weakening of trade preferences and special pricing arrangements, many countries' dependence on tourism continues to grow as other traditional productive sectors, such as agriculture and manufacturing industries, struggle against tough external competition.

TOURISM IS POSSIBLE FOR ALL COUNTRIES

Tourism is a commodity. Every country has something to offer - even the poorest nations can offer their heritage, traditional culture and natural sites, which today's adventurous tourists are seeking.

Despite this strong potential, countries often exclude developing the tourism sector's export capabilities within national export strategies. To be successful, each country needs to formulate and manage a tourism strategy which identifies and justifies its strategic objectives, priorities and targets. Sustainable tourism should be a key element of national export strategy of the majority of developing and transition economies.

Most tourism is dependent on private sector initiatives, with the majority of operators being small and medium-sized enterprises (SMEs). Because the sector is very fragmented, and firms compete for business, cooperation between them doesn't come naturally. Export strategy-makers need to provide encouragement for collaboration to develop the industry. Fragmentation also means that standards vary greatly. For a country to be successful in developing a sustainable tourism industry, governments need to implement a regulatory and support framework.

Know The Trends

As with all service sectors, it pays to know the market. In a report on "A New Tourism Scenario - Key Future

Trends," Auliana Poon of Tourism Intelligence International identified 12 trends classified into three categories: supplier; consumer; and destination.

Supplier Trends

- Cheaper, shorter, faster.
- Closer to home.
- Internet helps customize holidays without raising costs.
- Increased polarization (e.g., mega/micro, luxury/budget, safe/unsafe) with less middle ground.
- Travel agents are reinventing themselves.

Consumer Trends

- Maturing, educated travellers.
- Independent travellers.
- Rise of the "bourgeois bohemians" who spend freely for uplifting experiences.
- Travellers seek to nourish body, mind and soul.
- Value for money.

Destination Trends

- Enough is enough - move away from mass tourism development to more sustainable models that preserve environment and culture.
- Travellers are moving away from products towards experiences.

These trends reveal a shift in global tourism. There are a growing number of busy travellers with a great desire to learn, with no money to waste, but much to spend. The inability of international tour operators to provide them with a more personalized service has influenced a change in behaviour. They travel independently, looking for charming small providers of accommodation and using local agents to book travel activities.

These travellers would rather spend time in one place instead of moving around. They are looking for areas rich in activities where it is easy to integrate with the local community and enjoy the experience of a lifetime. Think cultural activities, adventure, explorations and educational experiences. Service providers' creativity plays an important role in attracting tourists.

For example, a country such as El Salvador could easily attract these types of travellers by offering a combination of appealing activities, such as diving and exploring caves in a volcanic crater lake, learning Spanish by living with a local family or producing pottery from volcanic lava using the ancient process of applying aniline dye.

Travellers who enjoy experiences such as these are happy to spend time and money if, at the same time, they are contributing to environmental conservation, poverty alleviation and cultural preservation. These highly educated and successful professionals are constantly seeking the enrichment of mind and soul. The "bourgeois bohemians" are top earners. They spend freely and obtain pleasure from the righteousness of a product, rather than price or brand name. They often favour operators that promise socially responsible tourism.

Building a Strategy

The building blocks of a successful tourism strategy include integrating the private sector and fostering collaboration among SMEs. One tactic is to segment the strategy regionally to attract the new type of traveller. Fair trade is also applicable to services.

ITC has produced a tool to help developing and transition countries develop a strategy for the tourism sector. International consultant Ken Robinson designed ITC's strategy template, which includes nine critical steps:

- Review the national environment for tourism.
- Review tourism performance.
- Assess the adequacy of national tourism-related data.
- Assess strengths and weaknesses relative to key competitors.
- Review the current focus of any tourism strategy.
- Assess resources, to support the implementation of a tourism strategy.
- Draft a national tourism vision statement.
- Consider infrastructure assets and potential key attractors.
- Review the economic environment affecting tourism.

FORUM ON INTERNATIONAL TRADE AND TOURISM

Tourism is a major sector of the global economy, with global receipts from international tourism surpassing most other economic sectors. In many developing and least developed countries, tourism activities are many times more important than manufacture or agriculture in terms of participation and economic activity. At the same time, however, tourism is a highly vulnerable economic activity, dependent on a number of factors, some of which are beyond the control of developing countries. Global events (related to international politics, health-related risks, climate factors, etc) may have a detrimental impact on the performance of the sector. Other factors, however, are policy-dependent and in this connection adopting a coherent developmental framework for trade in tourism services becomes a crucial issue, particularly for those countries with high economic dependence on tourism.

Purpose: In the above perspective the event will feature a series of panels focusing on the following aspects:

a. Lessons from existing experiences on the liberalization of tourism to support export competitiveness, and implementation of policies that ensure spill over effects on local communities and poverty eradication;
b. Models and schemes to develop and monitor market intelligence
c. Areas for increased south-south tourism trade flows taking advantages of FTA and RTAs
d. Possible cooperation in infrastructure-related projects, including in third countries,
e. Implementation of the Lisbon Declaration;
f. Inputs to the host country's efforts to launch a innovative integrated strategy for the Tourism sector.

Expected outcome: The outcome of this event would shed some ligth on some national experience in order to provide insigths on how policies and a new genaration of innovative policies and strategies could be developed in more coherent manner to lift performance and development in tourism destinations of devloping countries.

Impact of trade liberalization on the equitable distribution of benefits in tourism destinations of developing countries. Competitive strategies to ensure development gains, poverty eradication and trade benefits in developing countries tourism destination. The impact of anticompetitive practices in the erosion of gains in the value added chains of tourism services. Models of market intelligence and innovative approaches to improve markets penetration, monitoring and assessment of performance of tourism destination of developing countries at the national, regional and interregional level Analysis of national experiences.

Economic Impacts of a Heritage Tourism System

US history has often served as a theme for tourism. Within southwestern Pennsylvania, a system of historical sites depicting the region's cultural and industrial heritage was formally organized in 1988. The Path of Progress included the renovation of 20 historical sites at a cost of $88.2 million. A five-year study monitored the growth and economic impact of 13-completed sites within the nine-county region. By 1998, the 13 sites had an annual attendance of nearly 1/2 million visitor days, with 74% coming from non-resident visitors. Regional expenditures by non-resident visitors were $15 million in 1998. Total regional sales impacts from these expenditures amounted to $33 million. Cumulative sales impacts from the entire system over the first 11 years of operation were $470 million, with 64% originating from non-resident expenditures and 36% from capital expenditures. A comparison of the original sites in 1988 to 1998 operations showed a net gain of $16 million in impacts from non-resident expenditures. More can be expected as the system expands.

The Impact of USA Economic Growth on Tourism

The launch of the World Travel Tourism Council's (WTTC's) annual economic impact research on Thursday, March 11 at ITB Berlin confirmed a 5 percent decline in global travel and tourism economy GDP in 2009. "And 2010 will be a flat year," said the council's president and CEO, Jean-Claude Baumgarten. "The USA is not likely to fare any better," Baumgarten added. "The economy has emerged from recession, with growth surging in Q4 2009. However, with the impetus provided by the stock cycle and fiscal policy set to fade, we expect quarterly growth to slow."

2010 is expected to bring a very gradual recovery in travel and tourism, with business travel and investment continuing to drag on growth," Baumgarten said. In terms of travel and tourism jobs in 2010, the picture is even gloomier this year, with WTTC forecasting a decline of 3 percent to 13.6 million - 9.8 percent of total employment in the USA. But travel and tourism economy employment could increase its share to

10.7 percent of total employment by 2020, or nearly 17 million jobs, if the policy environment is conducive to growth."

US travel and tourism has received very little government support since the beginning of the global economic crisis, despite its significant contribution to GDP, employment, and investment," said Baumgarten. "Think of all the support that has gone to the financial sector, even though its share of GDP is not that much larger." But this situation clearly cannot continue in the long term," Baumgarten warned, "and, indeed, it looks as though it may be about to change with the long overdue signing of the Travel Promotion Act. Increased international promotion and marketing are critical to attract growth from overseas markets and to ensure that the sector realises its long-term potential as a major generator of employment, driving economic growth."

WTTC strongly maintains that it is crucial for government policy to support rather than hamper the long-term development of travel and tourism. And this means that policymakers need to be wary about placing extra burdens on this previously dynamic sector at this crucial time, when profitability is already under severe pressure.

"Our latest research shows that, if the US government can ensure a favorable operating environment, the country will see a strong recovery in travel and tourism demand over the next ten years," said Baumgarten, "and this will also stimulate a recovery in investment, resulting in an annual growth of more than 11 percent in travel and tourism investment for the USA between now and 2020."

o Travel and tourism economy GDP is the broadest measure of the economic contribution of the travel and tourism sector to gross domestic product. It records the activity of traditional travel and tourism providers (e.g., lodging, transportation, etc.), plus tourism-related investment, public spending, and export of goods. It includes both the direct effects and the indirect effects via the supply chain of travel and tourism spending.

- o Travel and tourism economy employment comprises the jobs generated by travel and tourism economy GDP, the broadest measure of travel and tourism's employment impact.
- o Capital investment includes fixed investment expenditure by travel and tourism service providers and government agencies to provide facilities, capital equipment, and infrastructure for visitors.

The Impact of UK Economic Growth on Tourism

Using the Scarborough Tourism Economic Activity Monitor (STEAM), tourism activity was monitored from 2001 to 2003. This model defined direct and indirect tourism expenditure in the following sectors;

- Accommodation
- Food and Drink
- Recreation
- Shopping
- Transport.

Cross River Partnership (CRP) used the model to provide an analysis of the economic impact of tourism in central London including year-on-year fluctuations, which has helped shape its Tourism Strategy. Soon after this project started, figures were gained for 1999 and 2000 and a baseline year of 1995 was added.

The project has revealed that in 2003 the figures tended not to vary much more than a three per cent growth or decline on 2002 figures and that;

- The estimated visitor spend in the Cross River area was £3.7 billion
- The expenditure on visitor accommodation in the core area was £429 million, a decrease of 2% on 2002

- The total food and drink expenditure in the core area was £356 million, a decrease of 5% on 2002
- The total visitor days in the core Cross River area, including accommodation, day visitors and visitor friends and relatives, came to a total of 42 million days, a decrease of 5% on 2002
- Total direct employment in the Cross River area (accommodation, food and drink, recreation, shopping and transport sectors) came to 24,023 jobs.

THE IMPACT OF INDIA'S ECONOMIC GROWTH ON TOURISM

The developing world has immensely contributed to the economic boost that India is currently enjoying and it's tourism sector has not been left out of the share of profits either- a major achievement for the image of brand India build up by a successful financial system in place in our country.

Some economists credit this fiscal feature of success of Indian financial system to the income generated by the tourism segment, movements across the cross-section of rising business opportunities, agricultural and educational sectors opening up as well as novel and attractive packaging of brand-building for India that have in turn, benefited the travel industry as well. Besides this, strategic planning of excursion packages, eco-tourism, sports events that bring the spot-light on India and greater patronage by greater number of MNC's heading to our shores as well as diversifications of the Indian open industries norm have contributed to the growth of Indian economy and thereby, Indian tourism.

The WTO (World Tourism Organization) reports that as many as 698 million people traveled to a foreign country in 2000, spending over US$ 478 billion while on tour; if India too had a share in these results, then surely the impact of Indian economy as a contributor to rising world economy and its impact on tourism cannot be ignored. More of free spending of disposable incomes, greater markets opening up and better scope for industrialization and earning opportunities have led the way for India's economy to successfully launch the enhanced tourism sector.

What has contributed to the economic growth of India and the tourism sector at large are factors of industrialization, education, higher number of qualified professionals, opening up of foreign markets, liberal trade policies and better advertising and strategic marketing.

The above factors have been collectively responsible for boosting our country's economic reserves and the impact of India's economic growth on tourism is increasingly being felt in specialty sectors like spiritual tourism, spa tourism, student/senior citizen or family vacation plan segments in tourism as well as (surprise, surprise!) adventure tourism! Better amenities and modernization of roads, infrastructure in hotels, local lodging options, accreditation of genuine travel operators and guides etc., training being imparted by government and private sector individuals interested in developing specific regions for tourism promotion and encouraging global gains for India have all been strategized well. These policies put in place after significant contribution from field experts like market watchers, tourism ministry and education and foreign affairs ministry support systems are governed by the needs of tourists visiting India for a certain cultural flavor, yet, not be deprived of comforts, hygiene, security and conveniences that are world-class.

CHAPTER-14

SUSTAINABLE REGIONAL TOURISM

Sustainability is just one word and yet there exists over 300 definitions. The best-known definition of sustainability or sustainable development comes from the World Commission on Environment and Development and is outlined as: "forms of progress that meet the needs of the present without compromising the ability of future generations to meet their needs."

It is important to consider that sustainability is about more than just looking after our natural environment. It is also about considering the social and economic impact of what we do and how we do it.

The challenge for Australia is to encourage the development and management of tourism products and services that will provide economic and social benefits to local communities while protecting and enhancing our natural and cultural attributes.

Sustainable tourism is an industry committed to making a low impact on the environment and local culture, while helping to generate future employment for local people. The aim of sustainable tourism is to ensure that development brings a positive experience for the local people, tourism companies and the tourists themselves, but sustainable tourism is not the same as ecotourism.

Global economists forecast continuing international tourism growth, ranging between 3 and 6 percent annually, depending on the location. As one of the world's largest and fastest growing industries, this continuous growth will place great stress on remaining biologically diverse habitats and indigenous cultures, which are often used to support mass tourism. Tourists who promote sustainable tourism are sensitive to these dangers and seek to protect tourist destinations, and to protect tourism as an industry. Sustainable tourists can reduce the impact of tourism in many ways, including:

- informing themselves of the culture, politics, and economy of the communities visited
- anticipating and respecting local cultures, expectations and assumptions
- contributing to intercultural understanding and tolerance
- supporting the integrity of local cultures by favoring businesses which conserve cultural heritage and traditional values
- supporting local economies by purchasing local goods and participating with small, local businesses
- conserving resources by seeking out businesses that are environmentally conscious, and by using the least possible amount of non-renewable resources

Increasingly, destinations and tourism operations are endorsing and following "responsible tourism" as a pathway towards sustainable tourism. Responsible tourism and sustainable tourism have an identical goal, that of sustainable development. The pillars of responsible tourism are therefore the same as those of sustainable tourism - environmental integrity, social justice and economic development. The major difference between the two is that, in responsible tourism, individuals, organisations and businesses are asked to take responsibility for their actions and the impacts of their actions. This shift in emphasis has taken place because some stakeholders feel that insufficient progress towards realising sustainable tourism has been made since the Earth Summit in Rio. This is partly because everyone has been expecting others to behave in a sustainable manner. The emphasis on responsibility in responsible tourism means that everyone involved in tourism - government, product owners and operators, transport operators, community services, NGO's and CBO's, tourists, local communities, industry associations - are responsible for achieving the goals of responsible tourism.

OUR RESPONSIBILITY

In 2008 we established The Leading Travel Companies Conservation Foundation, a non-profit organization that's goal is to support the development of long-term, sustainable tourism globally. Our group of companies contributes US$1 million per year to support threatened communities, natural environments and historic sites all over the world. The Foundation supports the Venice in Peril charity and in 2010 funded the restoration of the Monument to Canova, in the Santa Maria Gloriosa dei Frari Church, where the famous sculptor's heart was interred upon his death and where some of the greatest art treasures in Venice are held.

Other projects have seen the Foundation support Conservation International to protect three million hectares of Atlantic Forest in Brazil, the World Wildlife Fund (WWF) to foster sustainable indigenous tourism in Australia's Kimberley region. We are also a primary sponsor of the Tourism for Tomorrow Awards which encourages tourism operators to develop and share leading sustainable tourism practices.

Every time we travel, whether by car, train, plane or coach, we are burning fossil fuels and contributing greenhouse gases into the atmosphere. And while there are many ways to travel while on vacation, we are pleased to advise that by choosing a Trafalgar guided tour, you are opting for one of the most environmentally friendly ways to go. This grid below shows you the amount of carbon dioxide emitted per kilometre for a passenger traveling on various forms of transport which clearly shows coach transport as emitting significantly less carbon dioxide than other forms of transport. With carbon dioxide being one of the main causes of global warming, it's good to know that buying an guided tour vacation is a better way to travel.

YOU CAN MAKE A DIFFERENCE

While there are many things you can do to lessen your impact on the environment while traveling, an easy way to make a difference is to 'carbon neutralize' your travel.

It's the carbon emissions in the atmosphere that are slowing warming our planet and causing climate change. Reducing these emissions is up to each of us and can be done by turning off appliances, driving less and buying local produce. For those emissions that can't be reduced carbon neutralising allows you to contribute to projects that are greening the planet in other ways.

Trafalgar has partnered with Sustainable Travel International™, allowing you the option to calculate the carbon footprint of your travel and contribute towards projects that will reduce the C02 emissions in the atmosphere on your behalf.

This voluntary scheme invites you to pay a contribution based on the amount of carbon likely to be generated from your travel. You can choose to offset your flight, coach travel or the energy consumed staying in your hotel accommodation.

WHAT ELSE YOU CAN DO?

There are many things you can do while traveling to minimize your environmental impact. Some of them you may already do at home but you can also do them while on vacation:

- o When you've finished with your vacation brochures, pass them onto a friend or recycle them
- o Buy local produce which reduces air miles incurred in transporting the food to a kitchen for final preparation
- o Respect the local culture and traditions where you are traveling through. Ensure your dress and behavior is appropriate for the places you visit. If you're unsure, ask your tour manager
- o Minimize waste by bringing your own water bottle and reusing it, and refuse or reuse plastic bags when shopping
- o Learn a few words of the local language and ensure the way you dress, eat and greet people is polite according to the local custom
- o Please don't pick plants and flowers, leave them for others to enjoy
- o At your hotel use water sparingly, take short showers instead of baths and hang towels for drying and reuse
- o Separate paper from plastic and try to recycle as much as possible
- o Throw any litter in the bin and keep the local environment tidy
- o Switch lights off & air conditioning off if you are not in the room or don't need them
- o Turn off your TV instead of leaving it on standby
- o Support a local environmental group and learn more about what you can do
- o Reduce your use and waste of precious resources such as water, food and energy
- o Leave as much packaging at home from goods you buy for your trip and recycle as much of this as possible.

True Test of Sustainability

Even if the "recession tourism" market fails to materialize, experts say, most destinations should be able to withstand the loss of revenue - provided the region is developed in a truly sustainable manner.

In other words, communities should not rely entirely on tourists, said William Powers, a senior fellow at the New York-based World Policy Institute.

"Tourism is one of several things you put in place, including sustainable agriculture, education, healthcare, land rights," Powers said. "You try to diversify."

Sustainable development efforts have often focused on the tourism sector as an alternative to ecologically destructive livelihoods such as mining and logging. If the recession leads tourism businesses to lay off workers, however, these and other extractive industries are not likely to provide renewed employment opportunities, due to the drop in global demand for the commodities.

Meanwhile, the upgrades that are often necessary for a tourism business to be considered sustainable, such as energy efficiency retrofits or solar panels, will likely be delayed until the global economy recovers.

"Companies will have to look at their costs on a whole host of levels," Spenceley said. "I'm concerned they may invest less in environmental responsibility and corporate social responsibility."

For Rainforest Alliance's Sanabria, the recession may provide a rare opportunity to reveal the true intentions of travel businesses that market themselves as sustainable.

"Those who see us just as a marketing write-up might cut [sustainability measures]. But that's OK. We only want people who see sustainability as important," he said. "It's a good test to see [which operations] are really committed."

Sustainable Tourism in USA

Organizations announce guidelines for sustainable tourism

BARCELONA (AP)-A coalition of 27 organizations called the Global Sustainable Tourism Criteria Partnership on Monday issued criteria for sustainable tourism at a conference in Barcelona.

The guidelines are available at Sustainable TourismCriteria.org. They focus on four areas: maximizing tourism's social and economic benefits to local communities; reducing negative impacts on cultural heritage; reducing harm to local environments; and planning for sustainability.

"Consumers deserve widely accepted standards to distinguish green from greenwashed. These criteria will allow true certification of sustainable practices in hotels and resorts as well as other travel suppliers," said Jeff Glueck, chief marketing officer of Travelocity, a member of the GSTC Partnership.

The partnership was initiated by the United Nations Foundation and also included the American Hotel & Lodging Association, the American Society of Travel Agents, the Caribbean Alliance for Sustainable Tourism, Expedia and the International Ecotourism Society among others.

The guidelines were developed in consultation with sustainability experts and the tourism industry and included a review of more than 60 existing sets of criteria already being implemented around the globe.

United Nations Foundation Chairman Ted Turner joined the Rainforest Alliance, the United Nations Environment Programme and the United Nations World Tourism Organization in announcing the criteria at the International Union for Conservation of Nature's World Conservation Congress.

SUSTAINABLE TOURISM ORGANIZATION

niting Conservation & Travel Worldwide: The Ecotourism Society's Objectives: The Ecotourism Society is an international non-profit organizaiton fully dedicated to finding the resources and building the expertise to make tourism a viable tool for conservation and sustainable development. The Society it documenting the best techniques for implementing ecotourism principles by collaborating with a growing global network of active professionals in the field. Why Joing the Society? The Society's mission is to further both individual and institutional capabilities to make this defninition of ecotourism into a reality. Through its membership program, the Society provides information resrouces, training opportunities, and access to an exceptional network of worldwide ecotrouism professionals which include tour operators, architects, conservationists, researchers, developers, lodgeowners, representatives of governmental and non-governmental organizations. The Ecotourism Society's membership is necessary to remain current in this dynamic field.

SUSTAINABLE TOURISM IN UK

The Fourth International Conference on Sustainable Tourism has recently taken place in the New Forest, home of the Wessex Institute of Technology (WIT). The meeting was chaired by Professor Francisco Pineda of the Complutense University of Madrid and Professor Carlos Brebbia of the Wessex Institute of Technology, UK.

The current economics issues have highlighted the importance of sustainability and heralds the end of the system on which modern society has been organised in the past. It also indicates the dawn of a new era with a more natural use of materials and energy. The scenario is set for a different type of society, one in which these conditions converge; planning and occupation of space; the material and cultural landscape being considered as resources and a suitable amount of leisure time becoming available.

The landscape is to be enjoyed is both the natural and cultural one. There are natural landscapes in the world which will require a higher degree of protection. Biodiversity should be cherished and the object of our constant attention. The cultural landscape will blend with this vision creating a process for constant education and knowledge production. It is in this context that cities and metropolitan areas seek the emergency of new perspectives. Traditional industrial landscapes are also an important source of education in a new technological world.

These ideas are the basis of the series of International Conferences on Sustainable Tourism which has now become a well-established forum for the discussion of new developments in this important field. The conference has been successfully held in Segovia (2004), Bologna (2006) and Malta (2008), before the present meeting in the New Forest, UK, took place.

SUSTAINABLE TOURISM IN AUSTRALIA

Holiday-makers and travellers will easily be able to judge the efforts being made by tourism operators to reduce or eliminate the carbon footprint of their operation with a new certification system being launched by Ecotourism Australia's new arm Climate Action Australia.

The Climate Action Certification Program is dedicated to ranking efforts to reduce carbon emissions. It is designed for all sectors of the tourism industry, regardless of size and level of carbon reduction already undertaken. It will include the tourism hotels, attractions, tours, transport, restaurants, travel agents, tourism commissions and industry bodies.

The pre-conference industry survey by Roy Morgan Research ranked climate change as the number one concern for the tourism industry. Forecasters and consumer research also suggest environmental concern is the most influential consumer trend for a generation.

This certification scheme will be a user-friendly, online questionnaire with on line instant help desk, and automatic filtering so businesses only deal with relevant questions.

The Australian tourism industry is straining in the highly competitive marketplace at present, with both domestic and international visitor numbers stagnating. Apart from being a practical, uncomplicated assessment, carrying the Climate Action Australia rating will give pro-active operators a competitive edge.

Chapter-15

'Governance' -How Regional Tourism is Organized

The force behind this very complex activity encompassing a wide range of relationships in tourism is a phenomenon of modern times. Understanding the meaning and the nature of this phenomenon and its various components is very essential. In order to understand tourism systematically, it is necessary to know the various components which together make tourism happen. Three of these are considered to be basic:

(a) Transport;

(b) Attractions / Locale;

(c) Accommodation

TRANSPORT

There can be no travel if there were no transport. Travel involves movement of people and this is possible only if there is some mode of transport. Connectivity is very vital for tourism development. This could be possible only if adequate transportation infrastructure and access to destination is efficient, comfortable and inexpensive. A tourist, in order to get to his destination therefore, needs some mode of transport. This mode of transport may be a motor car, a coach, an aeroplane, a ship or a train which enables a traveller to reach his predetermined destination.

Locale

The locale may include the holiday destination and what it offers to the tourist. The holiday destination may offer natural attractions like sunshine, scenic beauty or sporting facilities, etc. The locale, with its attractions and amenities, is the most important as these are very basic to tourism. Unless these are there, the tourists will not be motivated to go to a particular place. However, since interests and tastes of tourists vary widely, they might choose from a wide range of attractions available at various destinations all over the world. Tourist demands are also very much susceptible to changes in fashion. Fashion is an important factor in the demand for various tourist attractions and amenities. The tourists who visit a particular place for its natural beauty may decide to visit some other attractions due to a change in fashion. Peter has drawn up an inventory of the various attractions which are of significance in tourism..

Accommodation

Accommodation plays a central role and is very basic to tourist destinations. World Tourism Organisation in its definition of a tourist has stated that the tourist must spend at least one night in the destination visited to be qualified as a tourist. This presupposes availability of some kind of accommodation. The demand for accommodation away from one's home is met by a variety of facilities. The range and type of accommodation is quite varied and has undergone considerable changes since last half a century. There has been a decline in the use of boarding houses and small private hotels. Larger hotels are increasing their share of holiday trade, especially in big metropolitan areas and popular tourist spots. In more traditional holiday and seaside resorts in Europe and elsewhere, big hotels are keeping their share of holiday resorts. In recent years some changes have been reflected in the type of accommodation. There has been a increasing demand for more non-traditional and informal type of accommodation. The latest trends in accommodation are holiday villages. In recent years there has been an increase in the popularity of such accommodation.

Geographical Components

Robinson has brought out a list of components of tourism which have been termed as geographical components of tourism. These are brought out in the following:

1. Accessibility and location
2. Space
3. Scenery:
   (a) land forms, e.g., mountains, canyons, coral reefs, cliffs, etc.
   (b) water, e.g., rivers, lakes, waterfalls, geysers, glaciers, the sea.
   (c) Vegetation, e.g., forests, grasslands, moors, deserts, etc.
4. Climate Sunshine, clouds, temperature conditions, rain and snow.
5. Animal life :
   (a) wildlife, e.g., birds, game reservations, zoos.
   (b) hunting and fishing.
6. Settlement features
   (a) Towns, cities, villages
   (b) Historical remains and monuments
   (c) Archaeological remains
7. Culture : ways of life, traditions, folklore, arts and crafts etc.

Scenic Attractions

Scenic attractions, like good weather, are very important factors in tourism. Scenery or the landscape consisting of mountains, lakes, waterfalls, glaciers, forests, deserts, etc., are strong forces attracting people to visit them. Breath-taking mountain scenery and the coastal stretches exert a strong fascination for the tourist. The magnificent mountain ranges provide an atmosphere of peace and tranquillity. Tourists visiting the northern slopes of the Alps in Switzerland and Austria and the southern slopes in Italy and also the Himalayan mountain slopes of India and Nepal for the first time, cannot but be charmed by their physical magnificence. Great natural wonders such as the Grand Canyon in the United States, the Giants Causeway of Northern Ireland, the Niagara Falls, the Geysers of Iceland, the glaciers of the Alps, the forests of Africa, the mighty rivers, the lakes and the deserts are a source of great interest to many tourists and have become the basis of an expanding tourist industry.

Historical and Cultural interest characteristics exert a powerful attraction for many. Since many centuries these have had a profound influence on the traveller. A large number of tourists are attracted every year by the great drawing power of Stratford-on Avon in England because of its association with Shakespeare, or the city of Agra in India with its famous Taj Mahal or Pisa in Italy for its famous Leaning Tower. Thousands of Americans and Canadians visit Europe because of its long historical heritage; besides, many view Europe as their original homeland and have a sentimental attachment to it. Any foreign visitor to England must visit London not because it is the largest city in the country and the capital, but because of its historical associations and traditions and its many cultural attractions. In a similar way the visitor in France includes Paris in his itinerary as he does Rome and Moscow in a visit to Italy and the Russia respectively. Many countries which are developing tourist industries are using the legacy of their historical past as their major tourist attractions. In India, the world-famous caves of Ajanta and Ellora are an example.

These caves are India's oldest and most beautiful testimony of religious architecture and painting, and are man-made caves hewn out of rocky mountains, conceived and executed some 2000 years ago.

Accessibility

Accessibility is a very crucial factor as it is a means by which a tourist can reach the area where attractions are located. Tourist attractions of whatever type would be of little importance if their locations are inaccessible by the normal means of transport. If the tourist attractions are located at places where no transport can reach or where there are inadequate transport facilities, these become of little value. The tourist attractions which are located near to the tourist generating markets and are linked by a network of efficient roads and can be easily reached by air receive the maximum number of tourists. The distance factor also plays an important role in determining a tourist's choice of a destination. Longer distances cost much in the way of expenses on travel as compared to short distances. An example can be that of India. About two million and a half tourist arrivals for a country of the size of India may look rather unimpressive. However, if one looks at certain factors like the country's distance from the affluent tourist market of the world such as the United States, Europe, Canada, Japan and Australia, one may conclude that the long distance is rather one of the factors responsible for low arrivals. It costs a visitor from these countries quite a substantial amount to visit India for a holiday. It has been stated earlier that Europe and North America continue to be the main generating and receiving areas for international tourism, accounting for as much as 70 per cent and 20 per cent, respectively, of international tourist arrivals. The intra-regional tourism (tourism between countries of the same region) has an appreciable influence on the distribution of world arrivals. Of the total international tourist movements within Europe and North America, at least 75 per cent are intra-regional. In the Americas the United States and Canada alone account for nearly 50 per cent of all international tourist traffic in the regions, where intra-regional international tourist movements are also predominant. In Europe, intra-regional tourism accounts for over 70 per cent of international tourist movements. Easy accessibility thus is a key factor for the growth and development of tourist movements.

Amenities

Facilities are a necessary aid to the tourist centre. For a seaside resort, facilities like swimming, boating, yachting, surf-riding and other facilities like dancing, recreation and amusements are important for every tourist centre. Amenities can be of two types: natural, e.g., beaches, sea-bathing, possibilities of fishing, opportunities for climbing, trekking, viewing, etc. and man-made, e.g., various types of entertainments and facilities which cater to the special needs of the tourists. Excellent sandy beaches, sheltered in sunshine with palm and coconut trees and offering good bathing conditions form very good tourist attractions. Certain other natural amenities such as spacious waters for the purpose of sailing, or the opportunities for fishing and shooting are also very important.

Business Seminar on "Regional Development for Sustainable Tourism"

"Malta's tourism industry is facing major challenges but is still managing to register growth, but there is absolutely no room for complacency despite the positive results achieved this year," stated Prime Minister Lawrence Gonzi during his key note speech at the business seminar entitled Regional Development for Sustainable Tourism.

The event, organised by the Malta Business Bureau and the Malta Hotels and Restaurants Association, tackled a number of issues relating to the sustainability of the local tourism sector. According to Prime Minister Lawrence Gonzi" it is a challenging time for Europe's tourism industries and this also applies to Malta. If we are to continue on the success achieved so far, there is a need for a concerted effort by all stakeholder and at all levels - this is the only way that Malta's tourism industry will develop in a competitive and sustainable manner."

Dr Gonzi also made reference to the significant contribution of the tourism industry to the local economy and called on all stakeholders to face challenges with determination and, above all innovation and a clear drive to deliver the a quality product and service. "Innovation and a dedication to ensuring the best customer satisfaction will be the key to the future success of the industry - we need to capitalise on our uniqueness, on our culture, on our heritage, and on our Mediterranean environment," he stated.

The Prime Minister also highlighted the fact that the tourism industry is a clear example of the need to reconcile economic growth with sustainable development, and explain how government has, to date, invested over Eur 26 million in regional development projects. "Financial investment is needed for the industry to tap niche markets and for innovative ideas to become reality and for this reason, government has made funds available for this aim," he stated.

"However, this is only one part of the equation and we must all accept the fact that success will only be achieved if a national effort is made - all socio economic players have a part to play in ensuring that Malta's tourism industry remains competitive, and is above all, sustainable," Dr Gonzi concluded.

The audience was addressed by a number of other high profile speakers including Mr Michel Laine, (Head of Unit within the European Commission's Directorate General for Employment, Social Affairs and Equal Opportunities, who spoke about funding opportunities available to businesses operating within the tourism industry. Mr Laine highlighted the fact that Europe is the world's leading tourist destination, enjoying around 40 per cent of global tourist arrivals, which led to the tourism industry playing a key role in Europe's economic and social development.

Mr Laine also pointed out that Malta's dependence on tourism, coupled with the fact that the it does not have a very diversified tourist base, makes innovation and the targeting of niche markets all the more important for the sustainable development of the local tourism industry. "The European Union provides essential support when it comes to financing projects that will improve the tourism product - investment in infrastructure and in training and education are just two examples of the different types of projects that can benefit from EU funding," he explained.

Mr Francisco Calheiros, the President of LAG Vale do Lima (Portugal) and also President of TURIHAB, the Association of Manor Housing Tourism also addressed the audience and focused on the development of regional networks and how this innovative approach contributes to the development of the tourism industry across Europe.

Mr Calheiros explained how he was involved in an innovative project entitled 'Europe of Traditions', which brought ten European destinations together to offer a traditional and unique taste of their culture by offering accommodation at a selection of exquisite houses of historical importance.

He explained how this approach targeted visitors who wanted a different yet quality experience that would truly introduce them to the country's unique heritage, history and culture, allowing the host country to truly capitalize on their unique characteristics. Mr Calheiros also shared his extensive experience within the Portuguese tourism industry and highlighted the fact that a number of successful projects had come to fruition thanks to the financial assistance made available by the European Union.

Mr John A Huber, President of the Malta Business Bureau also addressed the audience and stated that it was necessary "to make an effort to re-create an image for Malta and to exploit our historical and cultural richness. To reach this desired objective it is important to use all the resources and the potential of all stakeholders interested in increasing the tourism based economy of the islands of Malta and Gozo."

He also said that "today's business world has become intelligent, interconnected and instrumental. Tourism still retains a soul; a human soul that us Maltese, us Mediterranean, us European endear and cherish. Hence my conviction of success in what we endeavor to do in no matter how courageous and ambitious it may be."

George Micallef, president of the MHRA spoke about EU funding opportunities that were being made available to the local business community. "EU funding is helping our industry to improve the product and standards and is expediting this process, at a time when disposable capital is in short supply, but the main concern remains the bureaucratic process involved to apply, which is further compounded by the administrative procedures imposed for eligibility."

Other speakers who addressed the audience included Ms Marlene Bonnici (Director General of the Planning and Priorities Coordination Department, Office of the Prime Minister), Ms Marie Louise Mangion (Head Tourism and Sustainable Development Unit, Office of the Prime Minister), Mr. Josef Formosa Gauci, Chief Executive Officer Malta Tourism Authority and Ms. Maria Joao Rauch (Expert on EU Funding, in the Fields of Local Development, Employment and Vocational Training) who moderated the panel discussion on 'Making Better Use of EU Funding'.

Bibliography

- "AJ Hackett Bungy". Bungy.co.nz.
- Aerial Extreme Sports (2008). History of Bungee.
- AJ Hackett (2008). History. Retrieved on 17 October 2008.
- AJ Hackett (2008). Welcome to Cairns. Retrieved on 17 October 2008.
- Bruce, Eric Stuart (1914). Aircraft in war. London: Hodder and Stoughton. pp. 8. http://www.archive.org/stream/aircraftinwar00brucuoft#page/8/mode/1up.
- Cameron, Ian (1990). Kingdom of the Sun God: a history of the Andes and their people. New York: Facts on File. pp. 174-175. ISBN 0-8160-2581-9.
- Chronology of the FAI World Hang Gliding Championships
- Cohen, Michael P., The History of the Sierra Club 1892-1970 (Sierra Club Books, San Francisco, 1988) ISBN 0-87156-732-6
- Cox, Steven M. and Kris Fulsaas, ed., ed (2003-09). Mountaineering: The Freedom of the Hills (7 ed.). Seattle: The Mountaineers. ISBN 0898868289.
- CRUZ FILHO, F. Murillo, Bartolomeu Lourenço de Gusmão: Sua Obra e o Significado Fáustico de Sua Vida, Rio de Janeiro, Biblioteca Reprográfica Xerox, 1985

- Cymerman, A; Rock, PB. Medical Problems in High Mountain Environments. A Handbook for Medical Officers. USARIEM-TN94-2. US Army Research Inst. of Environmental Medicine Thermal and Mountain Medicine Division Technical Report.
- Eric Larson, 2003 p135, The Devil in the White City; Murder, Magic, and Madness at the Fair that Changed America. Citing Chicago Tribune, Nov. 9, 1889.
- Hamilton, AJ. Biomedical Aspects of Military Operations at High Altitude. USARIEM-M-30/88. US Army Research Inst. of Environmental Medicine Thermal and Mountain Medicine Division Technical Report.
- Jungle Bungy Jump (2008). Phuket Thailand.
- Kockelman JW, Hubbard M. Bungee jumping cord design using a simple model. Sports Engineering 2004; 7(2):89-96.
- Lynn Thorndike, Renaissance or Prenaissance, Journal of the History of Ideas, Vol. 4, No. 1. (Jan., 1943), pp. 69-74.
- Mackinder, Halford John (May 1900). "A Journey to the Summit of Mount Kenya, British East Africa". The Geographical Journal 15 (5): 453-476. doi:10.2307/1774261.
- Mike Barber needed to fly 1% further than Ruhmer's 435 miles (700 km) in order to break the official FAI record; Barber needed to fly only 3 more miles for a total of 440 miles (710 km). Barber's flight remains the longest hang glider flight ever.
- Mountainous plateau creates ozone "halo" around Tibet
- Muza, SR; Fulco, CS; Cymerman, A (2004). "Altitude Acclimatization Guide.". US Army Research Inst. of Environmental Medicine Thermal and Mountain Medicine Division Technical Report (USARIEM-TN-04-05).

INDEX